## DATE DUE

BRODART

# François Mitterrand

# François Mitterrand

❖ ❖ ❖

## The Making of a Socialist Prince
## in Republican France

SALLY BAUMANN-REYNOLDS

PRAEGER

**Westport, Connecticut**
**London**

Copyright Acknowledgments

English translations of quotations from Mitterrand's *Ma Part de verité* c/Librairie Arthème Fayard, 1969, and *Politique*, c/Librairie Arthème Fayard, 1977, are published by kind permission of the publisher Librairie Arthème Fayard, Paris, France.

English translations of quotations from Mitterrand's *L'Abeille et l'architecte*, Flammarion, 1978, are published by kind permission of the publisher Flammarion, Paris, France.

Library of Congress Cataloging-in-Publication Data

Baumann-Reynolds, Sally.
    François Mitterrand : the making of a Socialist prince in
Republican France / Sally Baumann-Reynolds.
        p.    cm.
    Includes bibliographical references and index.
    ISBN 0-275-94887-0
    1. Mitterrand, François, 1916– .  2. Mitterrand, François, 1916–
—Political and social views.  3. Presidents—France—Biography.
4. France—Politics and government—20th century.  5. Political
leadership—France—History—20th century.  6. Socialism—France—
History—20th century.    I. Title.
DC423.B4     1995
944.083´8´092—dc20        94-37201

British Library Cataloguing in Publication Data is available.

Library of Congress Catalog Card Number: 94-37201
ISBN: 0-275-94887-0

First published in 1995

Praeger Publishers, 88 Post Road West, Westport, CT 06881
An imprint of Greenwood Publishing Group, Inc.

Printed in the United States of America

The paper used in this book complies with the
Permanent Paper Standard issued by the National
Information Standards Organization (Z39.48-1984).

10  9  8  7  6  5  4  3  2  1

# Contents

# Preface

In 1981, when François Mitterrand was finally elected president of France after two unsuccessful attempts to obtain the post, I was teaching French language, literature and culture at the University of North Carolina at Asheville. By then, it was already evident to me that this statesman was a type of national political figure that has never appeared on the American political scene. Like many of his U.S. counterparts, Mitterrand has training in the law and, at the level of action, is very pragmatic. However, at the more fundamental level of culture, he is very much "a man of letters"—that is, he is an avid reader of serious literature, a student of history, a self-conscious political philosopher, a prolific writer and powerful orator in his own right, and most recently a "philosopher king." Little of Mitterrand's writing, none of his speeches, and only a few books about him are available in English. It was my intense curiosity about the eleven books that he had written (without ghostwriters, it should be noted) and had published by 1981 (two more have been published since then) that furnished the impetus for this study.

In the United States Mitterrand remains at best poorly understood and virtually unknown, except among a small group of specialists. There are obvious reasons for this: First, the American media give scant coverage to French domestic politics; second, our educational curriculum pays little attention to contemporary continental European domestic affairs; and finally, linguistic and cultural barriers pose a dual problem for those Americans desiring to acquaint themselves with the French president. Mitterrand is a highly refined product of a distinct social, literary and political tradition, in a country that prizes its culture above all else.

This book is an attempt to show the American public why Mitterrand is such an extraordinary political figure. By examining his family and cultural background, his character, the historical circumstances and the distinctive French democratic system in which he has had to operate, this work tries to explain certain aspects of Mitterrand's political approach to an audience that views him largely as an enigma. It covers his youth, his wartime experiences, his participation in the Fourth Republic, his years in the opposition, and finally, his first presidential triumph. How Mitterrand won an unprecedented second seven-year term and how he has wielded national power undoubtedly constitute an important topic of research, but how he achieved that power in the first place is an even more compelling one because of its nearly total improbability; furthermore, his prepresidential career foreshadowed and helps explain both his ability to hold on to the presidency and the decisions that he has made during his two terms.

It is difficult to be objective about François Mitterrand. French people who have followed his career tend to either admire or despise him. The complexity of the issues involved adds to the challenge of fairly evaluating his actions. Nevertheless, though at a great geographical, historical, and even political distance, and in spite of his errors, weaknesses, and unconvincing arguments and claims, I have frankly found it impossible not to be impressed by this Sisyphus of French politics.

I wish to thank the National Endowment for the Humanities for awarding me funds to begin this project, the interlibrary loan staffs of the University of North Carolina at Asheville and North Carolina State University libraries for their friendly and efficient service, Georgette Elgey, technical advisor to President Mitterrand, for facilitating contact with the Elysée Palace, Julius W. Friend for his helpful suggestions and comments, Nina Neimark for her invaluable editorial assistance, and finally my husband, Russell, for his total support of this endeavor.

*Note:* All translations of French texts, unless otherwise indicated, are by the author.

# Introduction

Republicanism, socialism, Machiavellianism—a system, an ideology, an art—these are the three pillars on which François Mitterrand has constructed his political philosophy and career. Each embodies certain traditions deeply embedded in French society and carefully exploited by the French president. François Mitterrand inherited his republicanism from his family. He acquired his mantle of socialism relatively late in his career by the force of circumstances. But his Machiavellianism is an art that he developed to a fine degree very much on his own, little by little, throughout his life. It is the most defining feature of his political character and the source of his success.

In France it is considered a cliché to call any politician Machiavellian, especially a politician as masterful as Mitterrand. In this sense the term is naturally being used in its vulgarized, pejorative meaning. The biographers Catherine Nay[1] and Franz-Olivier Giesbert[2] cite this characterization of the French president. (Giesbert largely rejects the idea in his biography whereas Nay's portrait appears to be based on it.) It is time to stop taking the concept for granted, explore its fuller and more complex original meaning as elaborated by Niccolò Machiavelli himself, and then take a closer look at Mitterrand's career in light of that loftier concept.

The common, pejorative definitions of the word Machiavellian are well known: "preferring expediency to morality," "the employment of cunning and duplicity in statecraft."[3] While acknowledging the possible conflict between the requirements of virtue and those of effective leadership, the Renaissance thinker Machiavelli clearly distinguished between several different types of princes, and he established among them—albeit in a tone of amoral objectivity—a very explicit moral hierarchy. He asserted that history demonstrates that those who attain glory along with power, those who obtain the "favor of the inhabitants," and those who obtain that favor through their own efforts in the face of many obstacles last longer than and are superior to those who do not meet these criteria. One can infer that the prince who meets all of these criteria is the most excellent one of all.

Clearly, Mitterrand has met the latter two criteria, obtaining the favor of the inhabitants (that is, the voting majority) and overcoming a myriad of obstacles through his own efforts. It is the first criterion, attaining glory, that is the most difficult to assess. What does Machiavelli mean by "glory"? Certainly, the concept of military superiority is inherent in this term. But the glory of the prince cannot be only of a military nature, and in a democracy it has to consist of more than electoral victory. In the final chapter of *The Prince* Machiavelli refers to the political glory to which a prince must aspire; he exhorts Lorenzo de Medici to unify the Italians and eject the foreign oppressors (the Spaniards), to be his countrymen's "redeemer," to institute "laws and measures [that] will render him revered and admired."[4] Glory for the prince, therefore, also depends on his ability to defend the independence of his people and to promote general well-being and justice through good laws. Mitterrand certainly took on the role of socialist "redeemer," but only a book about his two presidencies can assess his full degree of "glory." This study is limited to the first part of that quest, the acquisition of power.[5]

Machiavellianism necessarily presupposes that princes (and not just hereditary ones) do exist—a premise that socialists cannot easily accept. That individual men and women are called upon to lead; that they possess sufficient force to do so; that they correctly refuse to submit to any outside earthly force in the form of a person, class, or "system of relations," sometimes even to reality itself as perceived by most others; that they stubbornly believe in their ability to shape events and history is a worldview that socialist purists prefer to ignore or, at least, minimize. Perhaps the most fundamental characteristic of a prince is his absolute refusal to submit to the power of any other human being or group, and this characteristic Mitterrand displayed incontrovertibly from the beginning of his political career. All this helps explain why it took him so long to be accepted as a Socialist by Socialists. The older generation of Socialist Party members considered his socialism to be only skin-deep, though it covered him from head to toe. They sensed that this Socialist pretender, in theory and in practice, was Machiavellian to the bone.

It is evident that Mitterrand was conscious of his princely vocation very early on and made others equally aware of it. He has always demonstrated supreme confidence in his ability to play a constructive role in French history. The French linguist Dominique Labbé used a metaphor from astronomy to describe the Socialist leader's princely demeanor:

> He sees himself fixed, unmoving in the center of the social universe, looking at the other planets revolving around him. This is why . . . he perceives himself, as well as his peers, to be distinct individuals who are endowed with . . . a unique,

irreplaceable . . . character, whose actions are undertaken consciously and in
total freedom.[6]

One should qualify this, however, by pointing out that Mitterrand has rarely
recognized a true peer on the national political scene. Indeed, only his epic
adversary, Charles de Gaulle, falls into this category. (Georges Pompidou,
Valéry Giscard d'Estaing, and Jacques Chirac certainly do not.) Generally, he
treats his political opponents as mere puppets or the cooperative agents of various interest groups or classes. This prevents him from exhibiting personal ven-
omousness, but not implacable disdain. The "planets" to which Labbé refers are
Mitterrand's friends and associates—generally one and the same group of individuals, who tend to be somewhat less unique than and not quite as irreplaceable as Mitterrand himself. He sheds his light on them, and they faithfully
reflect it. Occasionally, though very rarely and usually just temporarily, a
friend-associate has become a friend-rival. And in only a few instances have any
of them spun off altogether.

Republicanism as a belief system harmonizes much better with Machiavellianism than does socialism. At first glance, this might not seem to be the case,
because Machiavellianism was originally articulated in an essentially aristocratic
world (although the Florence of Machiavelli's time had been a republic for several hundred years) and republicanism is based on the principle of popular will.
However, there is no fundamental contradiction between these two concepts.
Indeed, one could say that, in a sense, republicanism is a generalized and
advanced form of Machiavellianism. While republicanism places even greater
emphasis on good laws as the most solid foundation of power than does
Machiavellianism and requires that the prince himself be subject to them, it also
presupposes that every individual is a kind of prince in his own domain, that
each has essentially the same basic rights and responsibilities of the aristocracy
of old (minus the idea of privilege), that each has a limited yet certain power
over his or her own destiny, and that each has, at least in theory, the opportunity to become *the* prince for a finite period of time.

Mitterrand's socialist tendencies can be linked more directly to his religious
background than to his republicanism, in spite of the fact that he himself
explains it historically as an extension of his commitment to the values of the
eighteenth-century Enlightenment. Mitterrandian socialism is the secular man-
ifestation of the fervent provincial French Catholicism into which he was
born—in particular, of its tendency to scorn money not only as an end in itself
but also as a legitimate means to an end. Although early on in adult life
Mitterrand renounced the overt expression of religion, he has consistently
adhered to the moral values of his religious upbringing, particularly those associated with faithfulness, charity, and struggle.

How can this antimaterialistic, religious attitude be reconciled with the fact
that French Socialists are the secularists par excellence? Mitterrand has made
use of the socialist explanation of man and history whenever it has suited his

purpose, but has always left himself an out. In the same breath he can categorically reject dogmatism and totalizing theories while exploiting the dogmatists'
arguments. What attracts Mitterrand to socialism, which he considers primarily
an economic philosophy, is not its deterministic explanation of man and history
but its preoccupation with social justice, economic egalitarianism, generosity
(the secular version of religiously motivated charity), and the moral nobility of
the meek; the French president always prefers to side with the perceived underdog. It is with socialist sensitivities, which he feels are not present to a sufficient
degree on the political right, that Mitterrand identifies most, not with its socialist ideology. In his princely fashion, he has dominated Socialist ideology, tolerated it, used it for his own purposes, but he has never let it dominate him.

The contrast between Mitterrand's political philosophy and economic philosophy is very striking. The former is based on the strong belief that the individual should possess and fulfill extensive political responsibilities at many different levels of society (for example, unions, professional associations, communities, regions, the nation). The latter is focused on protecting individuals from
economic threats and risks, ensuring their standard of living, and providing for
their financial security; the government is expected to assume a greater and
greater role for the individual, whose own responsibility in these areas becomes
more and more indirect and minimal. Mitterrand's socialism is very paternalis-
tic.

Mitterrand's prepresidential career can be divided into two parts: (1) from
the World War II years to 1958 and (2) from 1958 to 1981. Initially, the future
Socialist president acted like a team player, functioning in relationship to a particular group such as a political party or a cabinet, and his struggles were mainly
electoral or, as a minister, administrative. But as the 1950s advanced, he began
to penetrate the political battle zone of decolonization. He did so not as a vanguard fighting for decolonization or as a defender of colonialism, but as a lonely
voice in favor of a compromise solution—he sought a reformed, federalist colonial structure. His calls for compromise and moderation were drowned out, and
de Gaulle returned to save the empire for the colonialists and to restore order.
At the top echelons of power, which Mitterrand had already reached by the end
of the Fourth Republic, only a few isolated Socialist and centrist leaders, plus
Mitterrand and the Communists, opposed de Gaulle's highly irregular resump-
tion of power, thereby consigning themselves to an indefinite internal political
exile.

In 1959 Mitterrand was not only in exile but in quarantine, considered
untouchable by both the right and the left. The right accused him of selling out;
by refusing to vote for de Gaulle's return, he had made it clear which side he
was on. But the non-Communist left would not have him either, for he had
dirtied his hands in the Algerian crisis and, as a "corrupt" Fourth Republic
politician, had committed other suspect political acts. Thus, he seemed to have
no place to go politically. Yet twelve years later he was head of the reconstructed
French Socialist Party and ten years after that president of the Republic. To

achieve this he fought battles continuously for over twenty years on three different fronts: (1) the Socialist front, to gain mastery over the mass of disorganized, contentious militants and voters; (2) on the Communist front, to avoid being outflanked on his left; and (3) on the right-left electoral front.

The issues have changed dramatically over the years, but it is clear that economic matters have increasingly dominated decisive national debates. Mitterrand has changed, too, but gradually. The year 1958 marked a turning point in French history, but Mitterrand audaciously broke ranks with the times in order to remain true to his republican convictions and, in a sense, to the past, to the Fourth Republic. His positions on various issues did evolve over the years; however, at any given moment in time he maintained a Pascalian *point fixe*, usually setting it out in the form of a written document, such as a treaty, a constitution, a program, or an accord. These are the rocks to which he clings as the political waves come crashing in, but he continues to move slowly from rock to rock.

## NOTES

1. Catherine Nay, *Le Noir et le rouge ou l'histoire d'une ambition* (The black and the red or the history of an ambitious man) (Paris: Grasset, 1984), p. 51.

2. Franz-Olivier Giesbert, *François Mitterrand ou la tentation de l'histoire* (François Mitterrand or the temptation of history) (Paris: Seuil, 1977), p. 9.

3. *Oxford English Dictionary* (New York: Oxford University Press, 1979).

4. Niccolò Machiavelli, *The Prince and the Discourses* (New York: The Modern Library/Random House, 1940), p. 96.

5. It is well known that Mitterrand is a great student of the Italian Renaissance and, in particular, of Lorenzo the Magnificent, the grandfather of the Lorenzo for whom *The Prince* was written.

6. Dominique Labbé, *François Mitterrand: Essai sur le discours* (Grenoble: La Pensée Sauvage, 1983), p. 74.

# François Mitterrand

# Prologue

## ALGIERS, DECEMBER 2, 1943

An escaped twenty-seven-year-old prisoner of war (POW), living under the name of Captain Morland, arrives in Algiers to meet the fifty-three-year-old leader of the Free French, the man of June 18, 1940, General Charles de Gaulle. A veteran of World War I, de Gaulle himself was once an escaped POW. The purpose of the meeting is to discuss the possibility of de Gaulle's taking control of the POW Resistance organization created by the young provincial from the department of Charente, whose real name is François Mitterrand. The interview lasts about forty-five minutes. One historian will characterize it as "glacial."[1]

The general first chides the escaped POW for arriving in Algiers in a British airplane (Mitterrand has come via London), then mocks his undertaking to organize the escaped POWs into an internal Resistance group, comparing it to organizing "Bretons, grocers, or butchers."[2] This is followed, however, by the general suggesting that this same network merge with another POW organization headed by de Gaulle's nephew, Michel Cailliau. Mitterrand does not refuse flatly, but asserts that this cannot be done without a vote by the POWs themselves. Mitterrand expresses his concern about agents provocateurs, informers, and the general problem of trust in such clandestine organizations in the interior. Although he promises to bring the issue to a vote, he does not guarantee its outcome.

De Gaulle would prefer to keep Mitterrand, who is rightfully suspected of being a Giraudist,[3] under close watch in Algiers and tries to impede his departure. But the three-time POW escapee succeeds in returning to Paris, and the promised vote is put not only to the "Pin' Mitt'" network, Mitterrand's organization,[4] but to a gathering of the representatives of all three important POW groups, including Michel Cailliau's organization and the National Front (the POW network controlled by the Communists). The inclusion of the Communists, vehemently opposed by Mitterrand, was Cailliau's idea, although Henri Frenay, de Gaulle's comissioner of POWs, will later blame Mitterrand.[5] Nevertheless, Cailliau's plan to submerge Mitterrand backfires. The latter, backed by Frenay, takes effective control of the new organization, the National Mouvement of POWs and Deportees (MNPGD). In an act of spite, Cailliau withdraws.

## PARIS, NINE MONTHS LATER

On August 24, 1944, de Gaulle returns to Paris and immediately goes to the Hôtel de Ville to greet the Parisians and his stand-in government, which he appointed from Algiers. Outside, the crowd is going wild, while inside, confusion reigns. As secretary-general and acting minister of war veterans, François Mitterrand is present. De Gaulle climbs onto a window ledge to shouts of "Vive de Gaulle!" and "Vive Leclerc!" (Many do not know which general is responsible for their deliriousness.) There is constant shoving from within. De Gaulle grabs the window casing and two men unseen by him, one of them Mitterrand, grab his legs, thereby preventing him from being pushed out of the window. Three days later, on August 27, de Gaulle officially receives his acting government. He shakes hands with each minister, asking his profession. To François Mitterrand, the youngest and last, he mutters, "You again!" and turns away.[6]

Several days later François Mitterrand is dismissed along with every other acting minister except two, Robert Lacoste and Alexandre Parodi. Thus ends François Mitterrand's active role in de Gaulle's provisional government, and thus begins the epic conflict between two great Machiavellians, one already well established and the other just beginning to carve out his destiny.

## NOTES

1. Claude Manceron, *Cent Mille Voix par jour* (A hundred thousand votes a day) (Paris: Laffont, 1966), p. 70. Manceron could only have known about this interview from Mitterrand himself.

2. Franz-Olivier Giesbert, *François Mitterrand ou la tentation de l'histoire* (François Mitterrand, or the temptation of history) (Paris: Seuil, 1977), p. 59.

3. General Henri Giraud (1879-1949), a Pétain loyalist, was copresident with de Gaulle of the French Committee of National Liberation in Algiers. Equipped and supported by the Americans and fiercely opposed by de Gaulle, he led the French Army in North Africa.

4. Maurice Pinot was commissioner of POWs in Vichy before the creation of Pierre Laval's government. Although a Pétainist, he opposed collaboration and went underground with Mitterrand after the Nazi occupation of the Free Zone. Together the two

men organized the largest POW Resistance organization.

5. Pierre Péan, *Une Jeunesse frânçaise* (A French youth) (Paris: Fayard, 1994), pp. 400, 407–8.

6. Giesbert, *François Mitterrand,* pp. 82-83.

# 1

## The Early Years, 1916–1944

In 1916 the Bolsheviks were preparing to take power in Moscow and tens of thousands of French and British soldiers were dying at Verdun defending France against German aggression in World War I. During that momentous year François Mitterrand was born in the small town of Jarnac about a hundred miles north of Bordeaux. Although practically every family suffered a human loss, that far corner of France was spared the thunder and carnage of the war. In the villages of southwestern France life went on in 1916—and for quite a while thereafter—much as it had in the nineteenth century. The sights and sounds of rural life and nature dominated the protected and pious nest in which the future president spent his childhood.[1]

Both of François's parents were devout Catholics as well as avid readers of secular literature. His father, Joseph, was a railroad employee who spent much of his time away from the family, staying for long periods in Angoulême, where he was station master. A taciturn man, he transported his "erudite library" from station to station.[2] When François was older, his father took over his in-laws' vinegar factory. His mother, Yvonne, of aristocratic background, bore Joseph five girls and three boys, François being the fifth child. She was an activist mother who carefully prepared each child's future. Coupled with her piety was a taste for writers of the romantic and postromantic eras such as Honoré de Balzac, François René de Chateaubriand, Alphonse de Lamartine, and Maurice Barrès, whose works she read aloud in the evening in addition to the newspapers of the day. She died when Mitterrand was twenty.

The Catholicism of François's parents did not most resemble the formalist, Jesuit tradition, but rather the more sober Jansenist one by which moral action mattered as much as obedience to rules.[3] Although they were pious, the members of François's immediate family were republican in politics; however, there were also some vociferous royalists in the Mitterrand extended family and social circle. Many devoutly Catholic families (including de Gaulle's) still felt nostalgia for the monarchy. Socialism and collectivist theories were roundly condemned. The elder Mitterrands' only apparent political activity was voting, politics being mainly a matter of discussion. Their social activism, as it was, was of a religious nature and consisted of regularly helping the poor in their community. François's father was a pillar of the Conférence St.-Vincent-de-Paul, a charitable organization, and his mother devoted a part of each day to the poor.[4]

Consistent with its preoccupation with poverty, the Mitterrand family displayed a corresponding moral disdain of wealth. As Mitterrand later recalled,

> One considered the hierarchies founded on money to be the worst sort of disorder. That money could take precedence over such values as fatherland, religion, liberty, dignity, revolted my family. It was the enemy, the corrupter one stayed away from.[5]

In France, as in Europe in general, the belief that money is fundamentally dirty has a long and complex history driven by both the teachings of the Catholic Church and the traditions of the aristocracy. Both traditions affected the Mitterrand family, and this belief stuck with Mitterrand throughout his life.

At the age of nine François was sent off to Angoulême to a Catholic boarding school for boys, the College of St. Paul, run by secular priests. This was normal procedure in a rural family that wished to prepare a child for a university education. Discipline at St. Paul's was relatively mild for a parochial school, but life was carefully regulated during the seven-month school year. The monkish routine was broken every year for five months when François returned home to enjoy rural summer life with a large tribe of siblings and cousins. François was an excellent student in the humanities, which the school emphasized; relatively little attention was paid to mathematics and the sciences.

During this eight-year period, the intellectually precocious François devoured books, assimilating much of the treasury of French literature. Blaise Pascal, Claude Saint-Simon, Romain Rolland, André Gide, Paul Valéry, Alfred de Vigny, Ferdinand Brunetière, the symbolists, Chateaubriand, Barrès, Stendhal, François Mauriac, Paul Claudel, Henri de Montherlant, and the contributors to the *Nouvelle Revue Française* were favorites. Mitterrand describes himself as studious, enthusiastic and dreamy during this period.[6] Others describe him as solitary, contemplative, shy, proud, and stubborn. He began thinking of becoming a writer, journalist, or statesman, three professions that have always been tightly intertwined in France, as the names on the young François's reading list suggest.

## FIRST STEPS INTO HISTORY

The train trip in September 1934 from Jarnac to Paris, where Mitterrand was to study law, represented not only a change in life-style and a new stage in life, but also a voyage in time. The train that deposited Mitterrand in the Latin Quarter of 1934 was a time machine that brought him out of the nineteenth century and into the twentieth. Adolf Hitler had just taken power; Benito Mussolini was ready to do so in Italy. The West was struggling with a worldwide depression. The French fascist leagues and Communist workers and students took to the streets regularly to fight out their political differences.

The provincial young man plunged into the ecstatic life of Paris with all the enthusiasm, energy, and curiosity of a brilliant eighteen-year-old; he brought with him firmly anchored activist Catholic values and the conviction that he would edify others through his example.[7] He soon adhered to a rightist political organization, the Volontaires nationaux, a student arm of Colonel François de La Roque's Croix-de-Feu.[8] François wrote that his political affiliation was made more out of necessity than desire—it was a way of establishing himself in the student community. Deeply patriotic, even chauvinistic, but still uncommitted, he was skeptical about politics as a worthwhile pursuit; he was neither a confirmed republican nor a declared antirepublican. Yet he was also irresistibly drawn to politics by virtue of its central position in public life—this was the area that captured everyone's attention. He actively participated (getting his picture on the front page of the newspaper twice) in two events emphatically on the wrong side of the barricades. First, he demonstrated against the presence of foreign students at the law school, and second, he protested against Professor Gaston Jèze, who had taken a public stand against Mussolini's takeover of Ethiopia (because Mitterrand believed that empire was part of the destiny of European nations, and he never questioned the means). By 1939 Mitterrand was serving as president of two distinct groups, the student section of the Conférence St.-Vincent-de-Paul and the literary section of the *Echo de Paris,* a right-wing newspaper for which he wrote a regular literary column. His primary interests were still activist Catholicism and literature, but he spontaneously identified with a politically reactionary milieu.

University life in France at this time did not require regular class attendance or daily study, since all hinged (and still does to a large extent) on successfully passing one set of examinations at the end of the school year. But the real school was the school of life to be found in the streets of Paris itself between All Saint's Day and Easter, and Mitterrand took full advantage of it: He attended political rallies of the right and the left, participated in demonstrations, conversed endlessly in the cafés, devoured books, read and wrote poetry, went to movies, concerts, the theater, parties, dances, played tennis, traveled home periodically, maintained a wide correspondence with friends, family, and former teachers in Angoulême, published newspaper articles, helped the poor in the suburbs of Paris, attended study groups, established social contacts of all sorts, and fell in love (with Marie-Louise Terrasse, known today as Catherine Langeais, a French television celebrity). His correspondence reveals that at times he was bothered by this breathless existence.

Mitterrand found life in Paris exhilarating but also felt the need to find some unifying purpose in his diverse activities. He wrote to his sister that he did not like being the "plaything of the outer world."[9] This letter also reveals his efforts to attain moral mastery over himself. The influence of Pascal is striking; the seventeenth-century moralist argued that man must always choose between uncertainties; that struggle is inherently morally noble; and that only spiritual love can provide the force necessary for the difficult tasks of life.[10] Mitterrand was a very earnest young man.

> Everything boils down to this: win or lose. One can never stay in the same place. . . . All morality rests on the value of each act. Anything that requires effort is great; only this effort is hard—what can help us to produce it? Only love. . . . Either one lives in the world or outside of it. If one doesn't reject it, it must be accepted. You have to want to conquer it.[11]

Through the Parisian maze Mitterrand carried his copy of Pascal's *Pensées*. On a questionnaire he indicated that the two works he would take to the army with him would be that one and Rabelais's "Abbaye de Thélème" (a Renaissance man's manifesto). (In fact, he took the *Pensées* and the *Imitatio Christi*, the medieval work on piety often attributed in the past to Thomas à Kempis. Later, he also named his firstborn—who lived only three months—Pascal.) But Mitterrand was determined to achieve a synthesis of the Christian and the worldly. Departing from Pascal and picking up Stendhal, Mitterrand's decision to accept the world as it was automatically meant, not changing it, but conquering it, making the spiritual and moral Pascalian quest appear to be a means to a temporal end.

The first political event to which Mitterrand deeply reacted was Hitler's annexation of Austria. He struggled with the age-old Machiavellian problem of reconciling Christian morality with politics, war, and diplomacy:

> In politics, only two approaches are conceivable: total surrender or absolute force. Surrender, which sacrifice requires, would be the most beautiful sign of grandeur. Individuals sometimes know how to sacrifice. . . . But voluntary renunciation, this offering of the right cheek after a slap on the left, is unknown to nations and really risks remaining so for a long time.[12]

This twenty-two-year-old understood both the temptations and dangers of accommodation, leading him to conclude that the highest political morality required the use of force—and the sooner the better:

> In the life of nations, as well as in the life of individuals, every retreat is a lost battle. A strategic retreat always masks a defeat; and the explanations meant to diminish the fault tend to define its causes; to reject responsibilities does not change the fact that man from his first fall pronounces his own condemnation.[13]

This article also reflects Mitterrand's visceral anguish and repugnance at the idea of yet another bloody conflict and the premonition of its inevitability.[14] The final words are those of a serious young man who feels morally implicated in all that goes on around him: "I know what sacrilege is being prepared, and in spite of myself, I feel a sort of shame, as if I were responsible."[15]

Mitterrand's studies led to two law degrees, a diploma in political science, a one-year certificate in sociology and another in French literature; he had begun a doctorate when he was called into the army.[16]

## SOLDIER, PRISONER OF WAR, ANTI-COLLABORATIONIST

In September 1938 Mitterrand was drafted into the 23rd Colonial Infantry Regiment, stationed just outside Paris. He rejected officer training mainly because that would have meant leaving the Paris region and Marie-Louise.[17] Eventually, he was assigned to second-class officer training and promoted to the rank of quartermaster-sergeant *(sergeant-chef)*.

A year later, England and France declared war on Germany, and Mitterrand was transferred to the Maginot Line, where the "Funny War" began. Mitterrand resented the fact that part of the army was digging antitank ditches all day while another part played cards or soccer or drank. He showed himself to be unsubmissive, even insolent. The detached, sophisticated political philosopher of the Latin Quarter soon became a soldier in spite of himself, with his primary concerns now revolving around the injustices and indignities of army life and the more general social injustices they represented to him.

> What would bother me, would be to die for values *(anti-values) that I don't believe in.* So I'm making a deal with myself. I'm deciding to live, God willing. I'm deciding that the cold and the mud must be tolerated. . . . I'm deciding *a debt must be paid.* [emphasis added][18]

It is not at all clear what precise values, other than military, he is referring to here. Nevertheless, he still feels that there is a "debt" he must pay; this idea of personal responsibility for historical events becomes a veritable idée fixe.

On May 10, 1940, the war in France began in earnest, and Mitterrand found himself in the midst of it near Verdun. For a month and four days he experienced the carnage, death, chaos, and terror of conventional warfare. Eventually, on June 14, the same day the Germans entered Paris, he was wounded, knocked out by the blast of a *Minnenwerfer,* and was carried for two days through the battle zone and then, as the French army retreated, from military hospital to military hospital.[19] One day he woke up to find German instead of French attendants. He was now a prisoner of war on his way to the Stalag 9A POW camp near Kassel in Hesse.

Wherever two Frenchmen find themselves, it is not unlikely that some kind of magazine will soon appear. So, in Stalag 9A (where Red Cross standards seem to have been respected for French POWs) *L'Ephémère* (The ephemeral) sprang up, and in it could be found the writings of Mitterrand. The Germans eventually discovered this sheet and suppressed it, but the copies that survived shed light on the conditions and state of mind of the prisoners. In those pages Mitterrand described the grueling POW experience, yet these emotions never gave way to despair. On the contrary, the young moralist seemed to look on the experience as his first serious test.[20] What the battlefront experience could not trigger in him one year of captivity did. He was no longer an individual resigned to his historical fate. Endless political discussions in the camps about which path France should take after the war not only helped pass the time, but generated in him new hope and the will to act.

At no point did Mitterrand believe that the Germans would not eventually be driven from France, and he now believed firmly that he would be a part of that process and the rebuilding of France. There was no question of resigning oneself to spending the years of struggle in a prison camp. Many prisoners managed to escape, and Mitterrand intended to be one of them. In fact, he escaped three times. The first two times he was caught; the third time he was successful.

But during the long hours of camp boredom, before his successful escape, Mitterrand's thoughts constantly turned to political philosophy, which he could only approach as the moralist that he was at heart. He took up the same maxims he had adopted before France's entry into the war and applied them to his camp situation to find the rudiments of a political philosophy. More than ever he was convinced that the improvement of society depended on the efforts of individuals and not on the belief in any -ism.[21] Mitterrand was apparently resisting many arguments put forth by his comrades. In other passages he describes how the prisoners chose leaders among themselves and how they developed a social contract of their own. The experience of captivity in a POW camp, a kind of sociopolitical microcosm evolving from scratch before his eyes, only served to reinforce his moral philosophy based on the primacy of the individual.

A passage written shortly after his escape, which describes how his transfer by cattle car as a POW followed the same route as Napoleon's march eastward—an irony not lost on the young humanist who had absorbed his history lessons well—develops more precisely the idea of France's "debt," or moral responsibility, for the war. He grapples constantly with the question: How did this all come about?

> France, in nourishing Europe with her fraternal ambitions, in imposing her warrior ardor, by spreading blood beyond her borders and in order to obtain impossible borders, had exhausted herself. I bore a grudge against this triumphal history which preceded unavoidably that slow march of a generation in cattle cars. I discerned the logic of events and asked myself if it was just that our misery was payment for misunderstood glories, or more exactly if it was just that

our downfall was imputed to us because, although we had abandoned our arms, all the rest had already been taken from us. I thought about the judgments that will condemn our debacle; people will incriminate the weakened regime. . . . Will they condemn the glorious errors?[22]

Hitler, then, is seen in part as Germany's answer to Napoleon, who, despite the "splendor," "glory," and "fraternal ambitions" he evoked, also made "errors" and ultimately brought about more "misery" than he was worth. Although each dictator left behind radically different legacies, both were arrogant expansionists and natural products of basically the same politicomilitary culture. If Napoleon had not existed, if the Treaty of Versailles and French foreign policy in the 1930s had been different, the war might have been avoided. But now, in Biblical fashion, the sons had to pay for the sins of their fathers. Mitterrand seemed so obsessed with the idea of individual and national responsibility that he gave practically no attention to the wrongs of Germany and the evils of Hitler, to which he rarely referred directly.

Although his explanation of the war never changed, Mitterrand's state of mind altered drastically during captivity. Thirteen days before his second escape attempt, his transformation from indifferent, bitter soldier to passionate patriot seemed complete. He rejected the role of rebel that some captives assumed. Having paid his share of the debt incurred by previous generations, he felt reborn and anxious to participate in the rebirth of France.[23] Just weeks later, by New Years Day 1942, after a third daring escape, Mitterrand was back in Jarnac, in the Occupied Zone, at the end not only of a long physical trial but also of a period of prolonged reflection. There was no shift in values, but an intensification of previously held ones. His return to France also confirmed a bitter premonition—Marie-Louise was no longer his.

Mitterrand's activities between the time of his return from captivity in January 1942 and the Liberation in August 1944 mark his steady ascent in the POW milieu as it evolved under the auspices of the Vichy government. Although his interests were more oriented toward social work than politics, he uncritically put his faith in Marshal Philippe Pétain and his corporatist National Revolution.

After a few weeks of rest, a family member obtained a low-level job for Mitterrand in Vichy at the French Legion of Soldiers. (From the beginning, family contacts with influential government officials frequently played a crucial role in Mitterrand's ability to network.) The Legion was a propaganda group promoting the National Revolution. Feeling useless (not disgusted),[24] Mitterrand resigned in April, shortly after the Germans had forced the reinstallation of Pierre Laval as vice premier. Soon Mitterrand was offered the choice of two jobs: one at the Commissariat for Prisoners of War; the other at the Commissariat for Jewish Questions, whose function was to implement the anti-Jewish laws of the National Revolution. This is proof, if need there be, of Mitterrand's awareness of the anti-Semitic nature of Pétainist ideology (in addition, his sister, Marie-Josèphe, was intimately involved with a former Cagoulard,[25] Jean Bouvyer, who would soon be an employee of this department in Paris). Furthermore, the two offers presumably reflect either what was thought to interest Mitterrand or what he was best qualified to do.

## MITTERRAND AND THE PRISONERS OF WAR

Mitterrand accepted the first offer, at the Commissariat for POWs, where he became head of publications. He wrote propaganda, censured articles, and created radio broadcasts promoting loyalty to Marshal Pétain aimed at repatriated and escaped POWs. In addition to his official duties, he engaged in extensive parallel activities involving making contacts with escaped POWs, falsifying identification papers for them, organizing them, and helping them find jobs. (One naturally wonders if some of the jobs offered to the POWs were not some of those taken away from the Jews.) All of these activities were known and approved of by Marshal Pétain, but not by Laval.

While the Vichy government under Laval was collaborating more and more with the Germans, Mitterrand remained uncritically faithful to Pétain. In January 1943 Mitterrand's mentor at the Commissariat, Maurice Pinot, was fired and replaced by a pro-Laval administrator, André Masson. Mitterrand and dozens of others quit in protest. Very soon Pinot and Mitterrand established contact with the pro-Pétain, anticollaborationist Resistance Army Organization (ORA) faithful to General Henri Giraud and Pétain; extensive but unofficial links were maintained with the Vichy government for the purpose of obtaining information. By March 1943 Mitterrand had established links with all the principal POW organizations associated with Vichy but also with the group led by Michel Cailliau, de Gaulle's nephew; this group was already closely associated with the various Resistance movements.

Conflict over strategy and personal rivalry between Cailliau and Mitterrand arose immediately. Cailliau advocated aggressive resistance, sabotage, close cooperation with the internal Resistance movements and political subordination to de Gaulle, all unacceptable to Mitterrand who insisted on less risky social work (such as aiding ex-POWs in finding jobs, lodging, etc.), information gathering, and independence of any group with a definite political commitment other than Pétainist. During this period he met with Henri Frenay, de Gaulle's commissioner of POWs from Algiers whose confidence he gained—Frenay was not impressed with the rash Cailliau. This later proved to be an important factor in the Mitterrand-Cailliau struggle for power. But Mitterrand's financial and material support still came from the Giraudist ORA, which was in turn financed by the English.

In the summer of 1943 Mitterrand engaged in open protest of Masson's leadership of POWs at two large public meetings, calling approving attention to himself from both Resistance groups and Pétain's personal entourage but dangerous notice from Laval, Masson, and the Germans. Henceforth, Mitterrand operated simultaneously on three different levels: (1) the official level represented by his work at the Allier Mutual Aid Center for POWS, covered by Pétain, (2) his parallel activities of organizing and protecting POWs, approved by the Pétain entourage, and (3) clandestine acts, or his progressive association with both Cailliau's group and Giraud's ORA, which involved some military training for his followers. Mitterrand was in contact with virtually every prisoner and Resistance movement with direct links to the Marshal, de Gaulle, or the Resistance, shunning only the group dominated by Communists. Playing a triple game, he was consciously preparing his entry into French history, prudently leaving the eviction of the enemy to others better equipped. By November 1943 his identity had been discovered and the Gestapo was actively tracking him.

In the fall of 1943 Mitterrand finally accepted the idea that he had put his faith in the wrong man. Pétain was obviously powerless. Giraud had recently severed all ties with the Marshal, but at the same time it was now obvious that Giraud himself had lost the power struggle with de Gaulle in Algiers. Out of necessity, Mitterrand also broke with Vichy and decided that it was time to obtain recognition and support from de Gaulle. He wanted this, however, without submitting to de Gaulle's authority—a feasible plan with the support of Frenay. He was also determined to remove Cailliau from any effective leadership role in a future federation of POW groups. Through Frenay, the meeting in Algiers described in the Prologue took place in December 1943 and Mitterrand achieved his goals. It was also during his stay in Algiers that Mitterrand met Pierre Mendès France for the first time, and he admired him from the start.[26]

In spite of Frenay's support, other Gaullists did everything in their power to impede Mitterrand's return to France. Even with the aid of the Giraudist network, it took weeks before Mitterrand arrived back in France, via England, to take the situation back in hand. In March 1944 the fusion of the "Pin' Mitt'," Gaullist, and Communist networks took place. The resulting National Prisoner of War and Deportee Movement (MNPGD) was financed by the National Resistance Council (CNR), the unified internal Resistance movement, which was Gaullist in political orientation (the CNR was headed first by Jean Moulin and, after his execution by the Gestapo, by Georges Bidault). Mitterrand, the faithful Pétainist, was now a Gaullist in spite of himself.

At the orders of Frenay, Mitterrand was assigned the primary leadership role and Cailliau a secondary one, but de Gaulle's POW commissioner was furious about the inclusion of the Communists and unjustly blamed Mitterrand for it. As could be expected, the entry of the Communists radically altered the political equation; now the struggle for influence shifted to the Communist-Mitterrandian opposition.

Mitterrand was present at the Liberation of Paris. On the morning of

August 20, 1944, he walked into the POW commissioner's Paris office and ejected at gunpoint Commissioner Moreau, Masson's collaborationist replacement; at noon, he lunched with a longtime family friend, the royalist mother of Jean Bouvyer whom he once described in a letter as one of his best friends.[27] Mitterrand's continuous connection with these old family friends with such dishonorable associations highlights the most disturbing feature of Mitterrand's war record; that is, his acceptance of the anti-Semitic nature of the National Revolution. Though unaware of Hitler's "final solution" until the end of the war, Mitterrand obviously knew of the open and active anti-Semitism of the pre-Laval Vichy regime—it was an integral part of the National Revolution that he had worked hard to promote, and he knew many who worked at the Commissariat for Jewish Questions. Though he might well have had inner reservations about certain aspects of this Revolution, he never expressed them publicly or, apparently, privately; he obviously believed that loyalty and unity behind the Marshal were the supreme requirements of the moment. Mitterrand was no worse than most, but Mitterrand the pretentious, rigorous, Jansenist moralist, who had long since felt called by God and history, is not to be compared to "most."

The Vichy government made regular, sincere, and mildly effectual efforts to defend the interests of the 1.8 million POWs in German stalags. As we have seen, there was even some contact between the POWs and France: letters were written, packages sent, and the Vichy government itself encouraged the creation of several prisoner organizations. But it is well established that Vichy made no similar gestures to help the Jews, in spite of Pétain and Laval's later claims at their defense trials. The Vichy government rendered life intolerable for the Jews of France—and not just refugee Jews. On its own initiative, starting in 1940, Vichy banned or severely limited to tiny quotas Jewish participation in the major sectors of French public, economic, and cultural life. It set up internment camps for "superfluous" foreign workers (both Jewish and non-Jewish). It accepted the expropriation by the Nazis of the property of French Jews in the Occupied Zone, protesting only the "Germanization" of this property, and then worked to gain control over it itself—efforts in which Bouvyer actively took part.[28] (Later, in the Unoccupied Zone, Vichy took over Jewish property directly.) During Mitterrand's tenure in Vichy, the government allowed and cooperated in the deportation of 65,000 Jews (most of them were foreign-born, but among those there were many naturalized French citizens whose citizenship had been revoked by the Vichy government; others were political refugees or pariahs from the East) in addition to 6,000 non-Jewish Frenchmen. Vichy did resist handing over French-Jewish World War I veterans and long-established, assimilated French-Jewish families. Its aim was not genocide, "only" cultural conformity. Nonetheless, its actions facilitated the pursuit and partial success of Hitler's "final solution."[29]

Considering Mitterrand's deep involvement in the events of the times, it is astonishing that his available writings contain no direct or explicit reference to the persecution of Jews as Jews in France during or after the war. Logically, the Jews could be included in the category of the deported, but the "D" in MNPGD did not refer to them but to deported workers. Several hundred thousand workers were sent to Germany, but their fate was generally not tragic. Most returned to France whereas only 3,000 of the 65,000 deported Jews left Germany alive after the war. Mitterrand cannot be accused of ever expressing anti-Semitic sentiments or personally condoning anti-Semitic policies or acts, and since the war years, he has on many occasions demonstrated sympathy for the Jewish people. Yet it is remarkable not to find, even after the war, evidence of explicit criticism of Vichyite measures aimed specifically at Jews, in particular those in the unoccupied zone, where they were under the authority—and presumably the protection—of the French state.[30] One of the risks of leaving behind so voluminous a written record of one's thoughts is that the neglect of such a compelling issue can be taken as evidence of one's indifference. Unquestionably, the POWs constituted the group with which Mitterrand most strongly identified, and he apparently felt little empathy for those whose suffering was beyond his personal experience. Also, no doubt because of the number of POWs, Mitterrand attributed tremendous political importance (which he overestimated) to the POW movement.

What is even more disturbing and puzzling is Mitterrand's continued personal association with or emotional loyalty to several individuals who dishonored themselves during the Vichy years, in particular René Bousquet (secretary-general of the police who was largely responsible for the deportation of thousands of Jews, including children) and his Vichy entourage (which Mitterrand employed in his Interior Ministry in the 1950s),[31] Jean Bouvyer, and Pétain himself, on whose grave Mitterrand has had a wreath placed annually since his death. The initial contacts can be attributed to family connections, historical circumstances, the need to gather information, or simple curiosity. But the personal loyalty that Mitterrand demonstrated to these figures throughout his life points toward a particular ethos—one based on a mix of absolute family or fraternal solidarity and Christian piety that dictates that one never abandon a lost sheep, especially one who has erred "sincerely."

Oddly, sincerity, or the strength of one's convictions, replaces the objective nature of an act itself as the criterion by which an individual's innocence or guilt is judged. For Mitterrand, the fact that one is "cultivated" can also attenuate immorality or criminality. Wrongs become "mistakes." Loyalty and forgiveness, convenient virtues, cover stubborn pride—for a man like Mitterrand it is hard to admit that one and one's friends were wrong. Also, loyalty toward Mitterrand goes a long way toward redemption.

## MARRIAGE

In the midst of his clandestine activities Mitterrand chose a wife. He saw a photograph of Danielle Gouze on a piano in a Paris apartment and decided then and there to marry her; she was nineteen years old. There was no time to spend on courtship during those unpredictable times. The two met a month after Mitterrand saw the photo, became engaged a month later, and were married in the fall of 1944. Very proud of his fiancée, Mitterrand used to introduce her by saying, "I'd like you to meet my anticlerical, democratic, and socialist fiancée."[32] The socialist label did not seem to bother the moralist; on the contrary, it is clear that Danielle's political pedigree impressed the as yet politically vague but adaptable young Mitterrand.

Danielle Mitterrand is, in fact, the daughter of anticlerical, socialist parents, both educators who lived in Cluny (in Burgundy) during the war. Because Monsieur Gouze was openly opposed to the Pétain government, he was dismissed from his academic position, causing the Gouze family great physical hardship. The Gouzes regularly gave shelter to Resistance leaders and held meetings at their home. For two months Danielle nursed wounded *Maquis* (Resistance fighters who suffered severe retaliation after attacking the Germans in the area too soon before D-Day) in an abandoned castle, for which, at the age of nineteen, she received the Medal of the Resistance. Thus, not only her politics but also her "activist" character were attractive to Mitterrand. Whereas Mitterrand himself "is not one of those who are on the left even before they realize it,"[33] Madame Mitterrand claims to have been there "instinctively."[34] Personally, she has been more intransigently to the left than her husband, but she has never been active in political life.

## MITTERRAND AND THE RESISTANCE

It was during these years that Mitterrand became disillusioned with the Church and open to a wide range of new ideas (although he continued to attend mass as late as the 1950s). During his POW and especially his later Resistance experiences he came into contact with a cross-section of French society that exposed him to ideas and types of people that he had never taken seriously before. Always intellectually curious, receptive, and vulnerable, Mitterrand began to reconsider the secularist and socialist ideas that permeated many of the Resistance groups, including his own. Besides, the National Revolution was obviously over, and Mitterrand had lost faith in the Church as a force for social and historical change; an ideological vacuum had to be filled.

The winter and spring of 1944 were the hottest months for the Resistance leaders on the Gestapo's hit list, including Mitterrand, and he narrowly escaped being caught just five days before D-Day.[35] After the Allies had landed and as the Germans were slowly pushed back, another wave of violence—a new reign of terror, of Frenchman against Frenchman—swept over France. Spontaneous revenge led to improvised legal procedures to mete out swift punishment to those thought to be collaborators. Mitterrand is remembered for his spirit of clemency during this time. His forgiving inclinations preserved him from easy vengeance. He refused to allow the liquidation of "S"—someone suspected of betraying Mitterrand to the Gestapo—asserting that there was insufficient evidence, and two cowardly caretakers, stating that "they must be miserable enough as it is."[36] Amid this madness, he retained his moral and legal scruples. As the spirit of revenge infected the POW movement, Mitterrand wrote to his troops:

> Let our minds be firm enough to accept the struggle and necessary sacrifices; let them be flexible enough also to remain faithful to the reality of our history. Though plunged in a whirlwind of ambition and calculation, France must keep a cool head.[37]

The historian Robert Aron gives Mitterrand credit for limiting the damage: "In Vichy among the Resistance organizations it was mainly the escaped POW movement, led by Mitterrand, that . . . assumed leadership of the crackdowns. It was, in general, not very bloody." But still bloody, one is led to presume, and one wonders, exactly what role Mitterrand played in these spontaneous purges.

Meanwhile, in Algiers, de Gaulle had approved a list of secretaries-general to act as temporary ministers in Paris until his government-in-exile could be transported from Algiers; he wanted to minimize the chances of a Communist takeover. Mitterrand was on this list as secretary-general of war veterans. Shortly after de Gaulle's return, however, Mitterrand was dismissed along with most of the other acting ministers, and Henri Frenay, a loyal Gaullist, was appointed minister of veterans. Frenay offered Mitterrand a permanent position as the secretary-general of his ministry, a fine beginning for an ambitious twenty-eight-year-old man coming out of the war. But Mitterrand refused the job. Clearly, he was not a bureaucrat but rather an independent-minded man of action. Furthermore, he was unwilling to give his loyalty to de Gaulle, which the position presumed, not because de Gaulle was insufficiently republican (at this juncture, his credentials in that department were better than Mitterrand's) but because Mitterrand required his own power base and independence. As important as a secretary-general might be, he takes orders from above; a "prince" never does.

Mitterrand found himself, politically speaking, in much the same delicate situation within France as France did within the realm of international power politics. Adrift, Mitterrand sought his own direction on the high seas of French politics, which were then dominated by Gaullists and Communists; caught between the United States and Soviet Union, France floundered about in the middle, searching for its own distinct democratic model.

For the moment, the MNPGD was the only group with which Mitterrand strongly identified, and it was also his only quasi-political affiliation. His POW movement was still politically ecumenical, including Gaullists, Socialists, Communists, their sympathizers, and all sorts of unaffiliated persons. A spirit of lighthearted, even joyous anarchy infused the ranks of the POWs, no matter what their political tendency, and youthful fraternity precluded the development of political tensions—for a while; however, the group was not politically governable. Nonetheless, it did possess a kind of emotional and moral unity that Mitterrand supported and promoted by writing articles in one of the POW publications called *L'Homme libre* (The free man). He rallied his comrades with uplifting words of encouragement in an effort to help them reinterpret their experience of captivity. For in spite of the joyful fraternity, many of the POWs suffered from a complex mixture of feelings, including guilt, bitterness, and a sense of failure. Mitterrand fought their demoralization.

For his role in the Resistance, Mitterrand received three awards: the Legion of Honor, the Croix de Guerre (war cross), and the Rosette of the Resistance. Probably because he had already displayed too much political independence of de Gaulle, Mitterrand did not, however, receive de Gaulle's Compagnon de la Libération award. (Many of those who did receive it had never lived in France under the occupation or the Vichy government.) In 1969, Mitterrand offered an explanation for this omission:

> The Gaullist dictionary, imitating the Stalinist dictionary, scratched out the pages that told the true story of the struggle against the enemy and identified service rendered to General de Gaulle with service rendered to France, while service rendered to France that did not contribute to the glory of General de Gaulle was deemed negligible if not suspect.

Mitterrand's political adversaries have made much of the fact that the Vichy government awarded Mitterrand the Francisque. Individuals who were judged to have served Pétain and the National Revolution in some special fashion received this award. Mitterrand received his in the spring of 1943 for his work in the Allier POW aid society. Accepting the award was awkward, but refusing it could have been dangerous. Mitterrand wore his cheerfully, as a joke—it was part provocation, part camouflage. In later years the Gaullists, despite de Gaulle's commendation of Mitterrand in his memoirs, and the Communists, who did not enter the Resistance until the Soviet Union was invaded, would try to exploit Mitterrand's having received this award. It is one of several sources of calumny that have plagued Mitterrand throughout his life and have greatly contributed to his political defiance and determination.

## NOTES

1. François Mitterrand, *Ma Part de vérité* (My share of the truth) (Paris: Fayard, 1969), pp. 19–20.

2. Claude Manceron, *Cent Mille Voix par jour* (A hundred thousand votes a day) (Paris: Laffont, 1966), p. 34.

3. The term *Jansenist* refers to the current in French Catholicism that developed, along with the Counter-Reformation, in the seventeenth century. Though the official movement was considered heretical by the Church and finally eliminated by the monarchy, Jansenist inspiration survived and spread throughout French society.

4. Franz-Olivier Giesbert, *François Mitterrand ou la tentation de l'histoire* (François Mitterrand or the temptation of history) (Paris: Seuil, 1977), p. 18.

5. Mitterrand, *Ma Part*, p. 252.

6. François Mitterrand, *Politique* (Paris: Fayard, 1977), p. 16.

7. Pierre Péan's *Une Jeunesse française* (A French youth) (Paris: Fayard, 1994), which came out several weeks after this book went into production, effectively fills in the previously large gaps in the public record of Mitterrand's life spanning the years 1934–1947, rectifies several factual errors, and dispels various rumors.

8. Colonel de La Roque was politically committed to the right but was not antirepublican.

9. Roland Cayrol, *François Mitterrand 1945–1967* (Paris: Fondation Nationale des Sciences Politiques, 1967), p. 25.

10. Blaise Pascal (1623–1662) was a Christian moralist linked to the Jansenist movement whose collection of aphorisms known as *Les Pensées* has become a classic of French literature. Mitterrand was strongly influenced by this work.

11. Giesbert, *François Mitterrand*, p. 26.

12. Mitterrand, "Jusqu'ici et pas plus loin" (Up to here and no farther), *Revue Montalembert*, April 1938, cited in Mitterrand, *Politique*, p. 4.

13. Ibid., pp. 4–5.

14. Ibid., p. 6.

15. Ibid.

16. Cayrol, *François Mitterrand*, p. 7.

17. Péan, *Une Jeunesse française*, p. 95.

18. Giesbert, *François Mitterrand*, p. 33.

19. There is a discrepancy in dates between Manceron's and Giesbert's versions. I have used Manceron's; see Manceron, *Cent Mille Voix*, p. 48.

20. Mitterrand, *Politique*, pp. 9–10.

21. Ibid., pp. 8–9.

22. Ibid., p. 14.

23. Ibid., pp. 10–11.

24. Péan, *Une Jeunesse française*, p. 118.

25. The Cagoule was an illegal, extreme right, paramilitary, terrorist organization active in the 1930s. Their members were antirepublican, anticommunist, and anti-Semitic—in short, pure fascists. In addition, as individuals in their various official capacities they played an active role in turning power over to Pétain and promoted the National Revolution; their declared enemies were then Gaullists, Communists, Masons, and Jews. Mitterrand had numerous social contacts in this group before, during, and after the war.

26. Pierre Mendès France (1907–1982) was one of the most admired French statesmen in postwar France. A lawyer and economist by training, he was elected deputy in

1932 on a Radical-socialist ticket. He joined de Gaulle's Free French at the beginning of World War II, and in 1953 he became prime minister. In or out of power, he served until his death as France's conscience.

27. Péan, *Une Jeunesse française*, p. 108.

28. Ibid., p. 226.

29. Robert Paxton, *Vichy France: Old Guard, New Order 1940–1944* (New York: Columbia University Press, 1982), pp. 168–84.

30. The author has been in contact with Georgette Elgey, historian and technical advisor to President Mitterrand, and because of her help has received information from the Elysée Palace. However, the author's request for enlightenment on this matter has gone unanswered.

31. Péan, *Une Jeunesse française*, p. 320. It is worth noting that in 1986 Mitterrand, Georgette Elgey, and René Bousquet all attended the small, private funeral of Jean-Paul Martin, Bousquet's friend and former assistant in the Vichy Ministry of the Interior. (Ibid., p. 318.)

32. Manceron, *Cent Mille Voix*, p. 82.

33. Ibid., p. 49.

34. Ibid., p. 76.

35. Giesbert, *François Mitterrand*, pp. 76–78.

36. Ibid., p. 79.

37. Ibid., p. 79.

38. Robert Aron, cited in Manceron, *Cent Mille Voix*, p. 82.

39. Mitterrand, *L'Homme libre*, Aug. 22, 1944, cited in Mitterrand, *Politique*, pp. 18–19.

40. Mitterrand, *Ma Part*, p. 30.

41. Cayrol, *François Mitterrand*, p. 8.

42. Péan, *Une Jeunesse française*, p. 295.

# 2

## A Young Minister at the Beginning of the Cold War

Journalism was the natural recourse for the ejected provisional minister of POWs. Already an experienced writer and political commentator, Mitterrand had by 1945 begun to work in a recognizable pattern of alternating periods of political action and political "witnessing." This pattern reflected a similar one in the career of de Gaulle, but since the political purposes of these two men were almost always radically opposite, when one moved up on the wheel of fortune, the other moved down. Mitterrand wrote for and edited *L'Homme libre* (The free man), later called *Libres,* the principal publication of the POWs, who were still his primary audience. The frustrated activist took his role of witness very seriously. Not content to be merely an objective observer of events, and being fully aware of the power of the word, he actively strove to influence the opinions and behavior of his readers.

For Mitterrand, the two most compelling spectacles of the Provisional Government period were the purge trials, in which Pétain, Laval, and others faced the accusing Gaullist state, and the debates of the Provisional Consultative Assembly where delegates were trying to chart a new course for French democracy. The young journalist found both of these processes more disquieting than regenerating, and his analyses revealed his own judgments of the wartime actors on one hand and his reactions to the constitutional dilemmas on the other.

The purge trials of Pétain and Laval crystallized public attitudes toward the principal wartime parties. Mitterrand devised his own moral ranking of the protagonists. This guilt-to-innocence spectrum started with Laval and his associates, ranged down through the establishment collaborators (such as the military police and the auto maker Renault), black market profiteers, submissive journalists, Third Republic defeatists (including Edouard Daladier and Edouard Her-

riot), the *attentistes* (those who waited the war out sitting on the fence), sincere
Pétainists, with whom Mitterrand had family and social connections (he neither
condemned nor defended Pétain himself), Free France (de Gaulle's movement
operating from outside metropolitan France), and the nonmilitary Internal
National Resistance Movement and the Internal French Forces (the domestic
military Resistance organization), and ended with the POWs, the deportees,
and the war dead. Not everyone's ranking resembled Mitterrand's. The
Gaullists claimed a higher position for themselves than Mitterrand gave them,
and the Communists displayed more wrath against cooperative journalists and
less against black marketeers (which invites speculation about some of the
Communists' wartime activities).

Mitterrand knew that there was a difference between justice and revenge
and that even among the collaborators there were nuances, various levels of
guilt, and moral distinctions to be made. The POW leader had no pity, however, for the German people—they deserved whatever reprisals would fall on
them.[1] Yet in the moral swamp of purge trials and reprisals, it was no longer a
time for fervor but rather for cool-headedness and restraint:

> Let us beware in our turn. Though we may accept the necessary methods, let us
> not get carried away by them. So often, actions end up by taking command of
> the mind. . . . The Resistance was much more than a refusal to see green uni-
> forms on our soil; it was also a refusal of the ways of war.[2]

The POW organization was still the only group with which Mitterrand
identified. In spite of the facts that few members were organizationally active
and that once peace had returned they shared only narrow, material interests,
they were strongly united emotionally, like most war veterans who have suffered
together. Politically, they could agree on only one thing—what they did *not*
want, which was a return to the Constitution of 1875. Mitterrand's own state of
mind at this time seems to have corresponded to the POWs' collective state of
mind; he knew more precisely what he did not want for France than what he
did want.

As the postwar examination of wartime activities yielded to discussions of
the future constitution, Mitterrand continued to chronicle and comment upon
the rapid turn of events. In particular, his writings represent an effort to clarify
for the POWs what was happening in the Provisional Consultative Assembly,
appointed by de Gaulle upon his return to Paris. The public debates concerning
these matters, which Mitterrand attended regularly, provided an extensive education in practical politics. Here he discovered the causal relationships, based on
party self-interest, between the political situation of each party and the constitutional positions it espoused. For example, the Radical Party preferred the
one-name ballot system reminiscent of the Constitution of 1875 because that
system favored the local notables who made up a large part of their party. (In
the one-name ballot system, each department is divided into several arrondisse-

ments, and each party puts up only one candidate for deputy.)[3] The "mass parties" preferred proportional list balloting because it highlighted platforms rather than local individuals, and it gave minority parties more influence than a majority system would. (In this system each party presents a list of candidates, frequently unknown in the area, to the whole department; they all subscribe to the same party platform. The number of deputies that a party will send to the National Assembly depends on the percentage of votes that the list receives and the number of seats that department is allocated.) The Provisional Government preferred majority list balloting (whereby all the candidates on the list become deputies of a given department if their party wins over 50 percent of the vote) because that would have strengthened its influence within the National Assembly.

Members of the government also wanted a presidential system whereby the two chambers of Parliament, the National Assembly and the Senate, would be subservient to the executive branch but would possess equal power; they thought that this system would divide and weaken the opposition. For the same reason, the Radicals, mass parties, and Resistance groups favored a parliamentary system whereby the executive branch would have to answer to the legislative branch and the "more democratic" (more representative of the population at large) chamber of deputies (the National Assembly) would dominate the "less democratic" Senate; the party bosses naturally feared the unwieldy dominance of the National Assembly less than a dictatorship of a strong executive.[4] Each party had its own distinct electoral and constitutional formula for democracy.

While Mitterrand was historically and morally *engagé,* politically he was not at all so. His numerous articles in *Libres* expressed both a healthy intellectual skepticism about the certainties expounded by Gaullism, capitalism, socialism, communism, and even Catholicism, and a kind of Gidean receptivity to the positive elements in all of these doctrines. Beyond the general republican values embraced by the Resistance, which he had pragmatically accepted with the disgrace of Pétain, he was uncertain about what constitutional, political, and economic arrangements would be best for France.

However, one can already discern a Mitterrandian ideology in embryo —albeit one based more on resistance to emerging negative tendencies than on attraction to positive forces. First, de Gaulle's opposition to political parties was clearly unrepublican in Mitterrand's eyes. Mitterrand resented the way Gaullists called on Frenchmen to unite and forget old quarrels and deep desires.[5] Second, Mitterrand had a deep-seated suspicion of the Communist Party, based on his experience in the Resistance. He had seen firsthand how their leaders, courageous as they were, always tried to take over any group in which they participated. Third, there was the perceived threat of what he called "Money, King Money," the "enemy who lurks":

Our International [which "unites millions of shackled human beings"] corresponds to the International of money. I too was a slave in the camps. And I am

not sure that I am still not one. . . . It is up to us to demonstrate that the one
who guards us ["King Money"] will be less vigilant than we.[6]

Mitterrand's distrust of monied interests and his natural sympathy for the
have-nots of society were based on moral principles and social prejudices rather
than on a socialist or Marxist explanation of history and economics, of which he
was skeptical. Mitterrand's only vision was that of the "harmonious synthesis of
. . . French political families brought together by captivity."[7]

The romanticism and idealism of Mitterrand's youth were still much in evidence in the leader that was emerging in the mid-1940s. Though cautious and
intellectually unsure of himself, he was not indecisive; as always, he required
room to maneuver. He was receptive, but not gullible. Ambitious, definitely;
opportunistic or cynical, no. The key word is *vigilance,* which recurs in many of
the articles he wrote during this period. Without knowing what was positively
best for France, Mitterrand stood ready to defend it against the dragons of
money, dictatorship, and foreign or Communist manipulation. It is not surprising that someone with such strong political interests, if not precise convictions,
combined with a taste for action and risk and an already tested capacity to lead
and inspire men would not be content to remain on the sidelines for long.

## YOUNG POLITICIAN

Mitterrand's decision to enter the mainstream of political life required him
finally to choose a party. The challenge was to find one that would allow him a
certain amount of independence and maneuverability. To Mitterrand, de Gaulle
appeared authoritarian and his followers subservient, and he felt that the
Radical Party, whose ideology was closest to his own, had been discredited by
its performance in Munich. The Communist Party (PC) was, of course, out of
the question. This left only the Socialist Party, or the French Section of the
International Workers Party (SFIO), the Christian democratic Popular
Republican Movement (MRP), or one of the small centrist swing parties, such
as the Democratic and Socialist Union of the Resistance (UDSR). Mitterrand
eliminated the SFIO because of the stifling power of its party bosses and the
MRP because he did not believe in the future of a party so closely tied to the
militant Christians; although he still considered himself a Christian, he had
become skeptical of the political role that the Church often played. Of the
swing parties, the UDSR, grounded in the Resistance movement, was the most
to his liking.[8] In joining the UDSR Mitterrand associated himself with the
socialist label for the first time. The term in this context did not have any precise political content, and he appreciated this party's tolerant, ideologically ecumenical approach. Furthermore, the UDSR was a new, young party whose
power structure was not yet fixed—a perfect situation for someone determined
to be his own boss and a leader in his own right. Always a defender of the party
system and always a hard worker on his own behalf, Mitterrand would never

have been a good militant doing the humble tasks required to strengthen a highly structured party such as the SFIO.

The Socialist Democratic Union of the Resistance was just what its name indicates—a catch-all, egalitarian, parliamentarian group of Resistance fighters who sought a political role. It was formed in June 1945 as the result of an agreement between three of the many different Resistance organizations—the National Liberation Movement, Liberation-North (an organization with socialist leanings), and the Civil and Military Organization (OCM, a conservative, bourgeois Resistance organization).[9] Ideologically, it ranged from socialism to Gaullism, and, in fact, until the late 1940s many members were also members of de Gaulle's Rally of the French People (RPF). It was a typical swing party in that its political importance far outweighed its numerical size, and it had virtually no grassroots membership. Writing in *Le Monde*, Jacques Fauvet commented:

> In the UDSR, the RPF is sometimes tempted to see a little betrayal, and the "third force"[10] would willingly see it as a big equivocation. It is suspected by each side of being a Trojan horse! It is very true that the UDSR is halfway between the rightist opposition and the government. . . . It is true that it accepts double membership with the RPF, and even with the "third force," and that it gives the impression of playing it both ways.[11]

While having no leanings toward Gaullism, Mitterrand initially occupied a center-right niche within the UDSR and generally a center-right position on the overall French ideological spectrum. The electoral alliances he chose in his earliest elections reflect this position.

The UDSR was extremely adaptable. In national elections it might enter into alliances with Socialists, Radicals, Gaullists, or any of several small conservative parties, depending on the local situation; however, electoral alliances with the Radical Party—under the leadership of Henri Queuille, a prewar Radical with a solid Resistance record—were generally favored by the UDSR throughout the nation. Candidates engaged in these alliances would be listed under the Rally of Republican Lefts (RGR) banner.[12] The Radicals and the Resistance leaders needed each other politically; the former furnished the electoral center-right constituency while the latter brought political respectability to the Radicals, who had lost theirs in 1938. Thus, Mitterrand found himself indirectly associated with some of the spineless leaders of the Third Republic whom he had so recently castigated, including Edouard Daladier who had signed the Munich Agreement in 1938; although Queuille was the real boss, Daladier was now the official president of the national Radical Party.

In June 1946 Mitterrand ran in the Second Constituent Assembly[13] elections in the fifth Seine district northwest of Paris, a conservative area, and failed to win a seat by a narrow margin. His loss was due to a split in the center-right Radical-oriented electorate. In November of the same year, when the first legislative elections were held (according to a proportional list system), he tried again, this time in the department of the Nièvre,[14] where Henri Queuille "parachuted" him to head the RGR list. (The term *parachute* refers to a political candidate being sent by the national party boss to run for office in a political jurisdiction where he or she is generally unknown.) Although Mitterrand was indeed unknown in this rural region southeast of Paris, he won a seat there with the help of old Pétainist and right-wing contacts who were known.[15] Over the years his constituency followed him from the right to the left; he held his seat, with only one short interruption, until he became president of France in 1981.

Of the four deputies, Mitterrand was the farthest to the right. His campaign platform was the most conservative and most opposed to the tripartite coalition government. (Consisting of Communists, Socialists, and Christian Democrats, the first elected postwar government had implemented a number of socialistic economic measures.) More precisely, the platform Mitterrand ran on was anticommunist, opposed to nationalization of industry and inflationary economic policies, and in favor of "law and order" (that is, putting down strikes, which tended to be led by Communists). Having acquired a small but very real chunk of political power, Mitterrand now perceived the "progressives" as irresponsible and even threatening.

The Cold War had begun in earnest, and Mitterrand quickly realized that the PC was the most serious threat to the reestablishment of a stable democracy in postwar France. In 1945 Mitterrand had demonstrated with Communist ex-POWs in the streets of Paris, protesting their treatment by the Provisional Government. However, a demonstration is not a strike. He opposed the tripartite system because he believed that it gave too much power to party bosses and not enough effective power to the National Assembly itself. He understood that tripartism had been brought forth by the fraternal and joyous idealism of the Liberation but also that the exultant wave of the recent past would break on the rocks of eternal practical problems and social divisions. The coalition was doomed, and the new deputy saw that the vast majority of citizens now sought a return to peace and normalcy.

Because the very ground rules of the future government were at stake, and a Communist takeover was thought possible even by many of the most cool-headed, the constitutional issues had greater political importance than economic ones. One of Mitterrand's first votes was against the Constitution of the Fourth Republic. Although it managed to pass, only a minority of the deputies (35 percent) voted for it while 34 percent voted no and 31 percent abstained. The Gaullists and Communists were among those opposing it, too, but for totally different reasons than Mitterrand: the Gaullists because they already had in mind a majority presidential system, and the Communists because they objected to its semimajority electoral system, which would inevitably diminish their numbers in the National Assembly (a certain minimum percentage of votes in any given department was required in order for a party to gain any seats in that chamber). Mitterrand and many of his Radical friends did not consider the constitution sufficiently parliamentarian. Although his wariness about the undue influence that party bosses could have on elected deputies later proved justified, the alternative he favored resembled the individualistic system associated with the Third Republic. Like most of Mitterrand's solutions this one fell back on a precedent.

The adoption of the Constitution of the Fourth Republic led to a new balance of national power. Overnight the country veered from a tumultuous tripartite government with an authoritarian de Gaulle commanding a coalition government of Christian Democrats, doctrinaire Socialists, and obstructionist Communists to a Third Force system whereby a delicate but cooperative balance was struck between the various nonextremist parties of the right, center, and left. After May 1947 the new semimajority electoral system effectively kept the PC and the Gaullist RPF—the two disruptive parties that did not accept the regime—if not out of the National Assembly altogether, at least out of the various Third Force coalition governments. The constitution was parliamentarian in that the Cabinet had to be formed from the majority in the National Assembly and was accountable to it. In theory it was a bicameral system, but the Senate had very little real power. Thus, the lower house dominated both the upper house of Parliament and the executive branch. The obvious dangers of authoritarianism, totalitarianism, and anarchy were averted, but not those of instability and stalemate.

Although Mitterrand had voted against the constitution—and against the semimajority list electoral system—he immediately accepted the new ground rules and applied them to his benefit. He ensconced himself politically in the Nièvre, winning several regional elections. In 1947 he won a seat on the city council in the departmental capital, Nevers, which he held until 1959. In 1949 he won a seat on the *conseil général* (departmental council) and was elected president of that body in the 1950s. In the early 1960s he became mayor of the small town of Château-Chinon in the Nièvre. He was extending his influence through every important layer of the national political pyramid.

It is difficult to imagine a comparable political career in the United States because here national, state, and local politics represent quite distinct jurisdictions, and politicians are generally not allowed to hold two or more elected positions at the same time; local influence does not necessarily lead to significant national influence and vice versa. In France, however, most real political and financial power flows from Paris, and it is possible for someone to hold the offices of municipal councilman, department legislator, and National Assembly deputy simultaneously. The accumulation and concentration of power is therefore extreme and results in a quasi-permanent political class. Successful French politicians resemble cacti in that many of them become so deeply and widely enrooted in the political layers of their highly centralized society that their national influence can be ended only by retirement or death.

The UDSR was a key splinter party in coalition governments, and Mitterrand, along with the much older and more conservative René Pleven, stood out immediately as an assertive party leader. In July 1947, Prime Minister Paul Ramadier appropriately appointed the recognized prince of the POWs to be the minister of war veterans—the position most similar to the one he had held in the Provisional Government and from which de Gaulle had ejected him. In this post, which he held throughout the years of the Ramadier government and into the early years of Robert Schuman's government, he effectively promoted and secured veterans' interests.

Recognizing Mitterrand's journalistic abilities, Schuman appointed him minister of information in 1948, putting Mitterrand at the head of the government-controlled airwaves. As a minister of information during the Cold War, Mitterrand had to walk a fine line between government "regulation" (censorship) and freedom of expression on airwaves that reached all the way into Eastern Europe. He rejected American requests for time to broadcast its message to radio-free Europe (inadvertently hastening, no doubt, the creation of the Voice of America), softened the government's militaristic-sounding press releases concerning the control of strikes (in particular, the press releases of Jules Moch, the Socialist minister of the interior who dealt forcibly with strikers), and reduced the time allotted to a Communist viewpoint. In all, he was the model of vigilance and acquitted himself honorably of the thankless task of limiting the abuse of this highly politicized French institution.

## ENTRY INTO THE COLONIAL "WARS"

In spite of his relatively high rank and the fact that he was also already an influential journalist, the ambitious young minister of information knew that his ministry was not the place where the future course of France would be decided. Where lay the future grandeur of the country? In an assertive, Gaullist-style independence? In NATO? In the Atlantic Alliance? In a united Europe? Mitterrand understood well the impracticality of seeking it in the first alternative. He also recognized the immediate necessity of following the second and third routes, but realized that these would never be adequate for attaining the lofty goals worthy of France. And while he supported the fourth position in the abstract, it represented only a vague dream fraught with too many entangling technical issues, dangers, and ancient rivalries and hatreds for a pragmatic politician to ponder seriously. For Mitterrand, France's future grandeur lay in her own backyard: Africa.

He truly believed, and just a few years later would put in writing, that

> [a] strongly structured central power in Paris, autonomous states and territories federated within an egalitarian, fraternal community whose borders will stretch from the plains of Flanders to the equatorial forests . . . is the perspective that it is up to us to develop and propose, for without Africa, there will be no history of France in the twenty-first century.[16]

This glorious vision of an imperial France could not have been less realistic, for England and every other Western European nation would soon shed their colonies. Yet Mitterrand persisted in conceiving of this beautiful realm where nineteenth-century empire and twentieth-century democracy; European, Arab, and sub-Saharan African; Christianity, Islam, and witchcraft; the industrialized, the nomadic, and the tribal would be reconciled, where France would again be able to assert itself as a great power and show the world the universal model of the most fraternal and cultivated civilization in the world. This fantasy was so real to the nostalgic student of nineteenth-century French history and literature that he could almost touch it with his fingers. Indeed, this proposal is an early example of a recognizable tendency in Mitterrand to think that if an idea can be described beautifully in words, it can, with a little effort, be made into a concrete reality. And so, he set to work to guide France on the path to twenty-first-century grandeur.

When Georges Bidault of the MRP became prime minister in October 1949, Mitterrand received no Cabinet-level appointment. This gave him the opportunity once again to bear witness, as a writer, to the course of French history, particularly in Africa. During a lengthy lecture tour of French-speaking sub-Saharan Africa, the romantic, idealistic Mitterrand discovered the exotic natural beauty and desperate poverty of those lands. With the eye of a politician he also perceived the political, economic, and cultural potential for development and the colonial successes, rigidities, and injustices. It occurred to him that here was an opportunity for France. Here also was an opportunity for Mitterrand.

A new prime minister, René Pleven, the right-leaning president of Mitterrand's own party, was sworn in in 1950 shortly after Mitterrand's return to France. At Mitterrand's request, Pleven appointed him minister for overseas territories, whose crucial responsibility was the administration of the western and central African territories, which later formed the states of the Ivory Coast, Senegal, Dahomey, Gabon, Guinea, Upper Volta, Mali, Mauritania, Niger, Chad, Togo, the Central African Republic, and the Congo Republic. (The remote island territories were also a part of this ministry.) The minister's goals were clear-cut—to seek liberal reforms in the sub-Saharan African colonies, but always within the framework of the French Union proclaimed in Article VIII of the Constitution of the Fourth Republic. This posed some difficulty, however, for Article VIII was replete with contradictions concerning the French Union, asserting simultaneously that (1) all nations within the Union were equal, (2) all individuals within the Union were equal, and (3) France administered the nations.

Most of Mitterrand's political colleagues did not share his sense of priorities, and because he was a junior member of the Cabinet, he had difficulty in making himself heard. During the years 1950-51 the Indochina War monopolized the Cabinet's attention where colonial affairs were concerned, for the French were unwilling to relinquish any of their colonies, even one as remote as

Vietnam. In the wake of its humiliating defeat in World War II, when many of the colonies were the sole territorial symbols of Free France, it was not surprising that France stubbornly held on to its territories. While this preoccupation with Indochina was to Mitterrand's advantage for the short term since it allowed him a free hand to do what he personally thought best in sub-Saharan Africa, it did not bode well for the long term.

Furthermore, there was no coherent policy, due in part to the multiplicity of ministries handling the various colonies. There were, in fact, three ministries concerned with colonial affairs in addition to Mitterrand's: the Ministry of the Interior was responsible for Algeria, because it was considered to be a department of France (like the Nièvre); the Ministry of Foreign Affairs oversaw activities in Indochina; and the Ministry of Associated States was in charge of Tunisia and Morocco. These ministerial distinctions reflected different degrees of control of the colonies by the mother country. This fragmented system, coupled with incessant ministerial crises, also prevented the formulation of a long-range approach to colonial affairs.

Like Algeria, the sub-Saharan African colonies enjoyed a modest degree of democratic participation in French domestic affairs. They elected deputies to represent them in the National Assembly and some local officials to represent them on their own councils on a basis of limited suffrage (few blacks were permitted to vote). There were Gaullists, Socialists, Radicals, Christian Democrats, and so on. In addition, the black African Democratic Rally (RDA) sent seven representatives to the National Assembly in Paris, although it is clear that the black population was underrepresented in the National Assembly, represented only nominally on local councils, and subjected to many other discriminatory social and economic policies. Because the RDA had become nationalistic, sympathetic to the Communists, and violent, many of its leaders had gone underground to avoid imprisonment. But the RDA deputies remained in the National Assembly and voted, usually in alliance with the PC; paradoxically, they had more of a say in the national and internal affairs of France than in those of their own land.

Another source of conflict lay in the perpetual disagreement over policy between the local colonial notables and the resident administrator, who was responsible to the metropolitan minister, in this case, Mitterrand. Immediately upon assuming his responsibilities as minister, Mitterrand became involved in the power struggle between these two political hierarchies. His involvement was occasioned by the publication of an article by two French West African priests in a journal called *L'Afrique nouvelle* attacking the high commissioner Béchard, who was under Mitterrand's authority. The priests were reporting on a lawsuit brought against the high commissioner by detractors who questioned his integrity. Béchard took the priests to court, and they were fined on the basis of an old law that forbade reporting such cases. The colonials, who were fiercely loyal to the priests, protested angrily, but Béchard, supported by a legalistic Mitterrand, reasoned that clericals were not above the law.[17]

This scandal pushed to the fore the increasingly urgent question of who had the ultimate authority in the colonies, the colonials or the national ministers. Although the minister for overseas territories was responsible to the prime minister, who was in turn responsible to the National Assembly—in which colonials were represented—the colonials viewed the ministerial rule emanating from Paris as obtrusive, dictatorial, and naively inappropriate. Mitterrand, in particular, appeared to them to be radical and even antipatriotic because of his sympathetic attitude toward the legitimate grievances of the RDA, considered criminal by the colonials, and because of his role in the Béchard scandal. From this period forward, the colonials, that is, all those in metropolitan France and in the colonies who believed strongly in direct rule over (not with) the indigenous populations—vowed eternal hatred toward François Mitterrand, who in turn defined himself progressively in opposition to them.

While the form of its rule was dictatorial, the content of metropolitan France's (in this case Mitterrand's) colonial policy for sub-Saharan Africa was significantly more moderate, liberal, and democratically oriented than that of the colonials themselves, who stood for vested interests and ultraconservatism. In the National Assembly Mitterrand was duly punished with tirades and a reduction of his ministry's budget. While the colonials and the ministry were competing with each other for authority, very little attention was being paid to the social and economic problems of the native peoples, which were actually the most pressing issues of all and which Mitterrand was sincerely trying to address. To complicate matters further, while colonials and administrators battled, local nationalism (supported by a Communist movement, adding yet another dimension to an already complicated picture) was growing ever stronger among the Africans themselves.

As their legitimate demands and complaints went unheeded and even denigrated by the white colonials, the black Africans became progressively radicalized by the RDA. Paris was too far away and too poorly represented in the colonies to do anything constructive about the abuses, exploitation, and discrimination. One of the most odious laws—the law allowing forced labor—had already been abrogated in 1946 (against the colonials' wishes), but by 1950 the situation had not improved much. The native Africans still received lower wages than the colonials for comparable work and lower prices for their agricultural products. They were not allowed to hold public office, and they regularly confronted humiliating discriminatory practices; for example, many businesses would not accept them as customers. This economic and political discrimination against the African population fueled the fires of communism and nationalism, originally two separate movements that shared a common enemy—the capitalistic colonials.

Mitterrand was aware of the faults of both the colonials and the RDA. Although he understood the reasons for the nationalist and communist proclivities of the frustrated RDA, he also criticized them as misguided, counterproductive tendencies that would hinder it in its pursuit of legitimate goals:

A simplistic nationalism, deprived of all historical context, was born and developed, nourished with disappointment and bitterness, sometimes with hatred, maintained by latent racism, and exacerbated by communist propaganda. Reasoning by analogy, disdaining hastily their own contradictions, cutting up the African world into arbitrary zones, inventing history, redesigning the contours of civilizations that long ago disappeared, young people exulted at the memory of a legendary past in which they sought justifications for a nationalist adventure. Throughout the ages, this had never been a fruitful path and, in fact, Europe . . . was [now] beginning to repudiate it.

. . .

[The Communist Party] had a fine time reorienting this desire for sovereignty toward revolutionary combat, especially since an absurd tactic of colonialism was to treat the most modest demands as Communist-inspired. The Communists took advantage of that confusion and, knowing full well that the stage of economic evolution of the sub-Saharan peoples offered a narrow field for the expansion of their own doctrine, they cleverly took up the nationalist banner. Its cells grabbed hold of every pretext to spout slogans.[18]

Mitterrand had an excellent intellectual grasp of the situation, but he had no means at hand to control any of these tendencies. He would manage to forestall some of them—a modest yet honorable achievement.

Mitterrand reasoned that if France would recognize the legitimate demands of the sub-Saharan peoples, which was morally imperative anyway, they could be lured away from the Communists and primary nationalism. This is exactly what he managed to do in the National Assembly during this period. In fact, in the RDA led by Félix Houphouët-Boigny, Mitterrand found a political ally (how valuable an ally it is hard to say) on both colonial and national matters. Mitterrand had averted Houphouët-Boigny's imminent arrest by French authorities and had made him promise to cease violence and to pledge allegiance to the French Union in return for France's implementing liberal reforms in the colonies.

The reforms to which Mitterrand agreed were based on the principles of a fair work code, the right of Africans to hold public office, and the enforcement of fair prices for African-produced commodities. Mitterrand gained the full confidence of Houphouët-Boigny, who switched his alliance in the National Assembly from the PC to Mitterrand's UDSR, thereby adding seven new RDA members to Mitterrand's group, making a total of twenty-three (less than 5 percent of the seats of the National Assembly). Simultaneously, Houphouët-Boigny persuaded his supporters to cease violence in the colonies. The RDA was legalized, reforms were enacted, and as a conciliatory gesture Houphouët-Boigny later became a state minister in the last four Cabinets of the Fourth Republic.

In public, Mitterrand promoted social and economic reforms as well as the enforcement of existing political arrangements—something that was very difficult to achieve since these two concerns were often incompatible. But in private, he could treat sub-Saharan Africa a little more cynically, a little more like a pawn in both national and international politics. On the national level we have seen that there was a modest harvest of deputy seats in the National Assembly to be reaped from the colonies. Mitterrand anticipated, rather naively, the day when de Gaulle's RPF would be evicted from colonial politics altogether and the liberal parties of the Third Force would predominate.[19] (It did not quite work out that way. As the end of the French Union approached, the Gaullist party became the last political refuge for the diehard colonials, and the natives lost all confidence in the liberals' ability to accomplish anything.)

On the international level, Mitterrand also saw things as working to France's advantage. In his memoirs Vincent Auriol, president of France from 1947 to 1954, recounts a conversation with Mitterrand in which the minister for overseas territories gloated over the progovernmental position of the RDA in the latest elections and the political submission of its leaders; Mitterrand contrasted their cooperative behavior with that of the antagonistic indigenous leaders in the nearby British African colonies, which gave him satisfaction. He believed that France could hold on to her colonies in Africa even if Britain could not, apparently not realizing that all the African colonies were part of the same domino game. (He was operating on the false assumption that what was not good for France's rivals was good for France.) Furthermore, Mitterrand believed that by deferring important political reforms, France could maintain its influence vis-à-vis the great powers. President Auriol quotes him as saying:

> I believe we must not implement the important reforms which Togo is asking of us, for it would result in all of French Africa saying: to succeed you have to be under the influence of the United Nations and Great Britain.[20]

Mitterrand's policies toward sub-Saharan Africa were not only part of an effort to promote greater social justice for oppressed peoples within the colonial framework but were also part of a far more complicated game of European power politics in which France strove to regain a position of dominance, especially vis-à-vis Great Britain.

Mitterrand's political subtlety worked against him in the short term. He was vilified by the more simple-minded colonials, who saw him as an antipatriotic *bradeur* (sell out). Although Mitterrand's reforms were on the line of progress toward colonial liberation that started with de Gaulle's own concept of a French Union, followed by Léon Blum's recommendations for liberal reform in 1946, Gaston Defferre's reform law of 1956 that gave autonomy to the sub-Saharan colonies, and finally total independence for all the sub-Saharan colonies under de Gaulle's presidency, the young minister incurred the wrath of the colonial Gaullists, MRPs, rightist Radicals, and the PC. The first three groups detested him for "antipatriotically abandoning" the colonies, while the last hated him for reinforcing "imperialist" control over them—that is, for enticing deputies away from the PC in the National Assembly and weakening Communist influence over the indigenous Africans.

Mitterrand was certainly being noticed now. In fact, his activities sparked so much uproar that in August 1951 a group of colonial Gaullists, MRPs, and Radicals insisted on his removal from the Cabinet. Although President Auriol sympathized with Mitterrand, he bowed to the colonials' demand and called upon the new prime minister, René Pleven, to dismiss him.[21] Mitterrand's own party leader thus had the opportunity to eliminate from his Cabinet the man who most threatened his ascendancy in the UDSR. This marked Mitterrand's first serious political humiliation. But larger trends were at work, too. While the colonial, not domestic, struggles of the 1950s led Mitterrand gradually away from the center right toward reformist positions associated with the left, a majority of the Cabinet members of the left and the right allowed themselves to be cowed by stronger-willed colonials of whatever party whose solution was classically reactionary—the use of force to maintain the status quo.

## NOTES

1. *Libres*, December 10, 1944, cited in François Mitterrand, *Politique* (Paris: Fayard, 1977), p. 28.

2. Ibid.

3. Napoleon I had divided each of the old provinces, such as Burgundy and Normandy, into two to four more manageable parts, called departments.

4. *Libres*, June 27, 1945, cited in Mitterrand, *Politique*, pp. 37–38.

5. *Libres*, March 17, 1945, cited in Mitterrand, *Politique*, p. 34.

6. *Libres*, October 26, 1944, cited in Mitterrand, *Politique*, p. 26.

7. François Mitterrand, *Les Prisonniers de guerre devant la politique* (Paris: Editions Rond-Point, 1945), cited in Franz-Olivier Giesbert, *François Mitterrand ou la tentation de l'histoire* (François Mitterrand or the temptation of history) (Paris: Seuil, 1977), pp. 81–82.

8. Giesbert, *François Mitterrand*, p. 90.

9. Ibid.

10. The term *Third Force* refers to any coalition government consisting of a mix of parties ideologically between the far-right Gaullist RPF and the far-left PC, such as the SFIO, the Radicals, the MRPs, or the conservative CNI.

11. *Le Monde*, May 15, 1948, cited in Roland Cayrol, *François Mitterrand 1945–1967* (Paris: Fondation Nationale des Sciences Politiques, 1967), pp. 16–17.

12. It is obvious that such terms as *socialist, republican, left*, and *radical* no longer had any precise denotations but still possessed strongly positive connotations.

13. The only job of this assembly was to write the Constitution of the Fourth Republic, after which it was immediately dissolved.

14. Since Mitterrand's first election, when the legislative jurisdiction had been the arrondissement, the electoral system had already changed. In the next election the legislative jurisdiction had become the department.

15. Pierre Péan, *Une Jeunesse française* (A French youth) (Paris: Fayard, 1994), pp. 523–25.

16. François Mitterrand, *Présence française et abandon* (Paris: Plon, 1957), p. 237.

17. Jean-Marie Borzeix, *Mitterrand lui-même* (Paris: Stock, 1973), pp. 47–49.

18. Mitterrand, *Présence*, pp. 172–73, 182.

19. Vincent Auriol, *Journal du septennat*, vol. 1 (Paris: Colin, 1970), p. 250.

20. Ibid., p. 251.

21. Giesbert, *François Mitterrand*, p. 113.

# The Colonial Reforms

# 3

## The Colonial Reformer

As wartime issues faded away and a new generation came to the fore, the centrist Radical Party and the conservative National Center of Independents (CNI), both of which had been strong during the prewar years, regained respectability and influence. In the National Assembly the Radicals were increasing their representation as the UDSR was losing ground. By 1949 the Gaullist members of the UDSR had pulled out of the party in order to devote themselves to building the RPF. Nevertheless, in 1951, with only 8 percent of the popular vote, the Radical and UDSR joint lists—which represented the crucial center of the ideological spectrum—won 11 percent of the National Assembly seats by virtue of the semimajority electoral system. This special electoral relationship between the Radicals and the UDSRs clearly benefited both parties.

The extreme ends of the ideological spectrum obtained far more positions in the National Assembly than the center, with the largest number of seats going to the left. The heavily represented parties of the far right (RPF) and left (PC)—who together made up about 46 percent of the delegates—questioned, for different reasons, the very legitimacy of the regime. Thus, the support of even a thinly represented swing party such as the UDSR was crucial.

In the 1951 elections, the voters of the Nièvre duly sent their adopted son to the National Assembly—along with a Communist, a Gaullist, and a Socialist. Mitterrand had campaigned again on a center-right domestic platform, calling for the reestablishment of social order.[1] However, René Pleven, the new prime minister and Mitterrand's arch rival in the UDSR, refused to appoint Mitterrand to the new Cabinet, choosing instead Radicals, MRPs, and CNIs. Mitterrand was not conservative enough to fit into his Cabinet.

At the government level, Pleven remained the most prominent UDSR party member. However, at the party level, Mitterrand was fast overtaking him in influence, and toward the end of 1953 Mitterrand was elected president of the party. The power struggle between Mitterrand and Pleven reflected the small party's dual political orientation. Pleven was preoccupied with trying to hold on to Indochina at any cost and promoting the European Defense Community (which would have created a supranational European army that included German forces), whereas Mitterrand was seeking to extricate France from Southeast Asia in order to concentrate on the more pressing problems in North Africa.[2]

Although he considered the colonial issues more interesting personally and more urgent politically, the deputy from the Nièvre consistently voted for measures promoting European unity. In 1951 he voted for the Schuman Plan, which established the Coal and Steel Community, precursor of the Common Market. This vote was consistent with his votes for the Marshall Plan and the North Atlantic Treaty Organization in the late 1940s. In 1953 he represented France at the Council of Europe; he later voted for the rearmament of Germany, bringing that country into NATO, and for the Treaty of Rome, which inaugurated the Common Market. Early on Mitterrand favored all serious efforts toward European unity.

However, Mitterrand was most committed to the development of the Franco-African community, with all its intrinsic contradictions, because he believed it to be more critical than European unity to maintaining France's position in international and European politics. He was right in judging that a strong Franco-African union would have given France greater leverage to orient European unity in the direction that France preferred; an imperial France could easily have dominated a defeated, isolated Germany and a Britain shorn of its empire. But Mitterrand was wrong in judging France capable of resisting the wave of liberation movements sweeping the globe.

Events were thrusting colonial problems into the minds of all French politicians. During the winter of 1952 economic and colonial problems created unbearable pressures from both the left and right, causing the collapse of the Pleven Cabinet in January 1952. The left had fought it for being too conservative on economic issues, while the right opposed it for being too liberal on colonial matters, particularly rejecting its conciliatory attitude toward Tunisian demands for more autonomy. Meanwhile, France's army was becoming more deeply engaged in the Indochinese conflict, although this was not yet in the forefront of public awareness.

Edgar Faure was then installed as prime minister and formed a Cabinet consisting of UDSR members, Radicals, Christian Democrats, and Independents. He chose Mitterrand, whom he held in high esteem, for one of the most sensitive posts in his Cabinet, minister of state for colonial affairs.[3] This gave Mitterrand direct responsibility for Tunisian affairs, which were starting to boil. The former minister of overseas territories took an approach to Tunisia very similar to the one he had successfully adopted for sub-Saharan Africa. The only trouble now was that he was being closely watched by nervous and suspicious colonials.

During the short-lived (three-month) Faure government Mitterrand came up with a comprehensive reform package, which was timid by later standards but scandalous by those of 1952. While Tunisia was theoretically still a sovereign nation "protected" by France according to the 1881 Treaty of Bardo, it had in fact become a French colony directly administered by French civil servants. The Tunisian rulers and people had little or no say in public and economic affairs.

Mitterrand proposed a return to the spirit of the Treaty of Bardo while at the same time taking into account French interests, which were deeply rooted in its protectorate. This development of new policy based on a preexisting document is characteristic of Mitterrand's management of political conflict; if the document is obsolete, at least it furnishes the opposing sides with a starting point from which to negotiate or, as in this case, to develop new reforms to be imposed from above. His proposals, deemed outrageous by the colonials, included dual citizenship for all native and European Tunisians, a single electoral college (the existing dual college system relegated the native majority to second-class status), universal suffrage, a representative assembly and an economic council (neither of which would have the right, at first, to initiate legislation), and bilingualism. France would retain control over defense, foreign affairs, internal security, and for a while, finances. The *résident général*, the appointed local agent of the French government, would exercise only "external" control over the bey (the native ruler of Tunisia).

While Habib Bourguiba, the head of the nationalist neo-Destour Tunisian Party, received the plan with great interest (in spite of the fact that it was never negotiated with any Tunisians), the representatives of the European Tunisians would have none of it. The plan died with Edgar Faure's Cabinet. More precisely, Mitterrand's plan itself helped provoke the attack that dealt the final blow, and the intransigence of the right on colonial issues coupled with that of the left regarding economic issues crushed the government.

Frequently, a newly formed government would be able to ram through the National Assembly the very measures that had contributed to the fall of the previous one. However, in the case of the conservative Cabinet formed by Antoine Pinay of the CNI, it was not Mitterrand's plan that sailed through the legislature but certain necessary, conservative economic policies that had been impossible under Faure's government. The reform process for Tunisia, though, was stalled indefinitely.

Indochina, where the politicomilitary situation was degenerating rapidly, was another matter altogether. France had seized Saigon in 1859 and declared Indochina a protectorate in 1884. By the end of World War II, nationalist pressures had exploded in the area, and France officially recognized Vietnam as a "free state within the French Union" in the Baie d'Along Agreement signed by France and Vietnam in 1949. This agreement did not end the fighting because the Vietnamese nationalists did not support Bao Dai, the Vietnamese leader installed by the French, and the French were still determined to control Vietnam militarily.

The fighting was currently eating up 20 percent of France's military budget, 8 percent of the country's total budget (although the United States still incurred 80 percent of the war's total cost). But Mitterrand's main concern was the justification for the war. He sensed that there was no clear national consensus about the objectives to be achieved. He dismissed the notions of a war of conquest or a war of liberation, viewing such goals as clearly incompatible with the declared policies of the French government. And he also strongly criticized NATO's (and hence the United States') concept of the Indochinese war as basically an anticommunist effort; according to Mitterrand, it was preposterous for a country of such limited resources as France to undertake such a war.

The Baie d'Along Agreement called for eventual French withdrawal, and Mitterrand always demanded that such written contracts between political entities, whether perfect or not, be respected. But Mitterrand's speeches in the National Assembly made no impression at all on René Mayer's Cabinet. (René Mayer was the colonial Radical from Algeria who had been installed as prime minister in January 1953.) It was at this time that Mitterrand and Pierre Mendès France came together on the issue of Indochina. For them, the war had to end as soon as possible, and this could best be accomplished by means of a negotiated settlement with the adversary.

After René Mayer's government fell, Joseph Laniel (CNI) formed one that included Mitterrand but not Mendès France. Laniel's Cabinet, which consisted of conservatives and centrists, lasted less than a year—from July 1953 to June 1954—and Mitterrand did not stay even that long; he resigned out of frustration after three months. During this brief period of participation, Mitterrand was appointed minister of state assigned to the new Council of Europe in Strasbourg—a position that required occasional appearances at the council, but little administrative or diplomatic responsibility.[4] Although Mitterrand's support was crucial for forming the coalition, Laniel's group, which espoused hard-line positions on colonial matters, was anxious to keep him as far removed from colonial affairs as possible. This governmental mission on the Rhine—a sort of internal exile—was probably designed to prevent him from meddling in colonial affairs. However, by virtue of the perpetual crisis situation in Indochina and North Africa and the very nature of cabinet government, Mitterrand continued to be vocal on these problems.

Laniel was a particularly weak prime minister. His Cabinet quickly became polarized around Paul Reynaud, another minister of state, and Georges Bidault, the minister of foreign affairs; Mitterrand, together with Edgar Faure, associated himself with Reynaud. Reynaud confronted Bidault for his hardline approach to Southeast Asia, and Mitterrand battled Léon Martinaud-Deplat, minister of the interior, who was associated with Bidault, over Tunisian and Moroccan problems. Faure, now minister of finance, fought with the conservative members of the Cabinet on financial matters.[5] For their part, the military leaders in Indochina, General Henri Navarre in particular, were indignant at Mitterrand's participation in this Cabinet.

By 1953 the Indochinese conflict had developed into a full-scale war in which the geographical position of France and the material resources that it could bring to bear were insufficient for the ambitions of the military and the conservative members of the Cabinet. Mitterrand, along with Mendès France, now called more and more loudly for negotiations with the Viet Minh and even the Chinese. While previously he had been against the internationalization of the conflict vis-à-vis China, he soon came around to accepting it. He saw the Korean War and Indochinese conflicts as interdependent, with the concluding of the former offering an opportunity to end the latter. If this failed, he felt France should negotiate directly with Ho Chi Minh and Mao Tse-tung.[6]

Mitterrand also fought in the Cabinet and the National Assembly to preserve the French presence within a federalist framework in North Africa. Tunisia and Morocco were in much the same position vis-à-vis France; that is, they were both protectorates—theoretically sovereign states ruled by their own leaders but "protected" by France. The protectorate relationship was supposed to be somewhere between the dependence of the Algerian departments and the independence of an associated state such as Vietnam. Mitterrand's principal criticisms of the protectorate concept revolved around the fact that France had progressively violated the spirit of the original protectorate agreements and had come to administer these states directly. He felt that the original treaties with Tunisia and Morocco—the 1881 Treaty of Bardo with the former and the Fez Treaty of 1912 with the latter—were still sound bases on which to build a modern federalist structure.

Because Mitterrand saw that nothing constructive could come out of this Cabinet, he soon resigned. Any thought of reform in the colonies was squelched, and only military solutions to colonial problems were sought in North Africa as well as in Indochina. At his resignation, Mitterrand was very aware of the ghosts haunting the civilian and military veterans of World War II: "The proposal to limit our military presence to the Hanoi-Haiphong line was rejected as if it were a question of the government shamefully leaving Paris for Bordeaux"[7] (an allusion to the hasty retreat of the French government after the 1940 German invasion).

Throughout the remainder of the Laniel government gridlock prevailed. But the inertia in Paris did not prevent the situations in Indochina and North Africa from steadily deteriorating. The native populations were becoming increasingly nationalistic and radicalized, while the European colonials defended their vested interests even more adamantly. The government finally fell in June 1954, brought down for the most part by events it could not control: strikes, the French debacle at Dien Bien Phu, and controversy over participation in the European Defense Community (EDC). It is probable that Mitterrand played no small role in its downfall. During this period the "liberal" milieu—represented by Mitterrand, Mendès France, and Jean-Jacques Ser-van-Schreiber and his associates at *L'Express* (for which Mitterrand wrote many editorials)—worked toward establishing a government that could break out of the gridlock.[8]

## THE MENDESIST PERIOD

Finally, in the summer of 1954, President René Coty appointed Pierre Mendès France prime minister, and Mitterrand helped him form a government.[9] Mitterrand wanted to form a single large new ministry for the French Union that would administer all overseas territories and departments; this would have given him sole jurisdiction over virtually all the French colonies in Arab and sub-Saharan Africa, as well as in Asia and the Caribbean. Mendès France rejected the idea. Mitterrand then requested and obtained the position of minister of the interior, which gave him extensive jurisdiction over Algerian affairs. In this post, he was mainly responsible for Algeria's internal security. His plans were to "remove unreliable personnel and change customs."[10] Mitterrand made it sound so simple.

Before the Algerian crisis came to a head in November 1954, Mendès France's government had three other pressing problems to address. He had been elected prime minister on the promise that he would end the Indochinese conflict within a month of taking office. The EDC issue and Tunisian affairs were also urgent. Mitterrand fully supported Mendès France in all these areas. The proposal for participation in the EDC was eventually killed, both Mendès France and Mitterrand taking a neutral position on the issue so as not to make it a vote of confidence or censure of the government. Although the EDC was defeated, shortly thereafter the National Assembly voted for integrating German forces into NATO as a more acceptable form of German rearmament. Mitterrand voted for this, too.

Upon entering office, Mendès France immediately began active participation in the Geneva Peace Conference. (The conference had begun during the Laniel government with Bidault representing France, but no progress had been made toward a settlement.) Thirty-three days later the Geneva Accords were signed, ending France's military presence in Southeast Asia. The accords divided Vietnam along the 17th parallel, granting North Vietnam to the Communist government of Ho Chi Minh and South Vietnam, which would remain part of the French Union, to the republic headed by Bao Dai. Although pleasing to the majority of the French nation, the agreement incurred the wrath of the colonials and the army. Bidault's major criticism of the Geneva Accords was that the American guarantee to support the non-Communist government of South Vietnam was not positive enough! (The United States did not actually sign the accords because it did not recognize Communist China, which did sign them.) Mitterrand also was not as grateful to the United States as one might have expected: "Not only did our allies become the vigilant guardians of the status quo, but, ignoring French interests, they drew political and economic advantages from it."[11] Furthermore, he felt that the United States and the Soviet Union were in a way two of a kind: "united by the same political goal regarding nonautonomous peoples, [they] struck the last blow [to any close relationship between France and Vietnam]."[12]

Having put Indochina quickly behind him, Mendès France hoped to be able to end the conflict in Tunisia just as smoothly. However, he wanted to do so without giving up the territory altogether, and this would prove to be more difficult than expected. Shortly after the signing of the Geneva Accords, Mendès France spelled out his Tunisian policy and the reforms he intended to enact—all of which were inspired by Mitterrand and the 1881 Treaty of Bardo. His policy called for substantial internal autonomy for Tunisia but insisted that France maintain control of military and diplomatic affairs. The colonial right put up fierce opposition to this policy, both in Paris and Tunisia, but in spite of the rightist outcries, Franco-Tunisian relations proceeded precisely in the direction Mendès France had laid out.

With the Indochinese conflict behind them and Moroccan and Tunisian affairs on hold, Mendès France and Mitterrand turned to what to them was most pressing: reform of the Franco-Algerian relationship. To their chagrin, the previous conflicts in Indochina, Morocco, and Tunisia turned out to be only dress rehearsals for the Algerian drama that was just beginning to unfold—France's real "Vietnam." The colonials had been forced to retreat militarily and/or politically from Southeast Asia, Tunisia, and sub-Saharan Africa. The Algerian "front," considered by the vast majority of French to be an integral part of France, would become the line from which no retreat would be tolerated.

The French had conquered Algeria in 1830 and had been there ever since. Waves of French settlers had populated the northern shores and created a prosperous, Western-style society. Europeans had in many respects improved the lot of the indigenous peoples, raising health standards and educating some of the populace. By the end of World War II, the native population had exploded by virtue of many of these improvements. Observing the material prosperity of the Europeans in which they had very little share, the North Africans began to realize how poor they really were. They had acquired enough French education to embrace the notions of liberty, equality, and fraternity and had seen what a French life-style could provide. Yet in Algeria, as in Tunisia, the European minority was willing neither to treat the Moslems as political equals nor to admit them into the mainstream of business and the civil service.

The Statute of 1947, which defined the position of Algeria within the French Union after the war, had been a compromise solution. Neither honestly applied nor flatly rejected by the parties involved, it crystallized many of the inherent contradictions and ambiguities of the notion of union itself. It declared that Algeria was a "group of departments" and conceded to them financial autonomy. It also established representative institutions but allowed the majority Moslem population to have only limited minority representation in them.

The real political decision-making still took place in Paris, and the ethnic French controlled the economy.[13]

As minimal as the constitutional concessions to Moslem Algerians were, they were never fairly applied. Regular and widespread election fraud prevented most Moslem nationalists from obtaining seats in the Algerian Assembly. The survival of *communes mixtes* (municipalities with Moslem majorities that were administered by Europeans) belied the democratic pretensions of the statute. In addition, discriminatory employment practices were the rule. These were just a few of the worst abuses.

As the new minister of the interior, Mitterrand had declared that he wanted to "remove unreliable personnel and change customs." Neither was as easy to do as he implied it would be. The European Algerian establishment offered frequently subtle and sometimes violent resistance to any change that threatened the status quo. The efforts of the minister of the interior to put the Statute of 1947 into effect were branded as selling out and were constantly thwarted.

Mitterrand tried to maintain a balanced posture, pushing for reforms on the one hand, and reassuring the Europeans on the other. In the fall of 1954, he proposed the suppression of the *communes mixtes,* incorporation of more Moslems into the civil service, and the creation of a local school of administration, all of which were unacceptable to the European colonials. It was absolutely necessary, however, to reassure them and to maintain their favor, because Mendès France's very slim majority in the National Assembly depended in part on the support of the European Algerian Radical deputies, who were led by René Mayer, the former Radical prime minister.[14] After an official visit to Algiers in October 1954, at which time Mitterrand bent over backward to reassure the colonials and offer hope to the Moslems, his public proclamations were optimistic. Privately, however, he was one of the first to warn of imminent violence.[15] The day after his return from Algeria, Mitterrand was notified by his intelligence service that a violent insurrection was about to break out.[16] A week later he posted an order for the necessary arrests to be made to prevent this. His letter arrived November 1, 1954—the day after the night of insurrection that marked the official beginning of the Algerian War.[17]

As minister of the interior, Mitterrand's first responsibility was to reestablish order. No possibility of independence was admitted. The Algerian National Liberation Front (FLN) was considered to be an outlaw organization, and no negotiations with it were permitted. Reinforcements were requested, and Mendès France granted them, bringing the total number of French troops in Algeria to 54,000. Mitterrand was present for "mopping-up" operations in the unsettled Aurès region where the rebels were hiding out. The civilian population in the area was "regrouped" (forcibly removed). Mitterrand approved the use of artillery and aviation for purposes of surveillance only; he refused to approve the harsher measures that the military wanted, including indiscriminate bombing and the use of napalm.[18] Mitterrand wanted to crush the rebel FLN, but actually drove more Moslems into it by also repressing the nonterrorist nationalist parties—the Movement for the Triumph of Democratic Liberties (MTLD), associated with the Communists, and the Democratic Union of the Algerian Manifesto (UDMA), the most moderate of the Moslem parties, led by Ferhat Abbas. Delegates from both these parties were no longer recognized in the Algerian Assembly. Ferhat Abbas, a key moderate leader, joined the FLN. Thus, dialogue between the Moslems and Europeans was effectively cut off.

At the same time, the European Algerians were blaming the French government for the outbreak, especially Mendès France and Mitterrand's policies in Tunisia, which had "infected" Algeria.[19] In the National Assembly, Mitterrand did what he could to calm all the parties, which included rejecting extremist demands from the left and right (independence, partition, integration, and so on) and calling for increased economic investment and political reform in Algeria as a response to the legitimate grievances of the Moslem Algerians. Mendès France supported him on all these points.

During this period, the use of torture by both sides became a glaring problem, and there was abundant evidence that the Algerian police, technically under Mitterrand's jurisdiction but virtually controlled by the French Algerian police at the local level, were guilty of some of the most heinous offenses. Mitterrand called for an investigation, which was promptly obstructed by the local police. He transferred several policemen to France, but many found their way back to Algeria.[20] He then called for the fusion of the upper echelons of the Algerian and French police forces. Despite his efforts, Mitterrand was never able to gain control of the local police.

In January 1955 Mitterrand proposed the creation of a team of select civil servants who would be faithful to him and whom he could send to Algeria to take the situation directly in hand. Mendès France refused to consider it and instead chose Jacques Soustelle, a Gaullist with a liberal reputation, as the new governor general of Algeria. Soustelle was thought to represent a liberal policy that was based on integration—a notion replete with intended ambiguities. Mitterrand was critical of Mendès France's modified Algerian policy as represented by Soustelle, which appeared to him to diverge from the federalist approach. Yet Soustelle claimed that his policy was not much different from Mitterrand's.[21]

While Mendès France and Mitterrand agreed on substance, differences in style became apparent. Mitterrand was provocative, aggressive, and impatient with the French Algerian leaders. He took special aim at a key French Algerian senator, Henri Borgeaud, in the National Assembly and the press. Mendès France, on the other hand, preferred a more calm, patient, and courteous approach with the recalcitrants, having faith that given time they could be persuaded to accept some reform.[22] Time was certainly against both of them, and Mendès France even believed that Mitterrand's extensive reform package and the brusque manner in which he wished to impose it on all parties precipitated the fall of his government.[23] After less than eight months, the CNI, the MRP, and some of his own Radical colleagues all withdrew their support. Ultimately, the campaign against the Jewish Mendès France became ugly with audible anti-Semitic overtones.

Even before their different styles began to show that these two leaders would not be able to work closely together over time, an element of distrust had already come between the young minister and the prime minister. It resulted from the "leaks scandal," which had unfolded in July 1954, just prior to the Algerian crisis.[24] In July 1954 Mitterrand was accused by a police commissioner of having leaked Cabinet meeting minutes to the PC during his participation in the Laniel government. Many on the right were anxious to believe the false evidence that was produced and to put Mitterrand on trial before a military court. It was a classic attempt by a fanatic faction to discredit an adversary through false accusations and innuendo; whether found guilty or innocent, the target is henceforth followed by the whiff of scandal, which corrodes the trust and respectability he or she has accumulated over the years.

By the end of September, the real source of the leaks was proven to be two collaborators of a National Defense secretary-general who had been present at the same meetings as Mitterrand. The two were considered merely the lackeys in the plot, but the masterminds behind it were never identified; the secretary-general was not held responsible either. Furthermore, the originators succeeded in carrying out their mission of humiliating Mitterrand and undermining the Mendès France government. Using the leaks scandal as a pretext, the military and political figures in league with the police attacked Mitterrand and Mendès France relentlessly.

Mitterrand was one of the last to know that he was being investigated for betraying the government, and Mendès France was, by his own admission, responsible for not informing Mitterrand about his being implicated. Mitterrand would never completely forgive him for this lack of confidence. Mendès France would explain the incident later as a misunderstanding that he regretted.[25]

Thus, in February 1955 Mendès France's government came to an end on more than one sour note. Both Mendès France and Mitterrand were distrusted and vilified by the right, and suspicion and disagreement over policy had sprung up between them. Although their political paths would continue to cross in the years ahead, each traveled his own road, with Mitterrand continuing to fight in the front lines of the political wars and Mendès France progressively retreating from them while remaining one of the most highly respected political figures of the era. Two such rigorously independent-minded individuals could never be tied to anyone else's cart for long.

In the colonial debates of the 1950s Mitterrand's reformist positions were among the most enlightened and humane; they were also among the most self-contradictory and unrealistic. Despite being lucid about Indochina, the closer he came to home, the more unrealistic he became. He tried his best, without success, to reconcile empire and democracy, an error he has recognized in later years. On a more practical level, he believed it was possible to separate domestic and foreign affairs in a progressively interdependent world. The colonials and Communists were, as fanatics often are, wholly consistent with themselves. The former saw no reason to change the prewar colonial system that had worked so well since before they could remember; it gave lip service to democratic principles, comfortable positions to the cooperative Arab elite, and effective control of the economy and administration to the colonials. The latter, in favoring immediate and total independence, were supporting the creation of a Soviet client state dominated by Communists.

Mitterrand was actually more of a cultural than a political imperialist. He would have preferred some form of republican federalism that would have allowed minimal French political control with maximum French "presence." Proud of his country's intellectual and artistic past, he was as anxious to export Pascal, Rousseau, and Gide (as well as a wide range of French institutions and services) as the Soviets were Stalinism and rifles and the Americans corn flakes and toothpaste. The irony of this is that it was in the French universities of the 1930s, 1940s, and 1950s that the colonized elites learned their Marx, Lenin, and Engels along with Voltaire and Rousseau. The former three, who proved to be far more powerful influences than the latter two, found their way to Hanoi, Phnom Penh (Cambodia was a French colony from 1864 to 1949), Tunis, Algiers, and Rabat via Paris more often than by way of Moscow. For example, a Cambodian farmer's son named Saloth Sar, whose family was connected to the Cambodian royal family, went to Paris in 1949 to study electrical engineering; after returning to Cambodia in the 1950s as a dedicated secret Communist prepared to practice revolutionary social engineering on a grand scale, he became known to the world later as Pol Pot. So, while the French exported the European ideas and ideologies of freedom and revolution, the Soviets and Chinese exported the firepower with which to implement them and end French political and cultural imperialism for good.

During this period of Mitterrand's career, it was his embrace of republicanism that was most in evidence. Mitterrand had put the prewar Croix-de-feu ideology far behind him, but socialist ideology and programs played no role in the development of the economic reforms that he proposed (although some Socialists supported them); he wanted to level the playing field already in place, develop infrastructure, and create more national institutions, such as schools and deliberative bodies, to better serve the whole population. What he desired most for the colonies and for the Franco-African Union was that France live up to its constitutional promises and establish an exemplary republican federalism, creating a new kind of empire—a noble but impossible mission.

This nostalgic and idealistic goal went hand in hand with a progressively refined Machiavellianism. By providing the French Union with a federalist framework, Mitterrand hoped to strengthen the hand of France on the European and international political stages as well as increase his own domestic power base. Just as he had established his initial base using the untapped forces of the POWs during and after the war and had enlarged it somewhat by bringing the abused African RDAs under his wing in the National Assembly, so did he hope to gain the confidence of Moslem Algerian representatives and thereby expand his influence further. By taking on the legitimate causes of neglected groups of have-nots while rejecting their extremist demands, he could slowly accumulate his own political capital. These were noble political goals for France and Mitterrand, but ones that ran counter to the inexorable historical forces that were changing the political landscape—forces that were outside the control of Minister Mitterrand, the Fourth Republic, or even General de Gaulle himself.

## NOTES

1. Roland Cayrol, *François Mitterrand 1945–1967* (Paris: Fondation Nationale des Sciences Politiques, 1967), pp. 13–14.

2. Alfred Grosser, *La Quatrième République et sa politique extérieure* (Paris: Colin, 1961), pp. 128–29.

3. Charles-André Julien, *L'Afrique du nord en marche: Nationalismes musulmans et souveraineté française* (Paris: Julliard, 1952), pp. 228–29.

4. Grosser, *La Quatrième République*, p. 64.

5. Jean-André Faucher, *L'Agonie d'un régime (1952–1958)* (Paris: Editions Atlantic, 1959), p. 65.

6. Vincent Auriol, *Mémoires*, vol. 7 (Paris: Colin, 1970), p. 295.

7. François Mitterrand, "FM explique sa démission," *L'Express*, September 5, 1953, pp. 13.

8. Faucher, *L'Agonie*, pp. 100–101.

9. Franz-Olivier Giesbert, *François Mitterrand ou la tentation de l'histoire* (Paris: Seuil, 1977), p. 120.

10. Ibid.

11. François Mitterrand, *Présense française et abandon* (Paris: Plon, 1957), pp. 61–62.

12. Ibid., p. 9.

13. Roger Le Tourneau, *Evolution politique de l'Afrique du nord musulmane* (Paris: Colin, 1962), p. 362.

14. Ives Courrière, *La Guerre d'Algérie*, vol. 1 (Paris: Fayard, 1968), p. 295.

15. Ibid., pp. 293–302.

16. Giesbert, *François Mitterrand*, p. 127.

17. Courrière gives a different account of what Mitterrand knew at this time. He alleges that Mitterrand never even saw the urgent report that Léonard had sent to Paris a week before: "The minister will never read the thin sheets which the Governor General sent. A blasé civil servant classified them in the umbrella reports file, 'those which officials send in great numbers in order to cover themselves'" (*La Guerre d'Algérie*, vol. 1, p. 317).

18. Alistair Horne, *A Savage War of Peace: Algeria 1954–1962* (New York: Viking, 1977), p. 100.

19. Grosser, *La Quatrième République*, pp. 331–32.

20. Horne, *A Savage War of Peace*, p. 100.

21. Ibid., p. 106.

22. Charles-Robert Ageron, "Le Gouvernement Pierre Mendès France et l'Insurrection Algérienne," in François Bédarida and Jean-Pierre Rioux, *Pierre Mendès France et le*

*mendésisme* (Paris: Fayard, 1985), p. 339. "Everything indicates that Mendès France would have wished more diplomacy on the part of his young colleague" (ibid., p. 340).

23. Ibid., p. 337.

24. See Claude Clément, *L'Affaire des fuites: Objectif Mitterrand* (Paris: Orban, 1980).

25. Giesbert, *François Mitterrand*, pp. 147–48.

# 4

## The End of the Fourth Republic

Soon after the demise of the Mendès France Cabinet, Edgar Faure, Mendès France's rival for leadership of the Radical Party, formed a new center-right government in which neither Mitterrand nor Mendès France took part. This government lasted long enough to clear a few more hurdles on the road to decolonization. It restored the sultan of Morocco and granted Morocco full independence, and in Tunisia it signed the Franco-Tunisian conventions, paving the way for independence in 1956.

But Mitterrand was not happy. He postulated a North African domino theory of progressive independence—first Morocco, next Tunisia, then Algeria—and he sharply criticized Faure for following a path that would most probably lead to this result. The Franco-Tunisian conventions (which even the right accepted) shocked him less than the policy lurches of the "opportunistic right," mainly made up of colonial, conservative, and Gaullist deputies, who now acquiesced in a policy more liberal than the one for which they had pilloried Mendès France.

In the meantime, Mitterrand continued to exert his influence to persuade the government—particularly Faure, the Radical Maurice Bourgès-Maunoury (Faure's minister of justice), and Jacques Soustelle (who continued to be the governor of Algeria)—to negotiate a federalist solution with moderate Algerians such as Ferhat Abbas, the head of the most moderate Arab faction. Although Mitterrand had initially wanted a federalist solution for Tunisia and Morocco only and had insisted on much closer ties with Algeria, he had, after much hesitation, finally accepted this solution for Algeria, too. His exhortations seemed to have had no effect on the government. Soustelle, originally appointed by Mendès France to direct Algerian affairs, had started out as an assimilationist with a liberal reputation. In 1955 he had declared that his and Mitterrand's positions were not very far apart. But since then he had moved far to the right on Algerian policy, and his influence now greatly surpassed Mitterrand's.

After Faure lost his majority in the National Assembly, a new center-left coalition called the Republican Front campaigned against the center right. This new coalition consisted of the Socialist Guy Mollet, the Radical Mendès France, Mitterrand, and Jacques Chaban-Delmas (a left-wing Gaullist whom Mitterrand had known since the Resistance) and their followers. (Most of the Radical Party plus the MRP and the CNI made up the center right.) The main issues of the 1956 campaign were the electoral process itself, the domestic economy, and, of course, the Algerian conflict.

With an increasing awareness of the regime's fragility, the parties talked more and more about tinkering with the semiproportional electoral system in force, whereby any party obtaining at least 5 percent of the vote was represented in the National Assembly. The center left, including Mitterrand, favored a return to the one-name ballot (single-member district), which recalled the "individualistic," or personal, system of the Third Republic. Though this regime had proved more stable than the Fourth Republic, it had nevertheless been incapable of successfully confronting the international economic and political crises of the 1930s. The center right favored the opposite—a switch to an even more proportional system. The leading political figures perceived their party's self-interest to be the same as the nation's.

Only Mendès France seriously addressed the problem of systemic instability. He proposed a law that would have fostered a legislative contract lasting the full five-year term of the National Assembly. By requiring the immediate dissolution of the National Assembly and new legislative elections in the event that a party participating in the coalition government withdrew its support in the National Assembly, deputies and ministers alike would think twice before withdrawing from the coalition, and there would be improved chances for governments to last as long as a legislative term; under the current system deputies could topple the government with impunity. Mitterrand did not become an immediate advocate of Mendès France's proposal. Although many political figures listened with interest to Mendès France's idea, the National Assembly never seriously considered implementing it—it would have meant voting to give up some of its own power.

During the national legislative campaign of 1956 Mitterrand took up the current economic issues with more enthusiasm than usual. He criticized the three recent center-right finance ministers—Pinay, Faure, and Pierre Pflimlin—for (1) leaving tradesmen and artisans subject to the "polyvalent brigades," whoever they were; (2) leaving agriculture defenseless against massive importations; (3) organizing a lowering of prices "of which the rural people were the victims" with no benefit to the national economy; (4) refusing to suppress the salary scales, which restricted salary increases; and (5) not tackling the problems of a minimum wage and housing.[1] Mitterrand was on the side of the "little guy," and on both national and international economic issues he was already a protectionist. This seems to have been his first major foray into the economic "wars." But it was Algerian policy that most concerned him.

The election results produced no absolute majority. Guy Mollet (SFIO), called on by President René Coty to be prime minister, formed a weak minority government. Mitterrand supported Mollet over Mendès France for prime minister at this time because of accumulated personal differences (stemming mainly from the leaks scandal and electoral squabbles); in return, Mollet appointed him minister of justice. Mendès France was designated minister without portfolio. The generally liberal-looking Cabinet Mollet put together quickly polarized into two groups—real liberals and hard-liners. In spite of his good intentions, Mollet quickly yielded to pressure from extremists in the European Algerian community, many of whom were ideologically "progressive" Radicals, Socialists, and Communists. Robert Lacoste (the Socialist minister in charge of Algeria) and Maurice Bourgès-Maunoury (now minister of defense) increasingly took matters into their own hands, only to let power flow through their fingers to the local police and military forces, who exercised it to atrocious excess.

First, Mendès France resigned his Cabinet position, for he wanted to have no part in a cabinet that seemed to aggravate rather than quell the violence. Then Alain Savary (minister of Tunisian and Moroccan affairs) resigned over the Ben Bella affair which had demonstrated very dramatically that the Cabinet had abdicated its authority to the military in North Africa. (Mohammed Ben Bella was one of the principal leaders of the Algerian FLN and the insurrection in 1954. An airplane en route from Rabat to Tunis carrying several leaders of the Algerian FLN had been intercepted by the French Air Force and forced to land in Algiers where the passengers, including Ben Bella, had been taken prisoner. The Mollet Cabinet as a whole had not authorized this action but defended it after the fact.) Mitterrand was shocked, but Mollet persuaded him to stay in the government, and he remained quiet.

The only action of the Mollet government that Mitterrand audibly defended was its participation in 1956, with England and Israel, in the military effort to recover the Suez Canal from Gamal Abdel Nasser. Although he took no part in the planning, Mitterrand was called on to defend the government's actions before the Senate. He had no difficulty doing this since all but the Communists seemed to approve of them. Mitterrand compared Nasser's seizure of the canal to Hitler's invasion of Czechoslovakia.[2] Furthermore, the French did not mind inflicting a heavy blow on a North African leader who was strongly supporting the Algerian rebels. But here again the government was frustrated and humiliated—this time by the United States, which prevented the completion of the mission.

The bazooka scandal was yet another fiasco that Mitterrand overlooked to avoid further embarrassing the Mollet government. This botched attempt on the life of General Raoul Salan, commander in chief of the French armed forces in Algeria, resulted in the killing of the wrong officer. (Salan, who was thought by some to be too subservient to Paris, would later go over to the French

Algerian insurrectionist side.) Under police interrogation, the hit men explained that the purpose of the assassination was to set off a political brouhaha that would reach Paris, where members of the far right were ready to carry out a coup d'état with the support of the military.

The affair—in which Senator Michel Debré, Deputy Pascal Arrighi, and another young deputy, Valéry Giscard d'Estaing, were implicated by the perpetrators—was stifled with the cooperation of Mitterrand. The Ministry of Justice had done its job in Algiers and had presented to Mitterrand, the minister of justice in Paris, a voluminous file that included a request to lift the parliamentary immunity of Debré and Arrighi. Debré pleaded personally with Mitterrand to forestall that measure, and the minister of justice, having already consulted with Mollet, agreed—supposedly to conceal the decadence of the regime and also probably out of fear of provoking even more violent protest from the right.[3] The government's immediate goal had become quite modest—mere survival.

Mitterrand was politically compromised by his participation in this feckless government that accepted the increasingly violent activities carried out by its delegates while it simultaneously preached cease-fire and peace. The political scientist François Dreyfus has said that Mitterrand was responsible "for the repressive policy instituted against the Algerians as well as against the French who favored greater liberalism."[4] This is a distortion of the facts. During the period when Mitterrand was minister of the interior he had applied a nonviolent but repressive policy by declaring illegal even the nonterrorist moderate Arab organizations, but he was not against liberal reforms. And during his tenure as minister of justice he objected regularly to the increasingly violent methods of repression used. However, his influence was very limited, for the minister of justice oddly had no jurisdiction over the judicial affairs of Algeria.

Because the Ministry of Justice was not deemed effective enough in enforcing justice (punishing the Arab rebels) in Algeria, Mitterrand was pressured into signing over authority for all Algerian judicial matters to the military courts under the jurisdiction of the Ministry of Defense, headed by Bourgès-Maunoury. The pressure exerted by Robert Lacoste, Soustelle, Bourgès-Maunoury, the military, and the colonialists was enormous. Out of fear and weakness, Mollet accommodated them. But whether Mitterrand offered much resistance to this pressure, just gave up, or considered this a convenient way to wash his hands of the messy business is not at all clear. The terrorism, counter-terrorism, torture, summary executions, "disappearances," and "suicides" occurred more frequently after the military courts took over. During this period Mitterrand chose public silence—purportedly in an attempt not to weaken an already beleaguered government—and private, ineffective protest in the midst of the very ungentlemanly atmosphere of Cabinet meetings.

Later, Mitterrand would offer this explanation of why he did not resign:

> I did not want to settle into the position of the perpetual quitter. I believed also that I could weigh on the decision-making. It is generally forgotten that I had

no ministerial jurisdiction over Algeria once Robert Lacoste was the resident minister. But I had my two cents worth to offer in cabinet meetings. With Gaston Defferre, I defended positions that were not accepted. I ended up by comprehending the situation and refusing to remain in the government when, after Guy Mollet, his successor Bourgès-Maunoury asked me to stay on at the Ministry of Justice. Thus, it was over Algeria that I broke with the government.[5]

It is also quite possible that the minister of justice chose silent solidarity with the Mollet Cabinet because he felt that this posture could enhance his own chances of becoming the next prime minister.

Meanwhile, a new generation and a "new left" was already springing up to challenge the "modern left" with which Mitterrand and those politicians and journalists connected with Jean-Jacques Servan-Schreiber's *L'Express* were associated. Comprising many journalists, primarily those associated with Claude Bourdet's *France-Observateur*, it drew its intellectual inspiration not from any particular political party but rather from individual intellectuals and their publications. It included writers, philosophers, and some academics—many of them existentialist-inspired, non-Communist Marxists who clearly hated and feared the right more than they distrusted the PC (reflecting Khrushchev's purported "de-Stalinization" of the Soviet Union and the start of a thaw in East-West relations). Contributors to Jean-Paul Sartre's *Les Temps modernes* and Jean-Marie Domenach's *Esprit* were also considered part of the new left. Various small, regional, politically unorganized clubs and groups also injected into the public debate ideas that only a few years earlier would have been considered unacceptable because of their Communist origins—ideas such as the independence of Algeria and a union of the left. The political world, though, was still not ready to take these ideas seriously.

Mitterrand had contacts with some personalities in the new left circles and no doubt was familiar with their views. However, he was neither an "intellectual" politician (one who derives a policy or action from preset doctrine) nor an intellectual's politician (one who is favored by intellectuals). Very aware of the existing political constraints, he did not adopt any of the new left's ideas as his own. Moreover, his own strong reformist and federalist convictions, especially concerning Algeria, were too firmly enrooted in his mind to yield easily to the new winds. In 1957 his optimism was still inflexible. In response to Raymond Aron's 1957 book, *La Tragédie algérienne*,[6] in which the conservative commentator expressed his belief in the futility of the war and the inevitability of independence, Mitterrand commented, "I find him . . . too pessimistic and too skeptical regarding the chances for a homogeneous, political Franco-Algerian entity."[7]

As he saw new leftist groups springing up, groups that shunned both the PC and the SFIO, Mitterrand began to see the need for a union of the various factions of the left. Yet he continued to view the Communist Party not as a political partner or an enemy party, but as a rival party. In 1954, at the seventh congress of his own party he commented on his "anticommunist" strategy:

> We do not confuse the anticommunist struggle with constant bullying. We don't consider the millions of people who vote Communist as permanently lost to the nation. . . . The Communist Party undergoes a decrease in strength each time action is taken on the social level. It is on the level of ideas and accomplishments that one must fight Communists.[8]

He would never engage in direct ideological warfare with the PC.

## THE FINAL DISINTEGRATION

Mitterrand's stance vis-à-vis the last three governments of the Fourth Republic, in which he did not participate, was that of a critic speaking from within a loyal opposition. Prime ministers Bourgès-Maunoury (Radical), Félix Gaillard (Radical), and Pierre Pflimlin (MRP), all men of the center right, found themselves held hostage politically by the militant right, which dictated Algerian policy.

During the Bourgès-Maunoury and Gaillard Cabinets a flurry of proposals and counterproposals on Algerian reform flew across the hemicycle of the National Assembly. Some disintegrated in midair. Some made it to a vote. One actually passed. But there was no political will to implement any of them. Mitterrand's Algerian reform package, which called for (1) maintenance of the "indissoluble" links between France and Algeria, (2) equality of individuals, (3) creation of a federal republic uniting France, Algeria, and the sub-Saharan African territories (independence was not envisioned), (4) internal autonomy, (5) universal suffrage, and (6) respect for civil rights,[9] never made it to a vote. Bourgès-Maunoury's proposal was a hopeless hodgepodge of cumbersome and powerless political structures, and Mitterrand lambasted it in the National Assembly. Nevertheless, he then turned around and voted for it.

> The political context dominating the domestic scene at the time—the massive hostility of a faction that was traditionally opposed to any [political] evolution and that was accentuated, internationally, by scattered attempts made here and there to internationalize the Algerian affair—made me decide to vote for it.[10]

But it did not pass. Shortly after its defeat, Gaillard proposed an altered version of Bourgès-Maunoury's reform, which Mitterrand voted against because one of the amendments provided for an electoral system that would have been effectively under the sole control of the European Algerians. This was the only bill that did pass, only to be completely ignored.

Gaillard's government fell when conservatives who made up part of his own coalition withdrew their support. They opposed the "good offices" Gaillard wished to solicit from England and the United States to help repair relations with Tunisia, which had been damaged by the Sakhiet affair (when the French bombed Algerian rebel camps in Tunisia, killing many civilians). Mitterrand loudly blamed the right for most of France's troubles:

> The policy of force desired and practiced by the right resulted, as it has invariably for twelve years, in a compromise more ill-fated than the preceding state of affairs. . . . Such is the fine program of the policy of force: no money for arms, no intermediary for peace, no hope for men.[11]

On one level he was right, but what he failed to grasp adequately was the evidence that something more than the electoral laws and Article VIII of the Constitution concerning the French Union were flawed.

A month went by while five different political figures tried unsuccessfully to form governments. Finally, Pierre Pflimlin was called upon, and he was able to obtain a majority. Mitterrand was virtually the only Third Force party leader never called to be prime minister during the years of the Fourth Republic. This was no accident. Toward the end of this regime, he was seriously considered,[12] but there were two insurmountable problems. First, he had made it clear that he would include the PC in his majority, since it would have been impossible for him to form one otherwise. Second, the right had made it clear to President Coty that there would be "incidents" if he were chosen.[13] In other words, the right would have turned even more violently against the regime.

There is also some doubt as to whether Mitterrand could have obtained the majority needed for investiture even with the Communists. And it is unreasonable to think that if he had become prime minister he could have put down the revolt of the generals, snuffed out Algerian nationalism, and sufficiently strengthened the Fourth Republic to avoid the national tragedy that was in the making. In any case, it is extremely unlikely that his coalition could have lasted long enough to accomplish his goals. Time, military restraint, and broad political support—all of which were lacking—would have been necessary for both negotiations with the Arab Algerians (nothing in the records indicates that Mitterrand would have taken de Gaulle's road and held a referendum at this time) and constitutional reform.

Although the Communists might have remained in a Mitterrand Cabinet until dissenters had been removed and negotiations with the Arabs initiated, the Communists would have put pressure on the government to grant Algeria an easy independence. Furthermore, it is inconceivable that both the colonials and the military who supported them would have acquiesced in any of Mitterrand's negotiated federalist solutions for Algeria, or that the Algerians would have settled for anything less than total independence. And if the Algerian crisis had not ended cooperation between the Communists and the government, serious attempts to reform the constitution would have. The Communists favored an even weaker executive branch than the one in place, an all-powerful National Assembly, and more proportionality in the electoral system—all destabilizing measures. At best, Mitterrand might have been able to defer disaster. He could not have avoided it altogether. The Fourth Republic was on a collision course that no single individual, or party, could have stopped.

During the night of May 13-14, Mitterrand voted for Pflimlin, who became prime minister with a clear majority (274 to 129, with the Communists abstaining). At the same moment General Jacques Massu and his fellow military insurgents in Algiers were demanding publicly that de Gaulle form a "government of public safety" in Paris. A day later de Gaulle declared that he was "ready to assume the powers of the Republic." Events were moving faster than anyone in Paris could manage them. First, General Paul Ely resigned, and the Algerian army withdrew its support of the regime. The next day Jacques Soustelle returned to Algeria and joined the military insurgency. Two days later de Gaulle spoke again: "I am a man who belongs to no one and who belongs to everyone."[14] (Events took a turn eerily similar to the scenario that the perpetrators of the bazooka affair had described.)

Neither the government nor de Gaulle disavowed the insurgents' activities. The newly installed government, in fact, went to great length to rationalize the military rebellion. The Fourth Republic cabinets had always had a tendency to follow behind the military and cover its initiatives, of which they had had little or no previous knowledge. Mitterrand did well to point out the absurdity of the government trying to justify its confusion by claiming that the military insurgents were there to contain the Moslem insurrection and bring the rioters back to "republican legality." To Mitterrand's dismay, despite the fact that Pflimlin still had a clear majority in the National Assembly, by May 26 both he and President Coty had decided to ask de Gaulle to become the new prime minister. Since de Gaulle had been denouncing the regime since its inception, everyone knew that the offer actually meant the dissolution of the Fourth Republic.

The opposition, sensing that the very fate of the regime was at stake, quickly gathered mass support and marched across Paris to protest de Gaulle's advent and to "defend the Republic" (reports claim from 120,000 to 300,000 participants on May 28). Both Mendès France and Mitterrand, members of the PC, dissident Socialists, and the major trade unions participated. Conspicuously absent were Mollet and the Socialist party faithful, who were leaning toward support of de Gaulle.

Whether or not to vote for de Gaulle's investiture was one of the most anguishing decisions of Mitterrand's career. A decade later, in *Ma Part de vérité*, he published a particularly vivid account of his thoughts and feelings at that historic moment:

> Thus, on that afternoon of May 29 . . . I walked alone for long hours along the
> quays of the Left Bank. . . . I questioned myself, anguish-stricken. Should I

defend a political system incapable of restoring to France its rightful position or should I lend a hand to the plot that was going to destroy it? I searched in the teachings of times gone by for the lesson I needed. Everything suggested consenting to the liquidation of the Fourth Republic, of its do-nothing kings, its palace mayors, that scene of agony. Everything also led me away from this dictatorship, visible to the naked eye underneath its innocent-looking mask. . . .

Fight for what and for whom? But I felt a debt to these forsaken people [who mournfully protested the threat to the regime]; I felt to blame for their indifference. If they watched the execution of democracy like a spectacle which did not concern them, whose fault was it if not the mandarins who had used up the words and emptied things of their meaning? Now, I had participated in the enterprise, I had respected its way of doing things, I had not shouted loud enough to disrupt the proceedings.[15]

In the 1940s, when Hitler had "punished" the French for their "glorious errors" and their weakness, Mitterrand had felt deeply that he was paying a "debt" of a purely historical nature, but now his responsibility was admittedly more direct. He really had contributed to toppling governments, although he had not abused the rules as some had. Yet Mitterrand did not see the problem or the desired solution at all in the way those leaning toward de Gaulle did:

The disorder, the anarchy, the impotence of the Fourth Republic were not the result of an excess of democracy but rather the stifling of democracy. The parties that managed it—the SFIO, the Radical Party, and to a lesser degree the MRP . . . were dominated by bureaucrats who had closed the doors . . . through which fresh air could pass. The regular consultation at the grassroots level was only a ritual for approving decisions that had already been made. Serious business was taken care of at the highest levels, the disavowal of which was prevented by manipulating mandates at the time of conventions.[16]

If Mitterrand cannot be accused of manipulating the grassroots, it is only because the UDSR had none; it was a classic party of notables.

On May 31, a couple of days after his riverside reflections, Mitterrand participated in a meeting at the Hôtel de la Pérouse at which Fourth Republic notables were given the opportunity to question de Gaulle about his intentions. Others at the meeting included Daladier (the irony of whose presence was surely lost on no one at the meeting—after all, it was only fitting that he who had accommodated Hitler should finally accommodate the very Frenchman who had refused to accommodate Hitler), Pinay, and Mollet. De Gaulle showed himself to be a master of evasion. Mitterrand, the last to speak, was the only one present who voiced an explicit objection to de Gaulle's bid; he declared that he would not support the general unless he disavowed the military insurgency and the "committees of public safety."[17] The next day in a long and dramatic speech before the National Assembly that was constantly interrupted by shouts and clamor from the right, Mitterrand expounded the ideas on which he had based his "no" vote regarding de Gaulle's investiture. The violent circumstances, de Gaulle's refusal to disavow the military insurgency, and the lack of precise guarantees that democratic procedures would be respected determined his opposition. Nevertheless, he recognized the difficulty of defending the customs of the Fourth Republic:

> We will not fight for the rites, for the mores, for the quirks of this system which have been so thoroughly denounced. Moreover, some of the men surrounding General de Gaulle in his government are . . . particularly well qualified to take it apart. This system—they made it, they managed it, they are responsible for its undoing.[18]

And he was no less sensitive to the particular attraction exerted by de Gaulle,

> the man who has unusual prestige and incomparable glory, and has rendered exceptional services. The man of Brazzaville, who more than any other, signifies by his presence alone before this tribune a hope for peoples overseas. . . .
>
> Finally, General de Gaulle embodies authority, which is indispensable for directing public affairs, and that is not negligible. . . . When, on September 10, 1944, General de Gaulle stood before the Consultative Assembly resulting from the struggles outside and within the Resistance, he had by his side two companions called Honor and Fatherland. But his companions today, whom he has doubtlessly not chosen but who have followed him up to now, are named Force and Sedition.
>
> The presence of General de Gaulle signifies . . . that from now on violent minorities will be able to attack democracy with impunity and victoriously. . . .
>
> In theory, this evening General de Gaulle will receive his powers from the national representatives; in fact, he already holds them by virtue of the military rebellion.[19]

There is a gap between Mitterrand's private thoughts and his public pronouncement. Although privately he already feared dictatorship, publicly he continued to show respect for the former leader of the Free French. He condemned only the "circumstances," not the man.

No one was listening, however, and the National Assembly elected de Gaulle prime minister by a vote of 309 to 224. The opposition was made up primarily of Communists, dissident Socialists, Mendesist Radicals, and Mitterrandists within the UDSR. René Pleven and his followers in the UDSR voted for de Gaulle.[20] Mollet, Pflimlin, Pinay, and Chaban-Delmas also went over to the general. Edgar Faure offered very discreet opposition and eventually actively participated in Gaullist and post-Gaullist governments. Gaillard retreated from the forefront of politics. Mendès France, Mitterrand, and Bourgès-Maunoury were the most prominent non-Communist leaders of the Fourth Republic to resist the Gaullist tide.

The day after the election, de Gaulle, as expected, asked the National Assembly to grant him full constituent powers. Mitterrand sensed that de Gaulle intended to assume full plebiscitary powers as well. Like other parliamentarians with a sense of history, he feared a replay of the populist authoritarianism of Napoleon III: "Nothing is more frightening to us than direct dialogue between the government and the people without the representatives of the nation being given any chance to express themselves."[21] Nonetheless, by a vote of 350 to 161, with 70 abstaining, de Gaulle obtained full powers, including the power to submit a new constitution directly to the people for approval by referendum, quickly confirming Mitterrand's fears of a plebiscitary regime.

Throughout this period there is surprisingly little evidence of the vulgar Machiavellianism so often attributed to Mitterrand. Of course, he participated in the back-room machinations of coalitions and oppositions—that is part of the political game. Mitterrand was publicly silent at the time of the Mollet Cabinet mainly because he judged that a pragmatic silence would jeopardize the fragile political situation and hope for a federalist solution less than anything he could say. The tactic was ineffectual, but not cynical. There is no appreciable gap between Mitterrand's writings, speeches, and actions. While maintaining respect for the system and deference toward his elder colleagues, he was forthright and outspoken on specific issues in the National Assembly, the cabinets in which he participated, and with de Gaulle himself.

Mitterrand's rejection of de Gaulle in 1958 exemplifies a loftier kind of Machiavellianism. It was the political moral equivalent of de Gaulle's own rejection of Marshal Pétain in 1940 though in less dramatic circumstances. De Gaulle's position was quite different in 1958 from what it had been in 1940. He occupied the moral high ground in 1940, and circumstances were of a much graver nature to be sure; they extended to the international level and pitted de Gaulle against an evil much greater than the evils Mitterrand feared in 1958—evils that, in this case, de Gaulle preferred to exploit rather than combat. Both princes opposed the onset of a new regime but for very different reasons—de Gaulle opposed Pétain's regime mainly because of its capitulation to a foreign power, not on political grounds; Mitterrand opposed de Gaulle because he feared the establishment of a repressive, authoritarian regime at home.

Nonetheless, Mitterrand's decision involved greater personal political risk than de Gaulle's and required at least as much courage precisely because of the very ambiguousness of the situation in 1958. In 1940 de Gaulle had a relatively safe haven and powerful allies to resort to. His stance brought him instant prestige and political influence over Frenchmen—a life-time supply of political capital. However, in 1958 Mitterrand had good reason to believe that the effects of his decision would plunge him into political oblivion indefinitely and bring him no guarantee of future prestige or influence. And unlike de Gaulle in 1940, he had no powerful associates to turn to. There was no organized counterforce within which to work, no political figure equal in prestige to de Gaulle with whom he could take up the fight. The most likely candidate, Mendès France, while rejecting the new regime, was not adept at or interested in the kind of practical political activism that the situation required; besides, he and Mitterrand had drifted apart since the end of Mendès France's premiership. Although they frequently found themselves on the same side of an issue, their natural political rivalry and difference in style (Mitterrand's pragmatic flexibility along with personal aggressiveness versus Mendès France's intellectual rigor coupled with personal restraint and patience) and, to a lesser degree, interests (Mendès France was much more interested in the economic ramifications of policy) also kept them apart. There was no animosity between the two men, but no intimacy either.

In 1940 it was clear that de Gaulle had chosen the side of good and the ultimate side of history. In 1958, it also looked as if de Gaulle again represented the flow of history and the morally preferable (although the merits and demerits of each side were hotly debated) and that Mitterrand resisted the historical tide and the necessary Gaullist response. But continued fidelity to his notion of republicanism caused Mitterrand to refuse to yield to the relentless flow of events and to choose the least popular of two uncertainties. Although it cannot be said that his decision was either wise or visionary, there is no doubt that his resounding "no" to de Gaulle was the turning point and the single most important Machiavellian act of his career.

## NOTES

1. François Mitterrand, campaign statement from National Assembly documents, January 1956, cited in François Mitterrand, *Politique* (Paris: Fayard, 1977), pp. 368–69.

2. Franz-Olivier Giesbert, *François Mitterrand ou la tentation de l'histoire* (François Mitterrand or the temptation of history) (Paris: Seuil, 1977), p. 167.

3. Ibid., pp. 183–84.

4. François Dreyfus, *Histoire des gauches en France (1940–1974)* (History of the leftist movements in France) (Paris: Grasset, 1975), p. 165.

5. François Mitterrand, *Politique 2 (1977–1981)* (Paris: Fayard, 1981), p. 9.

6. Raymond Aron, *La Tragédie algérienne* (The Algerian tragedy) (Paris: Plon, 1957).

7. Interview in *Paris-Presse*, June 29, 1957, cited in Mitterrand, *Politique*, p. 130.

8. Interview in *Paris-Presse*, May 9, 1957, cited in Mitterrand, *Politique*, p. 369.

9. Mitterrand, *Politique*, pp. 128–29.

10. *Journal Officiel* (Assemblée Nationale) [abbreviated throughout as *J.O.* (A.N.)], no. 109 (November 29, 1957): 5,072.

11. Mitterrand, *Politique*, p. 150.

12. The idea circulated in the newspapers of the day, and several scholars concur: Giesbert, *François Mitterrand*, p. 202; Alexander Werth, *De Gaulle: A Political Biography* (Harmondsworth, England: Penguin, 1965), p. 23; Jean-André Faucher, *L'Agonie d'un régime (1952–1958)* (The agony of a regime) (Paris: Editions Atlantic, 1959), p. 213; and Mitterrand, *Politique 2*, p. 9.

13. Mitterrand, *Politique 2,* p. 9.

14. Mitterrand, *Politique,* p. 193.

15. Mitterrand, *Ma Part de vérité* (My share of the truth) (Paris: Fayard, 1969), pp. 56–58.

16. Ibid., p. 53.

17. *Combat,* October 22, 1962, cited in Mitterrand, *Politique,* p. 195.

18. *J.O.* (A.N.), no. 55 (June 1, 1958): 2,585.

19. Ibid.

20. Those saying no to de Gaulle "seemed to be suggesting . . . that the Fourth Republic was at heart sounder than it seemed, and that the right course was to take the risk of civil war in France as well as in Algeria, in defense of the Republic and of republican institutions" (Dorothy Pickles, *Algeria and France: From Colonialism to Cooperation* [New York: Praeger, 1963], p. 148).

21. *J.O.* (A.N.), no. 56 (June 2, 1958): 5,774.

# 5

# The "Desert Crossing"

In the legislative elections that followed the dissolution of the final National Assembly of the Fourth Republic, Mitterrand, along with Mendès France, Defferre, Faure, and Bourgès-Maunoury, lost his Assembly seat. Although swept from the national scene by the Gaullist tide, Mitterrand remained in provincial politics. He held on to his seats in the Nevers municipal council and in the general council of the department of the Nièvre. In addition, he was elected to the Senate (the upper chamber of Parliament, traditionally a retreat for older political notables whose careers are on the decline) and the mayoralty of Château-Chinon, a town of 3,000, capturing the latter post from a Socialist incumbent by engaging in an electoral alliance with the Communists.[1] But even though he still occupied positions of influence at many different levels of government, Mitterrand was now powerless at the national level. As de Gaulle's "desert crossing" was coming to an end, Mitterrand's was just beginning.

In 1958, for the first time in his life Mitterrand turned to the practice of law to help him support his wife and two sons. He joined the firm of Irène Dayan, the wife of his lifelong friend Georges Dayan, and maintained an association with the firm until 1965. Although Mitterrand, with his superb oratorical skill, had the potential to be a great trial lawyer, private law practice was much too narrow a field for him. His love of action, his preoccupation with public affairs, and his will to power could only find satisfaction in politics.

## THE OBSERVATORY SCANDAL

For a little over a year, the former minister of justice led a tranquil existence as a senator and practicing lawyer. Then abruptly, in October 1959, scandal again broke over Mitterrand's head. On October 7, a shady character named

Robert Pesquet (elected deputy in 1956 on a Gaullist ticket—he later joined the Poujadist[2] group) approached Mitterrand, who had only met him once before, at the Palais de Justice to warn him of an assassination plot against him. At first Mitterrand did not take Pesquet seriously. Every day for six days Pesquet begged Mitterrand to meet with him so that he could inform him of the details of the plot, but Mitterrand refused.

Meanwhile, during a time when rumors of civil turmoil were rife, Mitterrand received anonymous phone calls threatening his and his family's lives. Getting nervous, Mitterrand finally agreed to hear Pesquet out in a public place—the Luxembourg Palace—on October 15. Pesquet informed him that one night he would be chased down in his car and that someone would try to kill him. He could save himself by jumping out of his car and hiding in the Observatory Gardens, which were near his home. Pesquet pleaded with Mitterrand not to tell anyone of the impending attempt on his life or to reveal Pesquet's name because Pesquet's own life and family would be endangered. Mitterrand agreed.

That very night things went as Pesquet had predicted. Mitterrand was chased. He jumped to safety and watched as his car was riddled with bullets. The next day all of France was scandalized by the attempt, and Mitterrand was the object of universal sympathy.

On October 19 Mitterrand met with Pesquet to thank him for saving his life. During that week he also spoke to the police, but did not give Pesquet's name as Pesquet had requested. Four days later Pesquet called a press conference and claimed that Mitterrand had set up a fake assassination attempt to provoke raids on the right and to draw public sympathy away from Mendès France to himself. Sympathy toward Mitterrand immediately turned into snickers and sarcasm as the gullible public was taken in by Pesquet's story. Friends and supporters on both the right and the left deserted him. Mitterrand suffered total public humiliation, even worse than that which he had endured during the leaks scandal. It was a political horror story that transformed the former minister of justice into an untouchable even to his colleagues on the established left, and it marked the lowest point in his entire career.[3]

Only Jean-Jacques Servan-Schreiber and his friends at *L'Express,* along with the pro-Gaullist François Mauriac, were quick to defend Mitterrand. Even Mendès France took a few days to come to the aid of his former colleague. Witnesses said that they had never seen a more discouraged, depressed Mitterrand. On top of it all, Prime Minister Michel Debré, whom Mitterrand had not pursued at the time of the bazooka scandal, requested that Mitterrand's parliamentary immunity be lifted so that he could be indicted for contempt of court. Debré, taking advantage of his declared opponent's predicament, claimed that Mitterrand had shown contempt by not revealing Pesquet's name to the authorities when he reported the event to them. The Senate voted 175 to 27 to lift Mitterrand's immunity, and an indictment followed; however, investigation into the contempt charge and Pesquet's frame-up were both lost, perhaps intentionally, in the shuffle of judicial procedure. But, as in the leaks scandal, the damage had been done; one of the government's most vociferous adversaries had been humiliated.

No one was ever prosecuted in connection with this affair, not even Pesquet. Later, on two different occasions, Pesquet admitted Mitterrand's innocence, giving different versions of the assassination plot each time. In 1965 he implicated the right-wing extremist Jean-Louis Tixier-Vignancour and in 1974 Debré himself, but there was never any thorough public investigation of the events. (Debré is a much more plausible source of the plot than Tixier-Vignancour, who had nothing to gain by embarrassing Mitterrand. On the other hand, Debré knew that Mitterrand possessed damaging information implicating him in the bazooka affair and that he opposed de Gaulle's every move; he had much to gain by the success of this plot.) To this day no one knows for sure who was at the source of this scandal other than Pesquet. Although it would take Mitterrand years to rebuild public trust, he recovered emotionally in a relatively short period of time; characteristically, he bounced back with more determination than ever to oppose the Gaullist regime implacably and reclaim a leadership position on the left.

The task of regaining respect and credibility (which had been weakened already by Mitterrand's extended acceptance of the Mollet Cabinet) was extremely difficult, for every significant political organization on the left had ostracized him. His own party, the UDSR, was falling apart under the pressure of the new regime and the strain imposed by the Observatory scandal. Throughout the early 1960s Mitterrand was virtually a political pariah. Since he had never been a doctrinaire socialist, he was always ideologically suspect in the eyes of strict Socialists such as Guy Mollet and the SFIO leaders in general. Now even his moral integrity had been impugned. When he applied for membership in the newly formed dissident socialist party, the Autonomous Socialist Party (PSA, later called the Unified Socialist Party, or PSU), purists such as Alain Savary and Edouard Depreux (for whose Algerian doctrine he had fought) deemed him unacceptable. There seemed to be nowhere for him to turn.

## A TRIP TO CHINA

During this period he made trips to sub-Saharan Africa, the United States, Egypt, and China, and although he always traveled as a private citizen, his distinguished past entitled him to the honors of an unofficial representative of France. His three-week tour of China provided him with the opportunity to study a traditionally anti-Western society trying to become a Western-inspired socialist utopia.[4] The experience resulted in the book-length essay *La Chine au défi*,[5] which represents Mitterrand's first serious effort to position himself on the left. In general, his criticism of China's obvious evils is tempered by an equally obvious desire on his part to see the Chinese Communist experiment succeed.

Mitterrand's visit took place at the end of one of China's worst years since the birth of the People's Republic. A combination of floods, droughts, and primitive agricultural methods together with agrarian "reform" had led to a disastrous harvest. The population had narrowly escaped massive famine and had suffered from high mortality because of malnutrition and physical exhaustion from overwork.[6] Only a generous supply of goodwill and indulgence on Mitterrand's part enabled him to discern progress at this point in Chinese development. Mitterrand accepted the argument that communism, on its march toward socialism, can and sometimes must skip the long, drawn-out liberal "bourgeois" revolution. He recognized the human suffering that occurred along the way, but dismissed it: "It would be wrong to fixate on [the system's internment camps, etc.], a vice which is limited neither to China alone nor to people's republics."[7] Finally, "the intense faith [of the Chinese] deserves better than the response they are accustomed to hearing from this side of the earth."[8]

Mitterrand's greatest sympathy goes out to China as a poor, proud, underdog nation. He is sympathetic toward the social aims of China even if he does not like its methods. He portrays the contrast between Peking and Hong Kong all to the benefit of the former, the latter representing the extremes of opulent decadence and degrading squalor:

> The contrast between a too easy life and squalid misery, the permanent commercial boom and the disorder of speculation, the triumph of neon-lit artificiality restored in my mind China's true image, its real dimensions, its grandeur.[9]

Here Mitterrand's atavistic provincial Catholicism coincides with Chinese communism's moralistic scorn of the individual pursuit of wealth. The "austere" grayness of the "frontier capital" somehow possessed a moral grandeur that the brazen neon lights of Hong Kong could never evoke for Mitterrand.

## TAKING ON THE GAULLIST REGIME

The question now for Mitterrand was not where lay France's future grandeur, but where, after de Gaulle, lay the path back to a more democratic yet stable republic and—more urgent for Mitterrand, whose political career appeared to be over after the Observatory scandal—what active role he could play in national politics. He naturally fell into the role of witness. But the witness quickly turned into a critic—sharp and unrelenting—and the critic became an outspoken political "resistance fighter" opposed to the Gaullist state, which the left generally viewed as a kind of occupation.

In his numerous articles in such periodicals as *L'Express, La Nef,* and *Le Courier de la Nièvre,* in his speeches in the Senate and later again in the National Assembly, and in his book *Le Coup d'état permanent,*[10] Mitterrand expressed his objections—some valid, some not—to the general's regime along with his own alternative solutions. The lapses in Gaullist democracy were easy for him to recognize and had nothing to do with his recent trip to China; his critique was based solely on the French republican and legal tradition, not on ideological considerations. His two main areas of concern continued to be colonial policy, particularly the handling of the Algerian War, and the Gaullist transformation of French political institutions. Foreign policy as a whole occupied him relatively little, and he gave even less attention to domestic economic policy.

Mitterrand immediately objected to de Gaulle's constitutional referendum of 1958 on several grounds. One of the main objections was that it incorporated two separate questions into a single yes-or-no vote: At the same time that the French were being asked if they accepted the political structure proposed by de Gaulle for metropolitan France, both the French and sub-Saharan Africans were also voting on whether their colonies should join France in forming a Franco-African Community. This meant that if a Frenchman voted no on the structural changes, he was automatically voting to abandon the colonies. By the same token, if an African voted yes to the referendum, he or she was automatically accepting the political institutions called for in the referendum. This posed a dilemma for Frenchmen such as Mitterrand and for the Africans who wanted to participate in developing the rules under which they would have to live.[11]

Mitterrand voted no on the referendum, along with the Communists and other dissidents on the left. But 80 percent of the voters, including the majority of the members of the SFIO and the Africans themselves, voted yes. Only Guinea voted no, whereupon France immediately granted it independence (and pulled out all equipment and aid). The Gaullist government gloated over its success in creating a Franco-African Community, for which Mitterrand and the last few governments of the Fourth Republic had worked so hard but had failed to achieve. Mitterrand, of course, rejected the comparison: "A liberal policy . . . that you determine voluntarily is not the same as a liberal policy that you are forced to consent to because you cannot do otherwise."[12] (He forgot that he, too, had developed reforms for the North African colonies in which no one outside of his ministry had participated.)

In the early months of the Gaullist regime Mitterrand complained about the imprecision and ambiguity of de Gaulle's personal stance on the colonies coupled with the fanatic colonialism of his supporters. Later, he attacked the plebiscitary form in which the referendum had been presented to the French people, the unilateral manner in which it was presented to the Algerians, and its gaps, inconsistencies, weaknesses, and overall lack of feasibility. Yet despite the war, the torture, the terror, the political confusion, the ultraconservatives' fanaticism, and the ever increasing desire for independence among the Algerians, Mitterrand remained hopeful that some kind of federalist solution could be found: "[Moslem hopes] are now on the side of independence. To bring them back to the side of France, France must change directions. . . . Hope can still choose France, but it is losing patience."[13]

In September 1959 de Gaulle publicized, for the first time, the idea of self-determination, which infuriated the civilian and military ultraconservatives in

Algeria, and they were soon rioting and plotting against him. At the same time, as yet fruitless negotiations were going on in Melun, France, with the Moslem Algerians. In November 1960 de Gaulle visited Algeria and returned to Paris determined to conduct a referendum based on his idea of self-determination for Algeria.

While Mitterrand accepted the idea of self-determination as such, he was sharply critical of the fact that it was put forth as a referendum. The senator predictably called for a no vote. The whole Parliament had again been bypassed, which the senator contended violated Article 89 of the constitution. Most of all it was the content of the referendum with which Mitterrand found the greatest fault. If the process called for in the referendum were to be put into effect, all Algerians would have to vote by state, which meant that if the majority within a state voted yes, then that region would be "associated" with France; if the majority voted no, the state would become independent. The inevitable result would be the de facto partition of Algeria. Nevertheless, the referendum was put forward and passed with a resounding 75 percent of the vote. Like all the other plans, however, this one was never implemented; all knew it would never work. The conflict was far from resolved.

In 1961, after continuous turmoil, civilian and military opposition came to a boil culminating in a four-day coup attempt, known as the "putsch," and months of civilian violence. The rebellious generals were eventually caught and put on trial. Meanwhile, the French government was trying to negotiate a settlement with the Provisional Government of the Algerian Republic (GPRA). The GPRA would concede nothing to the French in their efforts to defend French interests in Algeria, including sovereignty over Saharan oil fields, which was France's last line of defense. To make matters worse, by 1961 the Franco-African Community had fallen apart, its Senate dissolved through the mail by de Gaulle; no one, African or French, had ever been seriously interested in working to create a real community. This further reduced the chances of integrating Algeria into even a loose federalist framework.

Deputies and senators continued to busy themselves by debating the government's meaningless proposals for self-determination, integration, partition, and so on. Mitterrand condemned all of the proposals. He even claimed that every effort of the Gaullist government to put down the Moslem rebellion and negotiate with the GPRA was based primarily on its preoccupation with reinforcing its own power: "You [Louis Joxe, the Minister of Algerian Affairs, representing the government] keep the war going just enough to prevent it from ending. To be sure, this clever, scientifically managed, uncertain state ultimately favors your plans and adds to your power."[14] Ignoring momentarily the realities of power politics, Mitterrand attributed a cleverness to the government it did not possess. Furthermore, his attacks, to the extent that they had any effect, worked to undermine the government's efforts to gain time and get the best agreement it could.

The violent attacks on the regime and de Gaulle personally by the OAS in no way mitigated Mitterrand's criticisms. He warned colleagues not to give in politically to the natural sympathy for any victim of an assassination attempt, noting that this was essentially a "duel where spoils are disputed."[15] He even went so far as to explain why the OAS generals' actions were, if not exactly acceptable, nonetheless understandable. In his Senate speech of July 1961, two years after the Observatory scandal, Mitterrand rubbed Prime Minister Debré's nose in the unpleasant mess:

> When one sees . . . General Salan somewhere in hiding and Michel Debré at Matignon, this perspective explains better than any plea . . . a certain lack of discipline, unjustifiable historically and politically; a certain revolt can be understood from a human viewpoint. That men felt called upon to prefer disobedience to perjury, whose fault, Mr. Debré?[16]

According to Mitterrand, at least the generals, who felt betrayed by de Gaulle, had been consistent with themselves. The Fifth Republic was only getting what it deserved in his eyes. Mitterrand gave no quarter to de Gaulle or Debré, who, when it came to Algeria, were hemmed in on all sides.

In 1962, giving up on Algeria, de Gaulle finally concluded the Evian Accords with the GPRA granting Algeria independence, including sovereignty over the Saharan oil fields. Mitterrand's opposition was still systematic. Faithful to his antiplebiscitary and pro-Franco-Algerian principles and also conscious that he was going against the current of French opinion, which now favored independence over continuing discord and violence, Mitterrand voted no on the accords, which were put to the French people in the form of a referendum. Mitterrand publicly claimed that, in this case, his reaction was based on an objection to the plebiscitary procedure rather than on the idea of Algerian independence itself; he could not condemn the substance of an agreement which the French overwhelmingly approved. The accords were passed with 90 percent of the vote (99.72 of the Algerians voted for them). For the senator, however, the substance of the accords was profoundly disappointing. Independence meant a historical rending, causing this avid supporter of the federalist solution unabashed public sorrow.

> Good luck then to Algeria, to the departing friend. But may she avoid spite and spare us her reproaches if for a moment . . . we turn our head to hide from her the pain that is grabbing us, and which hope itself . . . cannot alleviate.[17]

Mitterrand felt most bitter toward those Gaullist ultraconservatives who, after politically pillorying anyone who had sought to reconcile legitimate French and Algerian interests through peaceful negotiation and reform, abandoned every French position to Arab revolutionary nationalists. He found an unlikely partner in his grief—Michel Debré, who also had difficulty swallowing the abandonment of Algeria. De Gaulle forced him to resign as prime minister, and Georges Pompidou, de Gaulle's longtime trusted advisor on economic and financial affairs, became prime minister.

Thus ended the Algerian War. It was the final, climactic act of French decolonization, a ten-year drama that had dominated Mitterrand's political life up until then.[18]

The second field on which the senator from the Nièvre battled de Gaulle without respite was the constitution. In the early years of the Fifth Republic, Mitterrand was as critical of the way de Gaulle governed as he was of the content of his policies. Mitterrand feared and disapproved of de Gaulle's preference for a plebiscitary system, which was evident despite his hat tipping to Parliament and was reminiscent of the methods Napoleon III used to bypass Parliament and exploit his popularity among the masses. By claiming the right to set the National Assembly's agenda, the executive branch was attempting to rob the legislative of its theoretical prerogative to initiate legislation. Furthermore, debate was limited; except for the vote of censure, which the Assembly retained, both houses were relegated to consultative roles. In addition, great leeway was provided for the use of executive decrees. (Later as president, Mitterrand accommodated himself quite nicely to the constitutional loopholes that allow the executive branch to bypass Parliament.)

Remarkably, Mitterrand fought hard against de Gaulle's referendum of 1962 on the proposal to elect the president by universal suffrage. To him this was yet another dangerous extension of a plebiscitary regime and was incompatible with the "Latin" traditions of France.

> I believe there is a fatal risk of sliding toward authoritarianism, because of the too lively passions—among others the passion for power—which will spare neither the executive nor the too often changeable, demanding citizens. . . . I do not see how balance can be maintained.[19]

Throughout the Third and Fourth Republics the president of France had been elected by the members of both houses of Parliament, who expected the officeholder to fill the role of arbiter between parties and stay above party politics. The president had appointed the prime minister, who was the real executive authority, based on the balance of power in the National Assembly. (The Constitution of the Fifth Republic designated an electoral college of 80,000 national and local elected officials to elect the president.) Mitterrand disapproved of the election of the president by universal suffrage because plunging the president into national partisan politics would radically alter the relationship between the president and prime minister: Either the president would totally dominate the prime minister or there would be conflict between the two. Mitterrand deplored both possibilities.

In addition, he saw election by universal suffrage as further weakening the

National Assembly, which the president could still dissolve. Thus, in contrast to popular interpretation, the senator interpreted this innovation as in no way moving toward an American-style presidential system, because it would leave the president with powers no American president possessed—to rule by decree, to obtain full powers as need be, not only to negotiate but also to ratify treaties, to dissolve a legislative chamber, and to hold referenda.

Rather than looking for ways to reinforce the executive branch, Mitterrand began to favor the idea of a negotiated legislative contract, a modified version of the concept originally proposed by Mendès France. This, he thought, would more faithfully respect the "customs" and "national character" of the French. Throughout the 1960s the Gaullists could operate without a legislative contract because they had hegemony on the right—that is, their party dominated the other parties that formed the presidential majority coalition, which was always supported by a legislative majority. The left entertained the idea of contract government because it knew that unity on the fractious left would never be easy.

There is no doubt that Mitterrand was still nostalgic for certain aspects of the old party system, whereby ideas perceived as being in the international, national, or individual interest supposedly counted more than personalities.

> The important point for me is that, when choosing the executive, it is necessary to eliminate the passionate, irrational, accidental elements as much as possible. Voters must be called on to vote on ideas, programs, and general orientation before deciding on the man.[20]

In the 1950s Mitterrand had criticized this very system, when applied at the legislative level, as giving too much power to party bosses, and he had promoted the idea of returning to the individualistic single-member district system reminiscent of the Third Republic. Then, Mitterrand had liked the idea of elected officials being more personally accountable to their constituents than to their party bosses. Although individualism had seemed desirable at the local level, its application at the national level was not yet appreciated by the left in general.

De Gaulle received a resounding (62 percent) yes on the referendum instituting direct presidential elections. The 38 percent opposed to the referendum included Mitterrand as well as many voters who supported the Communist and non-Communist left, and even some centrists; but, as the figures suggest, the political elite was far behind public opinion on this issue. After the success of the referendum, Mitterrand's charges of dictatorship intensified. Even more moderate centrists began to worry about the tremendous concentration of power within the presidency. Previously, the form and content of presidential power had been severely limited. Now many moderates were beginning to believe that the country had gone too far in the other direction.

The French presidential electoral system instituted under de Gaulle, and still in use today, differs significantly from the American system (which Mitterrand has never viewed as a model for France). There are no intraparty primary elections (although the first ballot could be considered a kind of national primary), and there is no longer an electoral college for the presidency. In the multiparty, two-ballot system of France, the candidate who wins the final popular vote wins the election. The strength of the mandate depends directly on the extent of the popular vote, along with the size of the presidential majority in the National Assembly. By contrast, in the American system, which is universal but indirect, the intermediary body, the electoral college, tends to exaggerate the popular vote, reinforcing presidential power regardless of the situation in Congress. When presidential and congressional majorities clash, there may be a stalemate, but there is no political crisis or expectation of early elections to forestall a crisis. Until this clash of majorities occurred in France in the 1980s, it was greatly dreaded.

In 1962 Mitterrand, having regained the support of his former constituents in the Nièvre, won back his National Assembly seat on a redistributionist, domestically protectionist platform tailor-made to further the material interests of a very traditional constituency of farmers, artisans, small merchants, and senior citizens. He favored the "indexing of agricultural prices on industrial prices, acceleration of rural development, suppression of salary zones, health insurance for merchants and artisans, aid for the aged, and democratization of education."[21]

With the Observatory scandal four years behind him and with a voice in the National Assembly, Mitterrand was once again well positioned to bid for leadership of the left. But he still lacked one important asset—a strong party base. The UDSR was little more than a collection of friends, and all the major parties of the left—the PC, the PSA, and the SFIO—viewed this humiliated former minister of the Fourth Republic with suspicion and even scorn. Undeterred, the restored deputy exploited every opportunity to badger de Gaulle and his government anew. In April 1964 de Gaulle went into the hospital for a week, delegating his command over the nuclear strike force to Prime Minister Pompidou. Mitterrand used this as evidence that the parliamentary controls of the Constitution of the Fifth Republic were inoperative, for even de Gaulle's own constitution called for the president of the Senate, not the prime minister, to be second in command. The ever vigilant Mitterrand had memorized the new constitution, and though he did not like it, he was prepared to hold de Gaulle to the letter of it.

Measures taken in the areas of civil rights and judicial reform also encountered Mitterrand's disapproval. He objected to the increased centralization of the judicial system (which was achieved by eliminating the justices of the peace), the subordination of the judiciary to the executive branch (the executive could appoint judges, create temporary positions, establish special courts, overrule judicial decisions by decree, and advance the age of retirement), the concomitant removal of powers from the Council of Magistrates (the most senior magistrates in the nation), and the strict new rules of conduct to be respected within the courtroom. And he criticized the restrictions on the right to strike and on free speech in the media and in public, areas where de Gaulle's government strove to limit the activities of opponents.

After the eruption of OAS violence, de Gaulle had created the "courts of exception" and extended police powers considerably in order to expedite the prosecution of his opponents, and "laws of exception" were enforced retroactively. To Mitterrand these reforms were serious infringements of France's republican traditions and constituted a resurrection of the judicial practices of the monarchy. Another disconcerting feature was the *cabinet noir*, de Gaulle's personal police service installed in the Elysée Palace that directed a network of unofficial agents and agitators who specialized in disrupting meetings and rallies of opposition candidates.[22]

In his brilliant doctoral thesis, *La Gauche et la Cinquième République*,[23] Olivier Duhamel analyzes the strengths and weaknesses of Mitterrand's arguments on constitutional matters at that time. According to him, Mitterrand was on firm ground in denouncing multiple violations, especially during times of crisis, of what democracies agree to be proper constitutional law.

> The creation of a new category of ordinances, in violation of Article 38 . . . which requires a vote of Parliament to enable the government to enact measures in the legal domain, the use of the referendum to legitimate this delegation of legislative power to the president . . . and this delegation to create a court of exception which replaced another created by Article 16 but [considered] still too clement,[24] recourse to Parliament in order to maintain what the Council of State had annulled,[25] and to institutionalize a State Security Court, formed an impressive succession of unconstitutional acts capable of justifying the permanent coup d'état thesis.[26]

Beyond this, however, Mitterrand's critique contained misinterpretations of the political and constitutional implications of the regime. Politically, non-Communist opponents of the regime tended to think that it was headed toward the extremes of either collapse (Mendès France's theory) or dictatorship (Mitterrand's theory). But history belied both prognoses. After 1962, as Duhamel notes, one could observe, if not total correction of the regime's behavior, at least "institutional appeasement" and a decrease in infractions of civil rights.[27]

According to Duhamel, Mitterrand's main constitutional error resided in his perceiving the new roles assumed by the prime minister and president to be a form of growing "irresponsibility."[28] The term *irresponsible* here means not responsible to the legislative body and implies arbitrariness.

> The argument presupposes the concept of a constant quantity of power wherein none of its holders can win power without another losing power, while the direct election of the head of state augmented legitimacy, and with it, the absolute quantity of political power.[29]

The zero-sum logic of Mitterrand's "monist parliamentarianism" blinded him to the fact that the president could not assume "irresponsibility" since (1) he, not the prime minister, possessed the power of dissolution—and dissolution involved accepting the risks and responsibilities that the consequent legislative elections would create—and (2) he was ultimately responsible to the populace by virtue of direct elections.[30] But Mitterrand still greatly feared the susceptibility of the general population to demagoguery. It is not at all clear from the argument why the people should be trusted to elect mayors, deputies, and senators but not their national president.

Mitterrand spoke relatively little about Gaullist foreign policy, but when he did, he adamantly denounced it. As with colonial policy, he found that the problems lay as much in the form of policy as in the content. Problems of substance were doomed to arise out of a power structure that allowed a "reserved domain" to the president. The "reserved domain," which to Mitterrand was a perversion of the concept of the separations of powers, amounted to a presidential monopoly on decision-making in military, diplomatic, and defense matters. Supremely confident in his own judgment, de Gaulle consulted very little with others, even in private, on matters of international importance. Mitterrand's preference was not so much for wider consultation within the executive but for the more systematic participation of deputies in the decision-making process.

As for the content of de Gaulle's foreign policy, Mitterrand found it foolishly anti-American, anti-British, anti-European, anti-NATO, anti-United Nations, and in Mideast affairs anti-Israel. He considered it to be nothing more than retrograde nationalistic posturing—a policy of prestige, devoid of the necessary real power to influence events.

> De Gaulle disposes only of insignificant pieces, but he moves them. He has studied the weaknesses of his time and knows admirably well the passions and games that agitate men, the buttons that set the chancellory teletypes in motion. He knows that it is good to excite the imagination, mystify minds. Snubbing old friends, smiling at enemies gets the air moving between East and West. And isn't that a way of announcing that one exists?[31]

According to Mitterrand, this obsession with prestige led to an incoherent series of diplomatic initiatives in an effort to give France an influential role. All inevitably failed because they ignored the true state of affairs. To emphasize the incongruities, Mitterrand telescoped twenty years of Gaullist foreign policy to show the full extent of its lack of realism. There was the call for the autonomy of the Saar Valley after World War II; de Gaulle's constant hostility to the European Community in the 1950s; his efforts to create a United States–Great Britain–France triumvirate around 1960; the Franco-German alliance of 1962, which failed to draw Germany away from the United States; his "Europe from the Atlantic to the Urals" to counter the "yellow peril," followed by his recognition of China to defy both the United States and the Soviet Union; his wish for a Paris-Madrid-Rabat axis; and his courting of Latin America, Eastern Europe, later French Canada, and anyone else who appeared resentful of Soviet or American power. To Mitterrand, de Gaulle's policies seemed archaically nationalistic, in search of alliances in which France would dominate and defy the two superpowers, the United States in particular, the Cuban missile crisis notwithstanding (during these events de Gaulle stood firmly behind President John Kennedy, whom he liked very much along with his Francophile wife, Jacqueline, of French extraction).

> He punishes. . . . Behind Kennedy and Johnson, he is catching up with the shadow of Roosevelt and giving him a whipping. The Roosevelt of Casablanca. The Roosevelt of Yalta. The Roosevelt of Berlin. The Roosevelt of the UN. What Roosevelt did, de Gaulle will undo.[32]

Mitterrand thought it folly for France to withdraw from the unified military command of NATO, which de Gaulle did in 1966, and to think that France could go it alone (the premise of the "sanctuary doctrine") in the event of a nuclear war. De Gaulle believed that, with its nuclear strike force, France could maintain its freedom and independence vis-à-vis both superpowers and in the event of a nuclear war rely mainly on itself for its defense. This did not preclude cooperation with NATO, but it did put French commanders on an equal footing with NATO's American command. For Mitterrand this was a dangerous derivative of de Gaulle's nationalism, which he feared amounted to "To each his own borders, to each his own bomb."[33] Consistent with this viewpoint, Mitterrand was strongly opposed to the development of France's nuclear strike force at this time.

Mitterrand considered de Gaulle's foreign policy as only an extraordinarily grand façade concealing an ordinary level of national power. But Mitterrand realized—and no doubt found it particularly annoying—that the façade's real value lay in the dazzling effect it had at home; France was again playing a pleasingly controversial role on the world stage.

By voting no to de Gaulle in 1958 and remaining faithful to parliamentarianism, Mitterrand had bet on three losing causes—the UDSR, the Franco-African Community, and the Fourth Republic regime itself. He had, however, done everything in his power to perpetuate all these honorable though inadequate arrangements. The fraternalism of the Resistance could not last forever, and the more control Mitterrand was able to exercise over his party, the less it looked like a modern political party and the more it looked like a Mitterrand organization with little influence beyond his person.

History was not on the side of France in the colonial conflicts. Mitterrand was probably right in judging that today the Moslem Algerians would be better off materially and politically if their cart had remained hitched to France, although we know now that there were limits to the cultural Westernization of Moslem Algerians. It is equally plausible that metropolitan France would *not* be as well off as it is, that the political and economic strain resulting from Algerian development would have held back for a considerable period metropolitan prosperity, the solidification of stable democratic institutions, and progress toward European union.

The Fourth Republic regime was from its inception a flawed political machine. Today, it is still difficult to conceive of any alternative to de Gaulle in 1958 other than anarchy, civil war, colonial war, or all three at once. De Gaulle had the broadest consensus of any leader, and even he was sorely challenged by his own military and the Moslems. The majority of French people seemed to sense what Mitterrand, Mendès France, and other liberals could not see, that what the country needed was not only a strong leader but also a strong executive, whoever the leader, and national unity—not a new electoral system, a shaky parliamentarianism, or an empire of any kind. De Gaulle filled the executive power vacuum both personally and institutionally. In order to alter significantly the balance of power in his direction, Mitterrand would have to find other grounds on which to attack de Gaulle and the rightist majority.

## NOTES

1. Jean Poperen, *La Gauche française: Le Nouvel Age 1958-1965* (Paris: Fayard, 1972), pp. 131-32.

2. The Poujadists were far-right populists coalesced around the deputy Pierre Poujade, a butcher turned politician.

3. The most detailed account of this scandal is related in Philippe Alexandre's *Exécution d'un homme politique* (Execution of a politician) (Paris: Grasset, 1973), pp. 227–47. The main subject of the book is Jacques Chaban-Delmas.

4. Before he committed suicide, François de Grossouvre told several people that René Bousquet organized and financed this trip (Laurent Joffrin and Serge Raffy, "Les Mystères qui restent" [The mysteries that remain], *Le Nouvel Observateur*, no. 1558 [September 15, 1994]: 33).

5. François Mitterrand, *La Chine au défi* (China challenged) (Paris: Julliard, 1961).

6. This assessment of China's situation at the time is based on Maurice Meisner's *Mao's China* (New York: Free Press, 1977), pp. 248–67.

7. Mitterrand, *La Chine au défi*, p. 192.

8. Ibid., pp. 198–99.

9. Ibid., p. 74.

10. François Mitterrand, *Le Coup d'état permanent* (Paris: Plon, 1964).

11. *J.O.* (Sénat), no. 57 (November 25, 1961): 1995.

12. François Mitterrand, speech given at Twelfth UDSR Congress, January 1959, cited in Mitterrand, *Politique* (Paris: Fayard, 1977), p. 164.

13. François Mitterrand, "Front populaire, 'coalition immorale'?" *La Nef*, no. 27 (April 1959): 11.

14. Mitterrand, *Politique* p. 180.

15. François Mitterrand, "Forum," *L'Express*, February 25, 1960, p. 5.

16. *J.O.* (Sénat), no. 225 (July 5, 1961): 686.

17. Mitterrand, *Le Courier de la Nièvre,* June 30, 1962, cited in Mitterrand, *Politique,* p. 184.

18. France still retains a handful of small, remote territories.

19. François Mitterrand and Maurice Duverger, "Faut-il un président aux français?" *L'Express,* June 1, 1961, p. 16.

20. Ibid., p. 17.

21. Charles Moulin, *Mitterrand intime* (Paris: Albin Michel, 1982), pp. 157–58.

22. Mitterrand, *Le Coup d'état permanent,* pp. 251–58.

23. Olivier Duhamel, *La Gauche et la Cinquième République* (The left and the Fifth Republic) (Paris: Presses Universitaires de France, 1980).

24. Reference to the High Military Court, created by de Gaulle, which did not produce the desired verdicts.

25. Reference to the docile Military Court of Justice, which had been declared illegitimate by the Council of State.

26. Duhamel, *La·Gauche et la Cinquième République,* p. 67.

27. Ibid., p. 68.

28. Ibid., p. 33.

29. Ibid., p. 68.

30. Ibid., p. 69.

31. Mitterrand, *Le Coup d'état permanent,* p. 102.

32. Ibid., p. 110.

33. *J.O.* (A.N.), no. 108 (December 2, 1964): 5,774.

# 6

## The Leader of the Left

In December 1965, for the first time in their history, the French voted for their head of state in a direct election under universal suffrage. (There had been a direct election in 1848, but at that time only men had had the right to vote.) This unprecedented event represented an entry into uncharted waters of modern French democracy. Each major political figure of the day—de Gaulle, Guy Mollet (the leader of the SFIO), Mendès France (the former Radical, who had become a member of the PSA), Mitterrand, and Waldeck Rochet (the head of the PC)—approached the 1965 election very differently.

De Gaulle and his followers treated it as a plebiscite, a popular "coronation";[1] they fully expected a resounding first-ballot victory requiring little or no campaigning on the part of the candidate himself. This optimism on the right was inversely reflected as pessimism on the left. The left also believed that a crushing first-ballot de Gaulle victory was inevitable, but to them the election was no plebiscite. Mollet and Rochet, both apparently still unable to understand the new logic of the Constitution of the Fifth Republic, saw it as a ritual of minor importance, and because the triumph of de Gaulle was assured, it did not matter who ran against him. Mendès France refused to participate actively, for he considered the election, like the regime, to be illegitimate.

Mitterrand, on the other hand, viewed the election as a grand opportunity. This was a sudden reversal, for he had recently opposed both the way in which the constitutional change had been instituted—by referendum—and the constitutional provision itself. The overwhelming majority of yes votes revealed a new political age and an opportunity for Mitterrand to bypass the party bosses he scorned. Commenting on this period later in *Ma Part de vérité*, he wrote:

Since . . . 1962 I knew I would be a candidate. When? How? I could not tell. I was alone. I did not have the support of a party, or a church, or a counterchurch, or a newspaper, or a current of opinion. I had no money and I could not expect any from the usual discreet sources we all know about.[2]

In his typical fashion the pragmatic Mitterrand fully embraced the logic of the new political rules that he had so recently rejected.

Now he saw a chance to demonstrate his leadership ability and to measure his national political strength against France's national hero's, for Mitterrand considered himself an adversary worthy of the majestic de Gaulle. This was a battle where the lines could be easily drawn between the republicanism of Mitterrand and the arbitrary power of de Gaulle. Although victory was out of the question for Mitterrand at this point, his stake in the election was substantial—it amounted to his leadership of the left. In sum, here was a battle that the deputy from the Nièvre could relish.

The direct presidential election added two new political dynamics to France's multiparty system. First, by reducing the ultimate choice of president to two individuals (and two programs), it polarized public opinion; this left-right polarization would henceforth predetermine to a great extent the terms of political conflict. What surprised many was that polarization also tended toward the formation of two voting blocs of roughly equal weight. (The Gaullists believed, rather complacently, that polarization would reinforce their preponderance on the right and the right's preponderance over the left indefinitely.) Second, this process of equalization gave the center renewed importance. As the civil crisis provoked by the Algerian War subsided, extremist stances gave way more frequently to moderate positions, and the center-right and center-left electorate started increasing. The growth of television campaigning also contributed to these tendencies to a degree by making reasonable, moderate-sounding candidates appear more attractive to voters than extremists. More than any other consitutional measure, the provision for direct presidential elections served to mitigate the effects of multiparty fragmentation and the extremism it bred.

The left was totally unprepared to take advantage of the new political opportunities right away, for the parties on the left were disunited, disoriented, and in disrepute. Guy Mollet and the SFIO retained only 11 percent of the electorate; the Suez humiliation, the SFIO's disastrous handling of the Algerian War, and its early subservience to de Gaulle deprived that party of its former prestige. As for the PC, it was still relegated to a political ghetto by the non-Communist left. The PSU—which was a haven for "rigorous" ex-Socialists such as Edouard Depreux, Mendesist Radicals (including Mendès France himself), ex-Communists such as Jean Poperen, and a new generation of politically ambitious civil servants such as Michel Rocard—showed promise; however, for the time being, it was concentrating its efforts on formulating the proper doctrine. In general, the groups comprising the non-Communist left spent more time quarreling with each other over doctrine than opposing the Gaullist majority.

Based on his experiences at the local level, Mitterrand had adopted a more "understanding" attitude toward Communist voters than most of his colleagues on the non-Communist left. In 1959 he wrote:

> It is certain that, because democracy is the democracy of money . . . , you will
> see good people rush toward other systems, in which the notion of liberty will
> be lost for good. . . . International communism . . . will appear to be the only
> way for the weak, desperate, abandoned, . . . to get back, and that will lead to
> bloody days, when all forms of revolution will be applied. . . . You will see communism pick up the pieces and build its house.[3]

Mitterrand perceived the greatest threat at the national level as coming from the right, not the left. In national politics the fraternal memories of the Resistance and the international alignments of World War II often counterbalanced the animosities of the Cold War, which did not affect the daily lives of the vast majority of French people. Mitterrand realized that the preconditions for any successful national strategy for the non-Commmunist left were (1) unity at the party level, (2) a broader non-Communist electoral base (to score well on the first ballot), and (3) direct cooperation with the PC itself (to win on the second). (At this juncture, the extreme poles still outweighed the center, which was decisive in the final moments of an election but whose long-term support could not be relied on by either the left or the right.)

> The history of popular democracies proves beyond a doubt that when the PC
> participates in a government with a coalition of democratic groups, the latter are
> doomed to annihilation. A just democratic balance will depend in the future on
> the creation of a tightly structured gathering of socialist and republican forces.
> [Democrats] remain the opponents of communism's ideology and methods. But
> they feel that the danger that threatens freedom and progress today comes from
> elsewhere.[4]

Mitterrand believed that it was "a crime or simply stupid" to neglect the 4-5 million voters who usually voted Communist in national elections.[5] In his battle with the right over power, the political "capitalist" Mitterrand viewed these voters as an undervalued, underexploited political asset controlled by unworthy proprietors, the PC party bosses (though, with respect to the PC itself, it was more a matter of competing for market share). He appreciated the immediate domestic demands of the Communist voters and willingly adopted those aspects of the PC agenda that he could support in an effort to justify their voting for him and his acceptance of their votes. Mitterrand was the first prominent non-Communist politician on the left to adopt this strategy.

Ironically, the one thing that all the leaders of the leftist factions could agree on was opposition to the constitutional referendum instituting direct presidential elections in 1962. In the National Assembly they had formed a "no" cartel. Leftist and centrist groups from the PC to the MRP preferred some kind of legislative contract to direct presidential elections, and Mitterrand had concurred. To protest de Gaulle's referendum on the constitution, the Radicals initiated a motion of censure in the National Assembly. The motion won a clear majority: 280 out of 480 votes. Without a seat in the National Assembly, Mitterrand could not vote, but he had supported the measure. De Gaulle responded to the motion by dissolving the National Assembly and calling for legislative elections before the vote on his referendum. It was at this juncture that Mitterrand and many other anti-Gaullists took the opportunity to regain seats in the National Assembly (proving Duhamel's point that the president's prerogative to dissolve the National Assembly does not necessarily reinforce his power).

With his UDSR in shreds, Mitterrand had nowhere to turn for national support but to the political clubs that were now sprouting up all over France—clubs such as the Jean Moulin Club, the Jacobin Club, the Toqueville Catholic Circle, and '60s Citizens. Professionals in many areas, journalists, academics, businessmen, union leaders, and civil servants were meeting regularly to discuss the social, economic, and political future of France.[6] Not to be left out, Mitterrand formed his own club with a dozen friends, mainly from the UDSR, called the League for Republican Struggle. Gradually, Mitterrand's club would swallow up most of the others except the Jean Moulin Club. His most valuable ally was Charles Hernu, head of the Jacobins, civil servant, and Mendesist deputy in 1956. Like Mendès France and Mitterrand, Hernu had voted no to de Gaulle in 1958. Soon after joining the opposition to de Gaulle, he transferred his loyalty from Mendès France to the much more action-oriented Mitterrand.

In 1963 Mitterrand's league and Hernu's Jacobins merged to form the Center for Institutional Action (CAI). The club members, like the politicians, still harbored suspicions about Mitterrand, so they elected Hernu, not Mitterrand, as president. In June 1964 the CAI supposedly fused with fifty-four other clubs to form the Conventions for Republican Institutions (CIR), again headed by Hernu. Giesbert calls this story a bluff, saying that there were not really fifty-five clubs.[7] Gradually Mitterrand and Hernu transformed the CIR into a powerful political arm for Mitterrand. Its long-range goal was that of the left: to wrest power from the Gaullists and "republicanize" the constitution. Its immediate goals were to promote the union of the non-Communist left and, most original, to present a single presidential candidate representing the whole left, including the PC, in the 1965 presidential election.

At first, Mitterrand's friend, the SFIO mayor of Marseilles, Gaston Defferre, made an unsucussful bid to be the non-Communist left's presidential candidate based on a Third Force strategy. Mitterrand supported his friend's efforts, although he had no faith in his strategy. Defferre, an archfoe of Mollet, had also engaged in intense political rivalry with the Communists in Marseilles for years; a cooperative relationship between them was unimaginable. But the center right proved to be too troublesome, also, and negotiations broke down. The MRP and CNI leaders could not agree with the Socialists on school policy, the use of the term *socialist,* and how to respond to Communist candidates on the second ballot in future elections.

There clearly was a void to fill. The deputy from the Nièvre appeared to be the most willing and able candidate to fight hard in a losing battle. And he intended to be the single candidate of the left, not a Third Force candidate. Mitterrand had to meet three basic conditions to proceed, namely, obtaining: (1) Mollet's approval and the official endorsement of the SFIO, (2) Mendès France's support, and (3) unnegotiated acceptance by the PC. The situation looked propitious. Mollet did not want a Socialist candidacy after the Defferre fiasco, and Mitterrand did not seem like a long-term threat to him or his party. Mendès France, who was preferred as a candidate by his party, the PSU, refused to run; he was unwilling to participate in a process he believed illegitimate. And the PC did not want to run a candidate of its own, fearing that the results would be embarrassing. It preferred Mitterrand to "class collaborators" such as Mollet, Defferre, and Mendès France, all of whom were more overtly anti-Communist than Mitterrand.

When political life resumed in September 1965 after the long summer recess, Mitterrand acted fast. In declaring his candidacy he issued the first serious challenge to de Gaulle's power:

> It is up to political organizations as well as to individual citizens to make up their minds concerning the fundamental options that inspire my candidacy. . . . It goes without saying that for me it is essentially a matter of opposing arbitrary power, chauvinistic nationalism, and social conservatism with scrupulous respect for law and liberty, with a will to seize every opportunity to further European unity and the dynamism of expansion regulated by . . . a democratic plan.[8]

The next day the SFIO, the CIR, and the leftist Radicals formed the Democratic and Socialist Federation of the Left (FGDS), an official but loose union of the non-Communist left. Although the two events were clearly linked, the FGDS did not function as a campaign organization: "My Socialist partners insisted that this link be kept out of view. Undoubtedly they feared my dragging the federation down."[9] The FGDS was formed more with an eye to the legislative elections to be held in 1967.

Two weeks after declaring himself as the left's candidate, Mitterrand proposed seven policy "options" that together formed a thoroughly nonideological platform, with heavy emphasis on civil liberties: (1) reform of government institutions to prevent the accumulation of personal power; (2) reform of the judicial system, of public information and television services, and of labor laws and other regulations that infringed on local rights, with the goal of restoring and extending civil liberties; (3) creation of a European economic and political union that would include Great Britain; (4) conversion of the nuclear strike force to peaceful purposes and the signing by France of a nuclear nonproliferation treaty with an Atlanticist perspective; (5) antimonopolistic, decentralized economic planning (but with no mention of nationalization of industry); (6) fiscal and welfare reform; (7) increased investment in education. Mitterrand's concept of "options" was a compromise between the specificity of a platform, common program, or legislative contract, which direct elections logically called for, and the principle of a politically neutral president-arbiter, which was still engraved in the Constitution of the Fifth Republic.[10] All presidential candidates in the future would have to yield to the pressure to define their particular political aims: Ignorant of or indifferent to the theoretical intricacies of the constitution, the average voter simply wanted to know for what he or she was voting.

There were as yet no other serious declared candidates, and de Gaulle remained silent. The center was trying to persuade Antoine Pinay to run, but he hesitated. Eventually, Jean Lecanuet would run, and there would be a few marginal candidates—Tixier-Vignancour, Pierre Marcilhacy, and Marcel Barbu— all on the right or far right.

Mitterrand, who had been on cordial terms with Waldeck Rochet since World War II, was certain that Rochet's PC preferred Mitterrand to any of the other candidates. Regular though unofficial contact had been established between Mitterrand and the PC, and the key issue at this point was whether the PC would offer him public support without negotiations. A delicate song and dance followed. At first, the PC demanded a common program, implying a negotiated agreement, but when it became obvious that Mitterrand would not agree, it retreated to a position of merely requiring that the candidate present an acceptable platform. By obtaining in turn acceptance of its support, the PC achieved de facto recognition, a significant step toward more official recognition.

The Communist leader finally offered his party's unconditional support to Mitterrand.[11] The PC specifically appreciated in Mitterrand's options the desire to convert the nuclear strike force, liberalize the right-to-strike laws, enact fiscal reform in favor of the working class, attack monopolies, and "democratize" economic planning, the last of which lent itself to many possible interpretations. However, along with these options, they had to swallow acceptance of the Constitution of 1958, the idea of a European political entity, and continued participation in the Atlantic Alliance.

How could the PC support Mitterrand without reservations when the general thrust of his foreign policy was so explicitly European- and Atlantic-oriented? De Gaulle's anti-American foreign policy was better designed to please both the Soviet Communist Party and the French PC than was Mitterrand's. However, as Jacques Derogy and Jean-François Kahn state, internal politics took precedence over foreign affairs;[12] defense of the French workers' interests was more crucial to a respectable PC electoral showing than deference to Soviet interests. Since there was little danger of de Gaulle's foreign policy being dismantled anyway, here was an opportunity for the PC to strengthen itself internally. Mitterrand exploited this perspective by explaining that the expansion of the Common Market was in the interest of French workers because it would create larger markets.[13] The PC was willing to go along with Mitterrand's Atlanticism and economic prudence in exchange for participation in a coalition government; in any case, the Communists considered Mitterrand's options as only a basis for future negotiations in which they would demand acceptance of more of their positions.[14]

Although *Pravda* openly criticized Rochet for supporting Mitterrand, in retrospect, it appears that the Soviets allowed (rather than forbade or encouraged, as Jean Poperen has suggested)[15] PC support of Mitterrand because the chances of de Gaulle losing were very small, and there was political capital to be gained on the domestic level at no cost on the international level. The Communists' support of Mitterrand throughout the campaign was active, unambiguous, and monolithic—there were no public second thoughts or qualifications. The same cannot be said for any of the other parties on the left, except, of course, the CIR. Eventually, however, they all (though often grudgingly) ended up supporting Mitterrand.

Mitterrand had received the official endorsement of the SFIO in September, but on October 19, Mollet stated that he was ready to vote for the Independent Pinay on the second ballot. (At the time, the MRP was still trying to persuade this economically conservative former prime minister to run because he was "the only possible counterweight to Gaullist influence in the business community.")[16] The Radicals split, with René Billère's group supporting Mitterrand and Maurice Faure's group backing the centrist MRP candidate, Lecanuet, who declared his candidacy when it was clear that Pinay would not run. The PSU (the renamed PSA) was also ambivalent. Many of the purists in the party categorically opposed Mitterrand, but the majority of the militants, as well as Daniel Mayer and Mendès France, supported him. The Young Turk Michel Rocard proposed a compromise solution which passed: endorse Mitterrand, but do not participate in his campaign.

The intellectuals, journalists, and other opinion makers were perhaps the most skeptical of all about Mitterrand's ability to achieve a respectable result. Servan-Schreiber predicted that Mitterrand could not draw more than 20-25 percent of the vote. After all, the initial campaign polls showed him with 11-16 percent support. The writer/journalist Jean-François Revel (in the 1970s a sharp critic of Mitterrandism) offered Mitterrand his support, and *Le Monde, Le Nouvel Observateur,* and Sartre's *Les Temps Modernes* finally came around with various degrees of enthusiasm. But no one really believed that Mitterrand's union-of-the-left strategy would work.[17] Poperen explains the intellectuals' hesitance:

> Curiously, a purist minority of left-wing intellectuals [the PSU] joins the "modernist left" hard-liners [Servan-Schreiber and company] in rejecting the single

candidate of the left. But while the former lean toward de Gaulle or desertion, the latter eye Lecanuet. . . . The thirst for purity and, behind the great sentiments, the Caesarist reflex against the resurgent "republic of parties" push [the purists] toward de Gaulle.[18]

This relative lack of enthusiasm on the part of some key figures did not demoralize the left's candidate. On the contrary, it only increased his determination to disprove their assumptions.[19] Mitterrand admitted later that a *Le Monde* article by PSU member Pierre Stibbe denigrating his character played a large role in his decision to run.

Throughout his campaign Mitterrand made much of the fact that he was not the candidate of any party, coalition, or even newspaper. He was a "loner." Certainly individuals, such as Defferre and Pierre Mauroy, from within the various parties would strongly support him and mobilize local federations. However, his real campaign committee consisted of his longtime friends and supporters, many from the old UDSR: Georges Dayan, Georges Beauchamp, Roland Dumas, Charles Hernu, André Rousselet, François de Grossouvre, Claude Estier, Louis Mermaz, Marie-Thérèse Eyquem, and Mitterrand's brother Robert. The bulk of the army of local volunteers, who put up the posters, distributed the flyers, and so on, consisted of former members of the MNPGD, Mitterrand's wartime comrades.

After failing to persuade Pinay to run, the MRP and the center found their man in Jean Lecanuet, an *agrégé* (roughly equivalent to a Ph.D.) in philosophy, a former Resistance fighter, and a former deputy who was now a senator. Lecanuet wanted to identify himself neither with the right nor the left but with the future.[20] But it was difficult to tell whether this dashing, Kennedyesque figure represented a forward-looking new movement or a return to the Third Force mentality of the Fourth Republic. Both de Gaulle and Mitterrand perceived it to be the latter. Lecanuet defined his political orientation as one that would give "priority to productive expenditures to prepare for the economic future, social justice, regional decentralization, stimulation of private industry, and the construction of a European entity."[21] His principal supporters included the MRPs, Maurice Faure's Radicals, Pinay's Independents, some ex-Gaullists, farmers, politically organized Christian associations, and numerous influential members of the various clubs. The substance of his campaign was wise and progressive, and based more on common sense than Mitterrand's and de Gaulle's, but he lacked charismatic leadership, and his following was too narrowly center-right to enable him to seriously challenge either of the other candidates. Mitterrand saw that Lecanuet, because of his official Catholicism and capitalist orientation, would be more of a divisive force on the right than a direct threat to his candidacy.

A suspenseful, rumor-laden silence emanated from the Gaullist camp. No one knew whether the general intended to run. Many thought that he felt he had completed his task despite the fact that he had not groomed a successor. On November 4 he finally declared to the nation that he would in fact be a candidate:

> As long as I have the frank and massive support of the citizens . . . , the future of the new republic will be decided and assured. If not, no one can doubt that it will crumble then and there and that France will undergo—but this time, without any possible recourse—troubled times more disastrous than those which it experienced before.[22]

De Gaulle was saying, in other words, "Me or chaos," calling to mind Louis XV's prescient remark, *"Après moi, le déluge."* (Actually, the deluge would come before de Gaulle's departure. However, the public believed that a departure of de Gaulle at this time would mean a return to the chaos of 1957-1962 even though the Algerian War, which had triggered it, was over. With France out of NATO, in the event of chaos anything seemed possible.) This popular belief was not very flattering to de Gaulle's disciples or to the system that he had put into place, for, if the regime was so strong, why was de Gaulle indispensable?

To develop further his seven options, Mitterrand issued twenty-eight propositions, amounting to a veritable platform, which he had developed without any negotiations with the PC. Five of the options dealt with institutions, five with Europe and foreign policy, four with nuclear policy, three with social policy, three with labor policy, two with decentralization, one with freedom of speech, and one with national education. Though nationalizations were not ruled out, none were foreseen either. One of the most original aspects of Mitterrand's platform was the advocacy of feminist concerns such as the legalization of the sale of contraceptives (in particular, the pill), which had been declared illegal in 1920, and the principle of equal pay for equal work. Mitterrand had hit upon the perfect formula to maximize his power base: give every group a little something it wants, and offend no one on the left.

On November 20, only two weeks before the first ballot, the general began campaigning. The polls showed that the situation was serious; a runoff was probable. De Gaulle had tumbled from 67 percent to 46 percent; Mitterrand had jumped from 16 percent to 28 percent; Lecanuet had already mustered an impressive 18 percent. (The three marginal rightest candidates—Barbu, Tixier-Vignancour, and Marcilhacy—showed no significant percentages.) De Gaulle did not realize what he had wrought. He had not taken into consideration several factors: the *usure du pouvoir* (the erosion of power effect) so familiar to the French, who tire of the same official being in power for periods considerably less than seven years; the fact that an incumbent is always on the defensive; and the unusual degree of public interest in the candidates, the issues, and the electoral process of 1965. His nonchalant attitude was reflected in statements such as "When the French see all these survivors of the Fourth Republic appear-

ing one after the other on television uttering, each in turn, the same recrimina-
tions, they will get tired of it fast."[23]

The Gaullist camp was in fact divided in its tactical approach to the campaign. On one hand, de Gaulle himself viewed the contest essentially as the old
Fourth Republic versus the new Fifth Republic, as the above quotation suggests.
On the other, Pompidou saw it more the way Mitterrand did, as the right versus the left, with Lecanuet being a spoiler on the right. Pompidou's agents, portraying Mitterrand as representing "adventure" on the domestic issues and
"abdication" on the international ones, described him thus:

> He is not in a position to govern, except by surrendering.[24] He can abdicate in
> Brussels . . . , he can abdicate in the framework of the Atlantic Alliance, with
> the reservation that he can also abdicate vis-à-vis Russia. . . . [His policies]
> would lead us to economic and financial bankruptcy. Will a Communist regime
> come out of it with a definitive decline?[25]

On December 5 de Gaulle obtained 44 percent of the vote; Mitterrand, 32 percent; Lecanuet, 16 percent.

De Gaulle's tactics changed drastically between the two ballots. The popular
*rassembleur* (rallying force) came to the fore. André Malraux, a former
Communist-sympathizer more apt to hold up the fragile bridge between the
Communists and the Gaullists, replaced Pompidou as de Gaulle's main supporting actor, and the general himself was more active than ever. On television
he transformed himself into an earthy, sarcastic man of the people, jumping up
and down in his chair, mocking the Europeanists; he was making a clear bid for
the votes of the anti-Europeanist, working-class Communist voters. He was less
worried about offending the orphaned Lecanuetists, most of whom would vote
for him anyway, than retaining his working-class constituency.

Pompidou's comments now also played more to the working-class voter
than to the business executive. Speaking publicly at a Gaullist rally, the prime
minister assumed for his candidate some of the economic goals more often associated with the left:

> It is a matter of showing that in the face of the opposition's dazzling but dema-
> gogic promises, Gaullism can also open the paths to the future, but the promises
> it makes will be fulfilled because they are solidly based; the Fifth Plan
> [Pompidou's economic policy], for example, will allow each household in 1970
> its own car and its own television set. Furthermore, the regional development
> policy is designed to remedy the disparities that currently exist between prosper-
> ous areas and areas that are lagging behind.[26]

One would have expected Mitterrand now to concentrate his efforts on
attracting as many of the Lecanuet voters as possible. The pressures on him
from the center were in fact great. Lecanuet, Maurice Faure, Servan-Shreiber,
Jean Monnet, and Paul Reynaud all beckoned; they announced that as individu-

als they would vote for Mitterrand. Offering yet another example of historical irony, even the extreme right Tixierists (making less probable Pesquet's recent contention that Tixier-Vignancour was behind the Observatory plot), and embittered admirers of an erstwhile colonialist de Gaulle, such as Jacques Soustelle and Georges Bidault, declared for the left candidate. But knowing that he could not win on December 19 by maximizing his centrist vote at the expense of the Communist vote, Mitterrand refused to negotiate with the center; he was determined to maximize the left's progress on the "third ballot" still more than a year away—the legislative elections of 1967.[27]

On the second ballot de Gaulle obtained 55 percent of the vote, and Mitterrand won 45 percent. The breakdown of the vote was not as strictly right versus left as the percentages would indicate. Mitterrand received 1 million votes from the extreme right, and de Gaulle obtained 3 million workers' votes. Forty percent of the center electorate went to Mitterrand, including most of its leaders, and 60 percent to de Gaulle (the rank-and-file center being more conservative than its leaders). However, the consensus on the left was that this was a personal success for Mitterrand, who had established himself as the legitimate leader of the left. In fact, it was much more of a victory for Mitterrand personally than a relative victory for the left as a whole, for the proportion of leftist votes was not significantly greater than it had been in the legislative elections of 1962 (and was actually even smaller, since a significant fraction of the vote came from the extreme right). Poperen states that "the left did not figure out how to attract the shifting electorate, enlarged by economic mutations and demographic movements."[28] What was important, however, was the progress that the militants made toward working together in spite of the sectarianism of their leaders.

A sociological breakdown of the results of the December 19 election reveals a situation that augured best for the left, well for the center right, and ill for traditional Gaullists. De Gaulle was clearly more popular with the older generation, while Mitterrand and Lecanuet were favored by the young. Traditional Gaullism was beginning its decline as a rallying majority force. A viable, rejuvenated center right, symbolized by Lecanuet and the rising star Giscard d'Estaing, was evolving. Young, modern, and dynamic, it would in the long run pose a serious political threat to both the traditional right and left. But it was evolving slowly among the elite, and as yet was poorly organized politically and unable to communicate its concerns quickly and widely. Mitterrand's extreme popularity in stagnant, depressed rural areas and among the working class, the old-fashioned artisans, and the mass of anxious young adults augured well for his political career in the next few years. Those who felt left out of or not yet actively involved in the new prosperity often turned to Mitterrand, who was not finished adding to his constituency.

Although Mitterrand had known that it was impossible to beat de Gaulle in 1965, he believed that a leftist victory in the 1967 legislative elections was possible. In his concession speech, he insisted:

The result obtained today confirms my certainty that the time is coming when republicans will win out. From now on all my efforts will tend to contribute to making the legislative elections the decisive encounter that will save the Republic from the adventure into which it is plunged by a cheap Gaullism.[29]

The tasks required for a legislative campaign, however, appeared no less daunting than those of the presidential campaign. As preconditions for a leftist victory in 1967, Mitterrand had to maintain his preeminent position on the left, augment the number of non-Communist left voters, solidify the FGDS, bring about an electoral agreement acceptable to both the FGDS and the PC, and make the agreement stick.

## THE "THIRD BALLOT"

His immediate problem was to strengthen his hold on the FGDS, to which he had been elected president at its inception in 1965. Although Mitterrand and Mollet did not have serious disagreements about either the overall strategy of the union of the left or doctrinal matters, an intense power struggle was already underway. First, Mollet suspected Mitterrand of not being a "true" Socialist because he was not born a Socialist; to him one did not become a Socialist gradually in middle age. Second, Mollet had no intention of giving up his control of the left's evolution, hence his clinging to the status quo. But Mitterrand had young friends within the SFIO who were just as interested as he was in change, among them Pierre Mauroy, Jean-Pierre Chevènement, and Georges Brutelle.

Although the candidate of the left had won 45 percent of the popular vote in the presidential election, his CIR was far outnumbered by the Socialists in party membership. Since representation on the federation's national committee was proportional, the Socialists and Mollet in particular tried to hold Mitterrand hostage and weaken his authority. One solution was to fuse the federation parties into a single, fully integrated party. But Mollet resisted all such obvious attempts to weaken his authority, and René Billères, president of the Radicals, opposed the obliteration of his party. Another solution was to augment the number of card-carrying CIRs to offer a counterweight to the Socialists. The CIRs achieved this by audaciously issuing a membership card to anyone who attended a CIR meeting.[30] As a counterattack, Mollet had Socialist Jean Jaurès clubs created throughout the provinces; these competed directly with the CIR for members. A row ensued. Mitterrand threatened to quit as president of the FGDS if the CIRs were not granted their "just" place within the FGDS. Mollet and Billères backed down.

The president of the FGDS imposed other procedures on his colleagues, frequently resorting to the threat of resignation as the ultimate means of persuasion. The discreet and assiduous listener of the pre-1965 period now displayed the self-confidence of an established leader, and some rivals accused him of being an autocrat. From the standpoint of electoral unity, the measures he dictated made sense: He demanded that the FGDS list only one candidate per district, that the president (himself) have authority over all nominations, that after the elections there be only one parliamentary group for FGDS deputies, and that the group create a countergovernment, or shadow Cabinet (based on the British model), over which he would preside.

Throughout the first half of 1966 Mitterrand engaged in some complicated political acrobatics—building up the CIR, holding on to the SFIO and Radicals, not alienating the center, and finally resisting the impatient entreaties of the PC for an immediate common program without closing the door to an electoral alliance with them, for without that alliance victory in March 1967 would be impossible. In June 1966 he stated categorically that the PC was the "natural ally" of the FGDS, thus ending internal debate and external befuddlement on the matter. In December 1966 the FGDS and the PC concluded an electoral agreement that stated that each would withdraw candidates with poor chances of winning on the second ballot to give the well-placed candidates of the other the best chances of beating the rightist candidates. There was still much mutual distrust between the PC and the parties of the FGDS, and many on all sides doubted that the agreement would be respected. The fact that there was no agreement on issues—even within the FGDS the Radicals disagreed with the SFIO and CIR on most economic issues—made it much more difficult. The FGDS also engaged in an electoral agreement with the PSU, which meant that there would be four separate legislative programs among the allied parties of the left—those of the PC, the SFIO-CIR, the Radicals, and the PSU.

Of all the issues covered in the party platforms, it was the practical economic policy proposals that elicited the most interest. The battle terrain kept shifting, and the fact that these were legislative elections only exaggerated the phenomenon. Voters wanted to know more than ever the economic future that the candidates had in store for them. Mitterrand adopted the broadest frame of reference yet from a strictly leftist perspective. In opposition to Pompidou's "order versus disorder" dichotomy Mitterrand set "economic privilege versus social justice." Both leaders took prosperity for granted and laid claim to representing the forces of economic change, progress, and expansion.

The only institutional problem that attracted attention in the campaign was the issue of what the president would do if the opposition prevailed, a question that arises in legislative elections when it appears possible that the legislative majority will not coincide with the presidential majority. Would de Gaulle resign? Would he dissolve the National Assembly and call for new legislative elections again? Would he appoint a prime minister and other ministers who reflected the new parliamentary majority? Or would there be a crisis, with civil unrest? These were the questions raised but never answered. De Gaulle purposely maintained silence on this point in the hope that the mounting anxiety would preclude such an unprecedented situation.

In the Parliamentary elections the right managed to retain its majority, although only by one seat, and thus the danger of an institutional crisis was averted. The left had reason to congratulate itself in spite of the fact that it did not obtain a larger share of the vote than it had in the 1965 national elections (its share seemed to be stagnating at around 44 percent), for it did win many more deputy seats, increasing its share from 146 to 194. The left's electoral success was due largely to the discipline imposed by the agreement with the PC. The agreement had been respected for the most part, and especially between the PC and the CIR; before 1967 Mitterrand had been the only CIR member in Parliament; after March 1967 there were seventeen, including Mitterrand intimates such as Louis Mermaz, Claude Estier, Roland Dumas, André Rousselet, and Georges Dayan. More and more leftists were recognizing that the single-member majority electoral system instituted by de Gaulle in 1958 put their divided parties at a grave disadvantage unless they entered into electoral agreements.

The deputy from the Nièvre was now the undisputed leader of the left, and he took it upon himself to act as a counterpresident. In August 1967 the FGDS reelected him as its president. Around the same time he issued a press release that consisted of a lengthy critique of de Gaulle's major policies and actions in which he placed less emphasis on institutional issues and more on social and economic ones, for the leftist economists and socialist ideologues were jointly exerting a strong influence on him. Economic privilege replaced personal power as the primary evil against which Mitterrand fought.

On the international level, although he remained faithful to the idea of a unified Europe that would include Great Britain, he now adopted relatively radical views of global politics, drawing parallels between "American economic imperialism" and "Soviet military imperialism" and praising "peoples' liberation movements" throughout the Third World. This was a clear break with his former views of the African national liberation movements. Only regarding Mideast affairs did he seem to preserve balance (beginning with the Six-Day War, he had disapproved of de Gaulle's pro-Arab stance). He also became more critical and impatient with the U.S. involvement in Vietnam, which was roundly criticized by de Gaulle, the PC, and the left in general. Only two years earlier, during the presidential campaign, Mitterrand had consciously played down the U.S. role in the Vietnam War, refusing to outbid de Gaulle's anti-Americanism; he had understood the American predicament better than he could politically afford to admit at the time. But now there was a clear break with the antirevolutionary, antinationalistic, reformist, colonialist positions of yore. Mitterrand's lucid and nuanced analyses of Third World affairs in the 1950s gave way to simplistic ideological interpretations of social conflict in the 1960s. In both foreign and economic affairs he traveled greater ideological distance between 1965 and 1967 than in any other two years of his career.

In regard to the specific problem of the arms race, he remained realistic in his short-term views—he continued to support adherence to the Atlantic

Alliance—but was overly optimistic in the long range, envisioning the "simulta-neous, progressive, and negotiated disappearance of military pacts" and the reuniting of Eastern and Western Europe. He could tolerate (though not hail) de Gaulle's withdrawal from NATO and continue to advocate converting France's military nuclear industry, not out of neutralist tendencies but out of faith in the perennial military superiority of the United States and its nuclear umbrella. Along with many others, Mitterrand was quite ignorant at this time of the disquieting trends in the strategic balance of military power between the United States and the Soviet Union and how that balance related to Third World "liberation movements."[31]

Yet it was not Mitterrand's foreign policy but his increasing emphasis on social and economic justice at home that hit the nerve of public opinion in the late 1960s. Calls for fiscal reform to favor income redistribution, attacks on the monopolies and the multinationals, and demands for more and larger entitle-ment programs and greater public-sector activity in housing and education were what more and more people wanted to hear; in the fall 1967 cantonal elections, the left received 49.8 percent of the vote. Whether or not Mitterrand's econom-ic insights were based on correct economic assumptions, one thing is clear: They were based on a correct perception, from a political standpoint, of the eco-nomic feelings of an ever increasing proportion of the French population at many different levels of society.

For there was still another complicating political force at work: the begin-ning of an ideological leftward drift across the whole political spectrum (and not just in France), exemplified by Pompidou's remarks on the ability of the right to achieve the goals usually associated with the left. Gaullists were showing more moderation, and the right and center began to co-opt some of the left's social goals (social security, national medical insurance, unemployment insurance, etc.), inclining Mitterrand and the traditional left toward increasingly radical positions, especially in the areas of economics and foreign affairs. It would re-quire the triumph of the Socialists fifteen years later for this trend to begin to wane.

In February 1968 the FGDS and the PC signed an "expanded agreement" designed to help the leftist groups advance toward a common program. It was primarily a clarification of differences between the two groups than an actual agreement, but, more important, it served as a powerful symbol of their willing-ness to work with each other. Regarding the reform of political institutions, the PC and FGDS agreed to "return to the letter of the Constitution of 1958: it was a way of fighting against the regime."[32] This was one more example of Mitterrand's legalist approach to political action; unable to fight de Gaulle *on* his constitution, he decided to fight him *with* it. (Mitterrand now claimed that it was not the document itself that he most strongly objected to, but the way in which it had been implemented.) The formerly much maligned document became the basis for both opposition to de Gaulle and unity on the left. It was a typically Mitterrandian solution to the problem of finding common ground between differing parties that would have tended to go in very different directions in defining precise policies.

On the issue of civil liberties, both the PC and the FGDS agreed to expand the traditional rights guaranteed by Western democracies (including freedom of information, the right of habeas corpus, an independent judiciary, the right to strike, etc.). The problem here lay in the sincerity of the PC; Rochet was extremely circuitous in his responses to questions in this area. Mitterrand adopted an attitude of confidence: "One can doubt the sincerity of the Communists' intentions. But to base a political strategy on intentions one attributes to others is senseless. The important thing is to create the conditions that make others act as if they were sincere."[33] Objective conditions, acts, and documents are what really count, not the subjective problem of sincerity versus hypocrisy, good intentions versus bad; this nonidealistic insight always served as the basis for Mitterrand's leftist realpolitik (this has nothing to do the importance that Mitterrand attributes to sincerity when judging friends who have erred).

There was relatively easy agreement on social and economic matters. Both parties would work toward traditional socialist and social-democratic programs. A small number of nationalizations were recommended. The newly nationalized industries would somehow be run differently and better than previously nationalized ones; management methods would not be statist, and the newly nationalized industries would become a driving force for the whole economy (though in what way was never spelled out). Mitterrand lamented the "timidity" of the accord in this area;[34] it was not Mitterrand who held back on nationalizations but the more centrist Radicals within the FGDS.

As expected, the leftist parties disagreed strongly on important foreign policy issues. To cover over these difficulties, they fled together into a utopian future in which Eastern and Western military blocs would be replaced by a single collective nonaggression security pact that would include mutual assistance.

Dialogue with Socialists, Radicals, and Communists was one thing, but dialogue with the government and confronting public opinion was another. Mitterrand had shown that he could take the Gaullists head on in the National Assembly, but hastening the slow but perceptible trend in the public's demand for more "economic justice" would be the most delicate operation of all. Mitterrand acknowledged that France was facing many of the problems that all Western democracies faced, namely those of international competition and domestic unemployment, the latter increasing in the wake of modernization, which was nonetheless necessary for competitiveness. He was also lucid in his critique of French capitalism—its conservative tendencies, common corrupt practices such as price fixing, the lack of checks on monopolies, the timidity of banks and investors, the lack of support for both public and private research, and ever increasing state administrative control. Left to their own devices, the wealthy did not do what they were supposed to do; there were "more bond holders than speculators, more landowners than entrepreneurs."[35]

But instead of viewing the problem as not enough capitalism or not enough economic freedom and fairplay, he now adopted an explicitly Socialist perspective: liberalism (used in the European sense this term is roughly equivalent to the American concept of free enterprise) had run its course, could never correct itself, and would bring economic progress to a halt if not transformed; capitalism had "arrived at the normal stage of evolution, that of monopolies; it is inconceivable that this system could destroy its own foundations."[36] The influence of the socialist ideologues in the FGDS is obvious.

The counterpresident proposed statist solutions for France's economic woes. Under a government of the left, nationalized vanguard industries would somehow enjoy greater autonomy than had previously nationalized industries and would therefore demonstrate greater dynamism. The underlying assumption was that public funds would offer a greater supply of capital than the private financial market and that new state-appointed directors would provide more innovative, productive, and selfless leadership, putting the public interest ahead of the profit motive. Simultaneously, the government would "invest" more in public housing, education, and services. Since the fiscal burden on the working classes was to be reduced, too, one can only infer that businesses and the "rich" were to be more highly taxed to finance these programs and that this would prove acceptable and adequate at least until the expected industrial expansion bore fruit. The counterpresident never presented statistical data showing how it would be financially possible to realize this program.

Just as the nationalized industries would serve as a motor for French industry as a whole, so would progressively socialized France serve as such for the European Common Market as a whole:

The major objective [is] obviously global planning. Some will say that others are not disposed to allow themselves to be led where they do not want to go. But we believe in France and her value as an example, just as we believe in socialism and its locomotive force. One with the other. One through the other.[37]

Mitterrand was intellectually ill-equipped to withstand the ideological onslaught of his colleagues in the FGDS with whom he had chosen to do business. When rational argument failed him, faith and ideology took over. Like Joshua's seven trumpets, the future unqualified successes of France's socialist policies would cause the walls of money to come tumbling down.

The counterpresident had reason to feel supremely confident in his and socialism's foreseeable political future. He was the commanding voice of the opposition both within its ranks and vis-à-vis the majority. In addition, organized Socialism (the SFIO and other Socialist groups) and socialist philosophies in general were again gaining favor. Marx and other socialist philosophers were an integral part of the philosophy course that masses of seniors in the *lycées* were required to take, and they were studied even more seriously in the universities and *grandes écoles* by large numbers of students. The socialist-leaning educators of France were at the head of a rearguard area of knowledge—ideological thought and analysis—and were preparing an upcoming generation of leftist sympathizers. In early 1968 it looked as if there were still four good years in which to prepare the new generation of voters for the confrontation with an aged, demystified de Gaulle.

Yet there were still forces inhibiting the left's progress from within with which Mitterrand had to struggle. First, the persistent sectarianism of the three groups composing the FGDS—the CIR, the SFIO, and the Radicals—and among the FGDS, PC, and PSU delayed unity. Second, and more important, the very popularity of socialist and Marxist ideas among the politically minded university students rendered them impatient with their plodding elders and forced a violent, anarchic, and premature showdown with the Gaullist regime. This tidal wave of protest escaped entirely the efforts of the traditional opposition to contain, control, and exploit it and left the politicians of both the left and the right baffled and off balance. This in turn created an electoral backlash, further delaying electoral victories of the socialist movement on the national level. May 1968 was just around the corner.

## NOTES

1. Georges Suffert, *De Defferre à Mitterrand* (From Defferre to Mitterrand) (Paris: Seuil, 1966), p. 15.

2. François Mitterrand, *Ma Part de vérité* (My share of the truth) (Paris: Fayard, 1969), p. 68.

3. François Mitterrand, speech before the Twelfth Congress of the UDSR, cited in Mitterrand, *Politique* (Paris: Fayard, 1977), p. 373.

4. François Mitterrand, "Front populaire 'Coalition immorale?'" *La Nef*, no. 27 (April 1959): 12.

5. François Mitterrand, *Politique*, p. 410.

6. For a good overview of the club phenomenon see Jean Poperen, *L'Unité de la gauche* (The unity of the left) (Paris: Fayard, 1975), pp. 359–64.

7. Franz-Olivier Giesbert, *François Mitterrand ou la tentation de l'histoire* (François Mitterrand or the temptation of history) (Paris: Seuil, 1977), p. 203.

8. François Mitterrand, communiqué issued through the Agence France Presse, September 9, 1965, cited in Mitterrand, *Politique*, pp. 417–18.

9. François Mitterrand, *Ma Part*, p. 79.

10. Olivier Duhamel, *La Gauche et la Cinquième République* (The left and the Fifth Republic) (Paris: Presses Universitaires de France, 1980), pp. 257–58.

11. François Dreyfus, *Histoire des gauches en France (1940–1974)* (History of the leftist movements in France) (Paris: Grasset, 1975), p. 263.

12. Jacques Derogy and Jean-François Kahn, *Les Secrets du ballotage* (The secrets of the ballot box) (Paris: Fayard, 1966), pp. 138–39.

13. Mitterrand, France-Inter radio broadcast cited in Mitterrand, *Politique*, pp. 425–26.

14. Poperen, *L'Unité de la gauche*, p. 473.

15. Ibid., p. 461.

16. Claude Manceron, *Cent Mille Voix par jour* (A hundred thousand votes a day) (Paris: Laffont, 1966), p. 118.

17. Derogy and Kahn, *Les Secrets du ballotage*, p. 126.

18. Poperen, *L'Unité de la gauche*, pp. 476–77.

19. Giesbert, *François Mitterrand*, p. 207.

20. Jean Lecanuet, cited in Manceron, *Cent Mille Voix*, p. 157.

21. Ibid., p. 223.

22. De Gaulle, speech given November 4, 1965, cited in Manceron, *Cent Mille Voix*, p. 184.

23. Derogy and Kahn, *Les Secrets du ballotage*, p. 183.

24. *Abandonment* is the term that the ultraconservatives used against Mitterrand to condemn his reformist colonial policies.

25. Pierre Rouanet, *Pompidou* (Paris: Grasset, 1969), pp. 139–40.

26. Manceron, *Cent Mille Voix*, p. 265.

27. Derogy and Kahn, *Les Secrets du ballotage*, p. 246.

28. Poperen, *L'Unité de la gauche*, p. 485.

29. Mitterrand, cited in Manceron, *Cent Mille Voix*, p. 280.

30. Catherine Nay, *Le Noir et le rouge: L'Histoire d'une ambition* (The black and the red: History of an ambitious man) (Paris: Grasset, 1984), p. 291.

31. Mitterrand, *Ma Part*, p. 121.

32. Ibid., p. 104.

33. Ibid., p. 107–8.

34. Ibid., p. 112–13.

35. François Mitterrand, "Une Economie désarmée," *Le Monde*, February 29, 1968, p. 7.

36. Ibid.

37. Ibid.

The Mendès France Cabinet (1954). Front row: second from left, Mitterrand; third, Prime Minister Mendès France; fourth, President Coty; second from right, Chaban-Delmas. (Courtesy of Sipa Press)

The 1974 televised debate between Giscard d'Estaing (left) and Mitterrand (right). (Courtesy of Sipa Press)

Mitterrand, Marchais, and Fabre sign an updated version of the Common Program in March 1978. (Courtesy of Sipa Press)

The second Mauroy government, formed in 1981. Front row starting third from left: Rocard, Jobert, Mauroy, Mitterrand, Defferre, Charles Fiterman (PC), Chevènement, Yvette Roudy, Badinter. Second row: third from left, Savary; fourth, Delors; sixth, Cheysson; ninth, Hernu; tenth, Laurent Fabius (the second prime minister). Third row, first on left, Crépeau (MRG). (Courtesy of the French Presidency); Edith Cresson (the third prime minister).

Presidents Mitterrand and Clinton at the White House in 1993. (Courtesy of the French Presidency)

# 7

# May 1968 and the Recreation of the French Socialist Party

The student revolt of May 1968 took everyone by surprise, including the students themselves, who were overwhelmed by the power that sheer numbers gave them. However, signs of trouble had not been absent. The academic year had begun with protests over dormitory regulations, and it was punctuated with small anti-American protests over the Vietnam War. Marxist and socialist ideas permeated the universities. Students felt impotent in the face of the aloof intellectual authority of professors and the all-powerful Ministry of Education. Overcrowded lecture halls and cafeterias and inadequate housing encouraged the students' sense of overall alienation.[1]

Mitterrand's initial reaction to the outbreak of violence and police repression was prudence: "Even if the method used by the students is not the best, that does not mean that the minister of the interior's is good."[2] Mitterrand voiced his criticism from his seat in the National Assembly, using the events in the street as yet more evidence of the current government's inadequacies, failures, and injustices, his constant refrain being, "It is time, high time, that the government resign." (Here he is not calling for the resignation of de Gaulle himself but of Pompidou and his ministers.) Mitterrand viewed this primarily middle-class student unrest as an extension of the economic difficulties of the youth of the lower classes; to him the students' anxieties stemmed principally from the precariousness of their general economic situation, both present and future. This did not prevent him from also making use of the elitist rationale often applied to the student protest, claiming it to be a critique of the "consumer society which consumes itself."[3] Continually preoccupied with not "leaving the masses behind" and at the same time with keeping up with history, Mitterrand sought to marry the revolutionary rhetoric of the young with reassurances for his traditional, petit-bourgeois constituency:

> The freedom that we want begins very modestly with the destruction of all the
> special courts and laws established to silence the people, and ends . . . with the
> destruction of this society which must be blown to pieces . . . not in order to
> burn the farm or the house of the one who built it, but so that the one who lives
> in the house . . . feels . . . solidarity with the immense task of those who have
> nothing and suffer.[4]

Swept up by current events, Mitterrand indulged in the rhetoric of the moment.

While it is quite true that some of the student leaders were anxious to lead
the working class, an act they deemed the stodgy PC no longer capable or worthy of doing, the working class resented the patronizing attitude of these sons of
the bourgeoisie. The workers may have wished to see the consumer society in
which they made their living "collectivized," but they certainly did not want it
abolished. The general strike, like the student strike it followed, was not led by
the PC, which harshly condemned as counterrevolutionary the tidal wave of
middle-class protest that it could not control. At the same time, the
Communists, who could not allow anyone to outbid them on the left, sought
ways to take advantage of the strike; their workers would not go back to work
without concessions on wages and working conditions.

At the peak of the disorder, on May 28, the counterpresident held a press
conference calling for the formation of a provisional government. It would be
composed of ten ministers, "excluding no one, and without any out-of-date distribution of portfolios . . . , based on the union of the left"; in other words,
Communists would be included.[5] He foresaw a presidential election to be held
soon after and parliamentary elections to be held the following October. For the
formation of the provisional government he deferred to Mendès France, but he
made it clear that he intended to be a presidential candidate.[6]

This move was clearly in response to de Gaulle's presentation of a referendum to the French nation on the concept of participation, an obvious effort to
appease the nation with a few symbolic reforms hastily thrown together. But
more important, it was an attempt to rally popular support behind him. On
May 24 de Gaulle had declared on national television that he would resign from
the presidency if his referendum did not pass. It was this potential power vacuum that Mitterrand proposed filling.

Once again Mendès France and Mitterrand found themselves thrown
together politically and forced to make an awkward attempt to work out a solution; naturally, there were misunderstandings and disagreements based on their
differing interpretations of events. During this crisis it became immediately
clear that Mendès France enjoyed a broad base of popular and political support
that excluded only the Communists. He was virtually the only prominent politician respected by the students in revolt. He had met with them in the streets
(after advising Mitterrand not to) and had attended their massive rally at
Charléty along with the young Michel Rocard of the PSU. The business community appreciated his economic expertise, and the left remembered him for his

progressivism on colonial matters. But he and Mitterrand found it difficult to agree on the composition of the proposed provisional government, specifically on whether it should include Communists and a representative of the students.

While these negotiations were taking place, the press, the public, and the political community all were reacting violently to Mitterrand's initiative. He had consulted beforehand with non-Communist leftist leaders, and they had at first approved his move. Immediately following the press conference, much of the press corps and some leaders on the right such as Pinay, Lecanuet, and Marcilhacy had also approved of his actions. But there was a violently negative reaction among these groups when it became apparent that Mitterrand's proposal had made a very bad impression on the public. Mitterrand's press conference had been broadcast on national television in a highly edited form. The television staffs were on strike, and the stations were manned during this period by Gaullist strike breakers who did their best, according to Mitterrand, to make him look like a "sub-dictator" making an opportunistic power grab.[7] Although he was booed by the students as a fixture of the regime, albeit as a member of its opposition (Mitterrand did not exist politically for them prior to 1965), the right lumped him together with the student protesters because of his "understanding" of their frustrations. And his recent loud calls in the National Assembly for the government to resign amid the chaos made him look more like a force for disorder than order. His political position regarding these events was too nuanced for public opinion to grasp.

Public opinion was definitely against the idea of a new provisional government, and the Gaullists severely criticized it as an illegal initiative. But even today Mitterrand's critics recognize the propriety of his plan, if not its wisdom. Nay, for example, accepts the substance of Mitterrand's self-defense offered in *Ma Part de vérité* while criticizing his rhetorical excesses of the moment (in fact, both sides constantly accused the other of leading the nation into a dictatorship).[8] Mitterrand wrote in 1969:

> My duty was to neglect nothing in promoting the failure of the referendum and to foresee the consequences of that failure. In linking his future to the referendum, General de Gaulle shifted ground . . . ; I had to look henceforth beyond the referendum, accept the hypothesis of a presidential vacancy and the deep trouble that would ensue, demystify public opinion, and reassure it by proposing an alternative solution.[9]

This was of course based on the assumption that Prime Minister Pompidou would leave with de Gaulle, a probability but not a constitutional requirement. At the time no one thought to bring up the fact that the president of the Senate, the lackluster Alain Poher, was, according to the consititution, the next in line to succeed the president.

On May 30, just when debate over the referendum and the composition of the provisional government was raging, de Gaulle shifted ground again and canceled the referendum and announced new parliamentary elections to be held in June. He had already traveled to Baden-Baden to gain assurances of support from the French military stationed there. Upon reflection, he had decided that it would be more advantageous to dissolve the National Assembly and hold parliamentary elections rather than to hold a referendum immediately. The former action was likely to strengthen, even inflate, his real political power; it would take advantage of a growing backlash that would give him a more supportive majority (the current Gaullist Parliament had begun to quake). On May 22, two days before the referendum was announced, Mitterrand had himself called for new legislative elections.[10] Yet nine days later, the day after de Gaulle had announced them, he termed de Gaulle's cancellation of the referendum and dissolution of Parliament an "18 Brumaire" (referring to Napoleon's coup d'état of 1799). The backlash to the student revolt erupted throughout France and immediately brought hundreds of thousands of pro-Gaullists into the streets. Mitterrand quickly lost what was left of his national support, and he was even in serious danger of losing his assembly seat again to a strong Gaullist in the Nièvre.

It was during these tumultuous months of May and June that Mitterrand picked up on an old leftist idea that would be one of his most constant political themes throughout the 1970s (a theme already introduced in *Le Coup d'état permanent*), namely, the continuity between the socialist revolutions of the twentieth century and the political revolutions of the late eighteenth and early nineteenth centuries. In a speech before the National Assembly he called for "a new alliance of the fighters for individual liberty, heirs of 1789, and the fighters for collective rights and freedoms, heirs of the bloody struggles of the nineteenth and the first half of the twentieth centuries."[11] The idea that Marxist-inspired revolutions in the twentieth century were the legitimate and worthy heirs of the earlier revolutions would go long unquestioned by the left and constitute one of the ideological tenets of the French Socialist Party after 1971.

To this idea of a logical continuity between "collective rights and freedoms" and individual ones was added the parallel between Communist police oppression (the economic system did not come under criticism) and Western economic "oppression." This notion would also prove politically popular on both sides of the Atlantic, but no place more so than in France in the 1970s. These two ideas together constituted the ideological bridge between the middle class (including white-collar workers, civil servants, and some liberal professionals) and the Communist-influenced working class. In the famous press conference of May 28 he declared,

> It is a matter of founding socialist democracy and opening up to youth this exalting perspective: the new alliance of socialism and freedom. It is only up to our imagination and will that the Prague spring of 1968 finds its answer in Paris. And thus that France may be the first among the industrialized nations to attack the very social structures that it has endured up until now as have others.[12]

Selling the ideas of "collective freedoms" and the communist-capitalist parallel to a larger segment of middle-class France would be crucial to Mitterrand's and the PS's success.

De Gaulle was right: The results of the unforeseen parliamentary elections reversed the progress that the left had made in parliamentary strength in 1967. Mitterrand, using the American term, described them as a "hold-up" because Gaullists had scared voters away from the Gaullists' opponents with warnings of civil war. The ideas that Mitterrand and the FGDS represented had not significantly changed since the legislative elections of 1967, but the number of FGDS representatives fell from 118 to 57, and those of the PC from 73 to 34 (validating Mendès France's contention that the public held an extremely unfavorable opinion of the PC's potential role). Gaullists won 294 out of 485 seats; the right's coalition majority, with 358 seats in all, overwhelmed the National Assembly. Mitterrand was the only CIR reelected to Parliament. The Gaullists, Pompidou in particular, reaped the political benefits derived from the conclusion of the Grenelle Accords, which raised the minimum wage and ended the general strike.

Shortly after the August 1968 elections the FGDS suffered another strong blow, the violent Soviet suppression of the Prague liberalization movement, referred to above. Many Socialist and Radical colleagues got cold feet and again disavowed the union-of-the-left strategy; the PC, which openly defended Soviet behavior, looked more than ever like poor political company. The FGDS soon fell apart. During periods of personal discredit and leftist political disarray like this one, the political warrior always reappeared:

> In leaving the presidency of the Federation of the Democratic and Socialist Left this November 7th, I will not be shedding my responsibility, I will not be giving up the fight. At the appointed time, I will keep the rendezvous we have agreed to. . . . It is necessary [for the Federation to] surpass and transform itself.[13]

Once again, the deputy from the Nièvre temporarily retreated to regional politics, taking the opportunity to write and reflect on the domestic and international events of 1968, which resulted in the publication of *Ma Part de vérité*. In it Mitterrand reviewed his entire political career, but more important, he offered his interpretation of the tumultuous recent past—the student revolt, the legislative elections, the Soviet invasion of Prague in August, and the role of the PC in French political life.

He reserved his severest criticisms for the student movement, lambasting it for its irresponsibility and "the way in which [the students] wanted to settle all scores at once: with de Gaulle, with capitalism, with the PC, with social democracy, with the CGT [the General Confederation of Labor, the Communist-dominated labor union], with the university."[14] He realized that the surge of youthful frustration was too broad, anarchistic, and amorphous to be neatly classified as a socialist movement. Yet it was clearly an oppositional force with some socialist elements, and he recognized in it a potential source of future support.

Mitterrand's views on foreign policy as presented in *Ma Part de vérité* strongly reflected his interpretation of France's internal affairs and also confirmed his shift away from the overt American sympathies he entertained in the 1950s and early 1960s. Soviet Communist evils tended to be ignored, minimized, related to a comparable evil in the West, or explained away, as had been the evils of Communist China. He claimed, for example, that the circumstances of Soviet Communist domination were unique since the U.S.S.R. was an underdeveloped country; that Soviet Communism was forced to develop in a hostile world (ignoring the possibility that Soviet Communist aggressiveness might be the major cause of that hostility), and so on. He did not discuss the differences between power relationships within the Eastern and Western blocs. Mitterrand indicated that the "right" the Soviet Union exercised in Prague in August 1968 corresponded to the one that Mitterrand believed the United States would arrogate to itself in Europe in the event of, say, a Communist takeover in Athens—a gross analogy, since the circumstances (internal versus external, violent versus democratic) of this hypothetical takeover were not considered.

In fact, the Prague invasion required special treatment because of its inopportune timing in relation to Mitterrand's plans for the union of the French left. Rather than portraying the Soviet Union as a bully nation prepared to impose its will on its "allies" by whatever means necessary, Mitterrand drew a picture of a hesitant, uncertain Soviet Union divided by hawks and doves.[15] He seemed to project his own confusion about the meaning of this invasion on to the Soviet government itself:

> [The] arbitrator [between the doves and hawks] is the group in power, which consented to the invasion either out of conviction, or because it felt threatened by the liberal contagion, but for whom there was no advantage in giving in too much to the other clan.[16]

The group in power (Brezhnev and company) was an arbitrating power? Mitterrand liked to think that it acted more out of a sense of the "threat of the liberal contagion" than out of conviction and that this somehow made a difference. (Probably the "other clan" here refers to the hawks, but the language is not clear.) It is obvious that Mitterrand is trying to explain away unpleasant events that do not fit well with his emerging worldview and domestic political strategy.

Mitterrand further developed the popular concept of the Soviet Union as an imperial giant different from but basically no worse than the other "imperial" giant, the United States.[17] The two are only estranged brothers who behave similarly; the Prague invasion is compared to the American intervention in Vietnam.[18] Thus, for Mitterrand the image of the United States as a bastion of democracy was fading and being replaced by one of an exploiter nation. Although recognizing that the United States preserved internal political democracy, he now publicly voiced the opinion that the Vietnam War represented political and military imperialism, and America's relations with the Third World economic imperialism. America was depicted as the capitalist nation par excellence, and capitalism was the new enemy number one.

Yet Mitterrand admitted that he could "tolerate" the Atlantic Alliance while working toward his ideal of an independent, socialist Europe.[19] He contended that a capitalist Europe would be absorbed by American multinational corporations and that European capital would flee to the United States. This undesirable scenario could be prevented only by a socialist France and the "contagion of new ideas" that would spread from its good example. Mitterrand enveloped the centrist notion of European unity, which he had strongly favored since the end of World War II, in a net of fashionable leftist ideas.

Mitterrand spent much of this period speaking and writing about his emerging socialist philosophy. In order to be taken seriously by the Socialists, he had to demonstrate that he was, in fact, one of them even though he had never been a member of one of their major groupings. In the process, he redefined socialism. For Mitterrand the left had to be socialist and socialism had, by definition, to be synonymous with the combined concepts of freedom and justice.[20] His primary criticism of capitalism was that it was incompatible with social and economic "justice." It tended toward the creation of monopolies, multinational corporations that escaped national political control, the concentration of a dominant, privileged class, an anachronistic style of government based on decree, and a waste of financial resources diverted to prestigious but unproductive and inefficient enterprises. In short, French capitalism represented the essence of capitalism. The answer to this predicament was socialism.[21] On the other hand, societies that claimed to be socialist but did not tend toward freedom and justice were, by definition, counterrevolutionary.[22]

The influence of Marx remains problematical:

> My exposure to Marx was too limited for me to extract anything but an approximate sense of his ideas, but sufficient to move me from boredom to intense intellectual excitement, and I relied on his interpreters, whose disputes and mutual excommunications heightened my pleasure.[23]

By treating the ideological debate as an amusing game Mitterrand established ironic distance between himself and highly questionable concepts without disqualifying them altogether—a politically evasive and astute maneuver. Mitterrand never explicitly adhered to or rejected Marxist philosophy, but he did sanction the systematic use of it by members of his party, thereby "covering" it. On his own he made use of some of its terminology (including "the class struggle," "the appropriation of the means of production as a way to end the exploitation of the workers," "the alienation of the worker," etc.), which indicates that he did accept many of its basic assumptions.

Mitterrand's socialism has been characterized as personalistic, idealistic, philosophical, and sentimental in the French tradition of Claude-Henri Saint-Simon and Pierre-Joseph Proudhon. He admits that there is another, contrasting kind of socialism—the kind that exists in the real world.

> Socialism [should rest] . . . on a system of moral values, on an ethic that itself dictates both the ends and the means, on the respect of fundamental values. The fight for freedom requires faith, solidarity, and rigor. The longer and more difficult the fight, the more [socialism] runs the risk of confining itself to sectarianism, of developing a taste for power, and of ending with the negation of reality and discipline, with centralization, with bureaucracy, with "happiness no matter what." [Although] conceived to end oppression, socialism then becomes the oppressor. In this guise it is "scorpion-socialism."[24]

It is clear that Mitterrand understood the importance of not sacrificing morality to socialism. But taking his writings together, one finds an intended confusion of terms. On one hand, he suggests that morality will guide socialism; on the other, that socialism is the ultimate expression of that morality—in other words, that morality depends on socialism for its further development. If you are a centrist, the former viewpoint will reassure you; if you are a Marxist-Leninist, the latter will.

Mitterrand's socialism could still not be called such if it did not incorporate at least a few of the characteristic concrete features of traditional socialism, including economic planning, nationalization of industry, and redistribution of wealth. He also incorporated libertarian innovations associated with the new left, such as self-management and decentralization. At the same time, he did not deny the importance of a viable free market either, in order not to alienate the centrist Radicals. There was something for everyone on the left. With time, however, nationalization would emerge as the most crucial and controversial issue of Mitterrand's specific socialist proposals.

The events of May 1968 did not strongly affect the socialist philosophy that Mitterrand elaborated between 1969 and 1971. He had one foot in the socialist pond by the 1965 presidential election and by the 1967 legislative elections he was in up to his waist. He was playing to the traditional, established non-Communist left, which he was still trying to organize. While recognizing its political potential, he still felt ambivalence toward the radical student movement—its anarchistic spontaneity and its lack of political focus prevented it from being a viable political force. Besides, Mitterrand did not naturally attract the student radicals, who found others more appealing as their representatives. Some of these came from their own ranks, such as Alain Krivine, and others from leftist groups outside Mitterrand's orbit—in particular, Mendès France and Rocard from the PSU, the first established political party to reap political benefit from the May 1968 movement. In time, Mitterrand would bring the PSU and more and more of the 1968 student generation under his wing, but he was in no hurry. His immediate task was to organize the established left, which included the PC, and the latter was deeply suspicious of the "counterrevolutionary" student movement.

In 1969, the same year that *Ma Part de vérité* was published, de Gaulle finally held his referendum on regional participation; this was a hapless effort to respond to the public's increasing demand for less micromanagement of their lives by the central government in Paris, and more important, an attempt to regain the popular support that he had lost as a result of the political crisis of 1968. The referendum was defeated, leading de Gaulle to resign immediately from office as he had promised he would do if the French people ever ceased granting him their confidence. He retired from public life altogether and lived out the last year and a half of his life finishing his memoirs at his provincial home. What made this all so astonishing was that the electorate had just returned an overwhelming Gaullist majority to the National Assembly. Thus, de Gaulle turned out not to be a dictator after all; nearly continuous popularity was more important to him than either raw power or social order, which he always contended would disintegrate after his departure. But this did not happen either. The streets remained calm, and the thoughts of the politicians turned to the forthcoming presidential election.

Defferre wrested the presidential nomination from an SFIO still controlled by Guy Mollet. (Mitterrand did not dare run this soon after the 1968 disturbance.) Defferre campaigned on a platform not very different in substance from Mitterrand's in 1965, yet his strategy was still overtly anti-Communist. He went so far as to pledge to select Mendès France as his prime minister if elected. On the left, Michel Rocard was the PSU candidate, and Jacques Duclos was the PC's. On the right, Pompidou and Alain Poher were candidates, the former representing continuity and emphasizing economic strength, and the latter, center-right parliamentarianism reminiscent of the Fourth Republic.

The fact that Pompidou won surprised no one; he was largely credited with restoring order after the events of May 1968. What was surprising was the distribution of votes on the first ballot. Pompidou received 44 percent; Poher, 23 percent; Duclos, 21 percent; Defferre, 5 percent; and Rocard, 3.6 percent—a humiliating outcome for Defferre and the SFIO. The Communist candidate had been four times more successful than the Socialist and had come within 2 percent of being a run-off candidate. The election vindicated Mitterrand's inclusive strategy for the left and marked a turning point in the evolution of the SFIO. Mollet retired, but he continued to maintain control over the party through his close ties with the party's new first secretary, Alain Savary (who had resigned from Mollet's government during the Algerian crisis and had left the SFIO for a while to form the PSA in the late 1950s).

## MITTERRAND'S TAKEOVER OF THE SOCIALIST PARTY

Defferre's defeat quickly brought the vast majority of Socialists around to accepting the union-of-the-left strategy. In his book *Un Socialisme du possible*[25] Mitterrand tried to show socialists in general and the members of the Socialist Party in particular that in other matters, too, their theories and doctrines need not separate them from him, that in fact they must unite behind broad, generally accepted concepts. All major dichotomies, such as revolution versus reform, self-management versus planning, he dismissed as false problems. The primary problem was

> [the left's] internal balance of power. If a central, coherent, homogeneous kernel is formed within democratic socialism, it will exert a power of attraction . . . on the right and left, . . . on the undecided in the center and on communist voters. It will counterbalance eventual Communist advances and at the same time will attract socioeconomic groups that vaguely identify with the left without going so far as to accept the Communist system.[26]

All doctrine and policy proposals had to flow from this condition on which the eventual acquisition of power depended.

Along with the ideological and strategic debates on the left went the struggle for brute power. These different levels of conflict were not unrelated, but competing leadership styles often provoked confusing rapprochements. Thus, although Mollet and Savary favored, in theory, the union-of-the-left strategy, many of the younger proponents of union and even Defferre, the principal old-guard exponent of the Third Force strategy with whom Mitterrand had always enjoyed a cordial relationship in spite of their differences of opinion, turned away from Mollet and Savary to look for new leaders capable of rebuilding the SFIO and captivating national attention. For the renewal of the SFIO and non-Communist left did not at all mean a change of principles but, under a stronger rejuvenated leadership, a return to socialist principles perceived as having been sacrificed in the past to electoralism (the belief that one did what one had to to get elected). The French Socialists rejected the example of their German Socialist brothers, whose German Social Democratic Party (SPD) had openly renounced Marxism in Bad Godesberg in 1959.

Ideologically, the SFIO was divided into three main factions, or currents. The Molletists, who were considered the center of the party, tended to be its oldest members. Their socialist convictions and credentials were beyond question; on a practical level, however, they were noted for compromise and concession. Mauroy and Defferre represented the right wing of the party. Both were presidents of large urban industrial federations—Mauroy of the Federation of the North, around Lille, and Defferre of the Bouches-du-Rhône Federation, around Marseilles—and both were fierce rivals of the Communists at the local level. However, Mauroy now favored union on the national level; Defferre still did not. The left wing of the party, represented by Jean Poperen and Jean-Pierre

Chevènement, had by no means as much popular support as Mauroy or Defferre, but Chevènement's Center for Socialist Studies, Research, and Education (CERES) dominated the Paris Federation, which was extremely well-organized and influential and managed to intimidate others easily with its intellectual brio and policy rigor. The young Chevènement, an urbane, intellectual, and witty Parisian, accepted Mitterrand much more readily than did the older, more serious, working-class Poperen, who tended to ally himself with Mollet (whom he resembled more). More than Socialists care to admit, personality and background often play a greater role in political relationships than does doctrine.

Many of the Socialist leaders suspected Mitterrand of opportunism. Mollet said, "Mitterrand did not become Socialist; he learned to speak Socialism."[27] Even Mauroy, who considers himself "biologically Socialist"[28] is on record as saying, "There is no room on the left for a personal adventure."[29] Savary had voted against accepting Mitterrand as a member of the PSU several years earlier, but he and Mollet were not adverse to using Mitterrand if it were possible. Both the SFIO and the CIR recognized the political advantages of fusing their organizations, but the difficulty lay in deciding on whose terms such a union would occur.

In 1969, at the time of the Alfortville congress, the SFIO had invited Mitterrand to join as a simple member, but he had refused. Soon after, at Issy-les-Moulineaux, Alain Savary had returned to the SFIO from the PSU (accompanied by Poperen and his troops) and suddenly found himself elected to be the new general director of the "new Socialist Party." Mollet, who had previously threatened to resign from the party when Defferre obtained the party's presidential nomination against his wishes, officially retired from the leadership. For years Mauroy had been considered the dauphin, Mollet's chosen successor, but he had lost favor with Mollet because of his close ties to Mitterrand. At first Defferre had supported Savary, but he quickly realized that Savary remained too strongly influenced by Mollet and did not possess the leadership qualities required to transform the party. Pierre Bérégovoy (another PSU transplant and Mitterrand's future chief of staff and later a prime minister, who committed suicide in 1993), Poperen, and Savary all wanted renewal—but without Mitterrand playing a major role and without necessarily eliminating Mollet.

Mitterrand and Savary continued to send out signals showing their respective desire to fuse the SFIO and CIR. The two finally agreed, and preparations were made for a congress to be held at Epinay in June 1971, at which time the leadership of the new organization would be determined. There was mistrust on both sides. Savary saw Mitterrand as an opportunist; Mitterrand viewed Savary as a naive, dreamy purist[30] under the thumb of Mollet. The principal practical problem lay in agreeing on the number of mandates to attribute to the future CIR delegates; the more mandates the latter could obtain, the more electoral weight they could wield at the congress. Poperen called Mitterrand's claim of strength a successful bluff (and not Mitterrand's first), for he managed to obtain a number of mandates many times greater than the CIR's actual numbers justified; there were only sixty-one permanent members of the CIR (although it claimed to have 10,000) compared to approximately ˙55,000 card-carrying Socialists. The CIR would be the only group to dissolve itself officially at Epinay, but all sixty-one permanent members would remain faithful Mitterrandists.[31] Everyone understood that it was not Mitterrand's Nièvre constituency or the CIR entourage that gave him clout but the 45 percent of the vote from 1965 that still clung to him.

While official preparations and negotiations were taking place, so did parallel private—even secret—discussions over informal meals. Mitterrand, Dayan, Mauroy, Defferre, and Gérard Jaquet along with others developed a Resistance-style, clandestine network. Only Chevènement was not in on their discussions: he was considered part of the problem. Now Mauroy and Defferre both turned against Mollet with a vengeance, the former because Mollet had rejected renovation by denying him the leadership of the party, and the latter because he blamed Mollet for his and the Socialists' humiliation in the 1969 presidential elections and also because he resented Mollet's unwillingness to renovate the party. Mauroy expected to become first secretary of the new party, an administrative post that Mitterrand did not covet; the former FGDS president no doubt sought a different role—that of charismatic national leader supported by a large, modern organized party. After two unsuccessful presidential bids, Defferre appeared to be willing to embrace more modest goals now, such as a Cabinet post in a Mitterrand government. Mollet and Savary knew nothing of this three-way alliance. One of the things that the conspirators agreed upon was that their alliance should remain hidden during as much of the congress as possible. Rather than signing joint motions, they would formulate distinct yet similar ones; Mitterrand's name would appear on only one at the very end of the congress.

Votes on various motions to be taken at Epinay would determine the ultimate balance of power and leadership within the party, and the challengers intended to leave as little to chance as possible. They knew that they could muster about 45 percent of the votes on key motions, a proportion roughly equal to that of the Molletists. Small groups, including CERES and Poperen's faction, would make the difference, but since their far-left ideology kept them apart from the social democratic "conspirators," it was difficult for the conspirators to predict their actions, let alone control them. Furthermore, getting the various bosses to agree on an issue did not eliminate the problem of persuading the delegates, who held the mandates, to follow their recommendations.

Mitterrand did not neglect Chevènement and CERES during this crucial time, for he was aware of the decisive role that they could play. It was hard to imagine Chevènement, a former protégé of Mollet, entering into a coalition with Defferre, the symbol of what Chevènement called "social mediocracy." But he did owe Mauroy and Jaquet a favor for their support of CERES candidates against Molletists in a recent election.[32] On the other hand, Poperen, a former member successively of both the PC and the PSU, was a poor prospect of support for Mitterrand. Mitterrand and his cronies stacked the deck as carefully as possible, but the final deal could not be predicted with certainty since democratic procedures had to be respected at a congress bringing together about a thousand delegates.

Thus, at the outset of the Epinay congress Mitterrand had established certain unofficial alliances, but all the allies were not yet allied with one another. And it remained to be seen who would mobilize the crowd in the hall. An aura of drama and intrigue loomed over an unsuspecting congress.[33] To the few who were initiated, it was clear that the leadership of the party was at stake. But since a public display of the power struggles taking place within the party would have been considered indecent, they had to be cloaked in a pseudo-debate about the union of the left.

The delegates wasted no time in getting down to business. The audacious Chevènement immediately brought up the matter of the voting system to be used. Since no faction had started out with a clear majority, this was a crucial issue. A proportional voting system and a combination of majority and proportional systems whereby a minimum percentage would be required in order to gain representation were posed as alternatives. Chevènement's CERES defended pure proportional representation for obvious reasons: they would reap the full potential of their constituents' strength. Although they did not speak out, Mauroy's and Defferre's groups appeared to favor the majority system because it would maximize their dominant positions and enhance the possibility of their creating a majority. Mitterrand's CIR appeared to go along with this, too, although the proportional system would have been more in their best interest because they were a small group. Chevènement's position was genuine; Defferre's, Mauroy's, and Mitterrand's were all feints to throw off Mollet and Savary. The Mollet-Savarysts now spoke in favor of an altered proportional system, which would penalize small groups such as CERES.

The congress as a whole voted for the proportional principle (60 to 40 percent), but not for a specific system. Only when one of Mitterrand's CIR lieutenants, Claude Estier, spoke in favor of CERES's proposal of a purely proportional system was there an inkling of the new coalition. Probably only a few CIRs, including Estier and Pierre Joxe (the son of de Gaulle's minister for Algerian affairs and a Marxist), enthusiastically embraced the CERES members as partners. As Albert du Roy put it, "The CIRs made virtue out of necessity: to prevent Mollet's success they had to offer the keys of the party to CERES."[34] The final vote on the matter (51.3 to 48.7 percent) revealed publicly for the first time the reorientation of Mauroy's and Defferre's factions and a possible new majority coalition grouping the right and the left wings of the party against the center. The Mollet-Savarysts sensed that something was up, for there was no logical reason for Mauroy and Defferre to support CERES's more radical motion unless they were all uniting against the status quo. Still, it was hard to believe that Defferre and Chevènement could stick together on subsequent motions, let alone in a governing majority. During these crucial hours much depended on Mitterrand's subtle persuasive powers.

At a private dinner during the congress all the members of the conspiracy fraternized for the first time together: Mitterrand; CIR members Joxe, Dayan, and Roland Dumas; Defferre, Mauroy, and Jaquet, representing the right and center of the SFIO; Chevènement and Didier Motchane from the CERES faction of the SFIO; plus a few others. The ticklish problem of how to present motions concerning the union-of-the-left strategy was raised again: Who would write and who would sign what? To ensure success, it would be necessary to lull the Molletist and Savaryst groups into believing as long as possible that the conflict was over policy rather than men and to create the illusion that the new coalition was formed spontaneously and against its membership's will. Chevènement agreed to the plan previously decided upon: After each faction presented separate but similar motions, all would support a motion, composed by Chevènement and signed by Mitterrand, calling for a union-of-the-left strategy.

To prepare the thousand delegates for such a motion, to rally (over the heads of the bosses) the greatest amount of support possible in a short time, to rouse the enthusiasm of the rank and file, and to raise hopes of electoral victory in the struggle for power, the deputy from the Nièvre took to the podium the day following the historical dinner. No one was better suited to this oratorical task: "When it comes to charm, he excels, especially when success carries him away."[35] Speaking as merely a delegate from the Nièvre, Mitterrand easily won the crowd over to his thought and, more important, to his person—even Mollet, in spite of himself, joined in the standing ovation that foreshadowed Mitterrand's conquest of the new party in formation. In a sense, Mitterrand picked up where he had left off in 1965.[36] In contrast, Mollet's speech was lackluster and old hat, although his ideas and strategy did not differ significantly from Mitterrand's.

Subsequently, the *comité directeur* (the eighty-one-member national governing body of the Socialist Party) was elected, revealing the relative strength of each faction; no ruling coalition was formed at this level. Of the 81, 28 were Molletists or Savarysts; 23, Mauroyists or Defferrists; 13, Mitterrandists (former CIRs); 10, Poperenists; and 7, CERES members. The voting on the final motion of political orientation would determine for at least the next two years who supported whom (more than who supported what) and who would lead the transformed Socialist Party (PS).

After the presentation of the various motions, Mollet, in one last attempt to salvage Savary's (and his own) position, asked Mitterrand to join with him and Savary on a motion favoring the union-of-the-left strategy, leaving the right-wingers Mauroy and Defferre to fend for themselves. At the risk of appearing to be the disrupter of unity, Mitterrand refused, bluntly reminding

Mollet of the real stakes of the game—the leadership of the party.

As planned, the elements of the new majority coalesced behind the Mitterrand motion. Shocking many inside and outside the party, Mauroy's and Defferre's troops (after some arm twisting on the part of their bosses) shunned the more moderate union-of-the-left strategy of Savary's motion in favor of the more radical-sounding, CERES-inspired strategy of Mitterrand's. It was not a landslide victory by any means; Mitterrand's motion won out over Savary's by a vote of only 43,926 to 41,757 (51.3 to 48.7 percent), with over 5,000 abstentions and other missing votes. But a new majority had been formed with Mitterrand as its unifying force.

> The success of the conspiracy was total since its principal instigator did not have to intervene openly at any time [on motions]. Thus, he conserved intact his image as the loner, the "federator," the former presidential candidate of the whole left.[37]

Mitterrand became the head of the PS during his first week as a member of the party. At the last minute, Mauroy was forced by his mentor Augustin Laurent, who was about to retire as mayor of Lille, to choose between being first secretary of the PS or mayor of that city. Deciding that his local power base was more important to him politically, he chose the latter position. It was clear in any case that Mitterrand could muster the greatest degree of party unity, support, and enthusiasm. Although Mitterrand undoubtedly did not relish the administrative aspects of the job, he knew there would be others to tend to the details.[38]

The Molletists and Savarysts were bitter. They called Mitterrand's coup a "putsch," a "takeover," and (using the same American expression that Mitterrand had used when the Gaullists had taken the National Assembly by storm in 1968) a "hold-up"; many on the left, inside and outside the party, recalled the old image of Mitterrand as a conniving Fourth Republic politician—the image certainly fit reality in this case. Both the old guard and the purists condemned his conspiratorial methods and the lack of ideological coherence of his coalition. Amid bitterness, skepticism, and sarcasm Mitterrand and his associates moved their offices to the vacated premises of the Cité Malesherbes, the traditional home of the SFIO. The former young disciple of Colonel de La Roque had traveled far.

## NOTES

1. The author observed these problems firsthand during 1967 and 1968 at the University of Strasbourg.

2. François Mitterrand, Agence France Presse press release, May 5, 1968, cited in Mitterrand, *Politique* (Paris: Fayard, 1977), p. 478. The minister of the interior is in charge of internal security.

3. Ibid., p. 480.

4. Mitterrand, cited in Jean-Marie Borzeix, *Mitterrand lui-même* (Mitterrand himself) (Paris: Stock, 1973), p. 151.

5. Mitterrand, press conference, May 28, 1968, cited in Mitterrand, *Politique*, p. 494.

6. Ibid., pp. 494–95.

7. Ibid., p. 496.

8. Catherine Nay, *Le Noir et le rouge* (The black and the red) (Paris: Grasset, 1984), p. 308.

9. François Mitterrand, *Ma Part de vérité* (My share of the truth) (Paris: Fayard, 1969), p. 151.

10. *J.O.* (A.N.), no. 34 (May 22, 1968): 2,032.

11. Ibid., p. 489.

12. Mitterrand, press conference, May 28, 1968, cited in Mitterrand, *Politique*, p. 493.

13. Mitterrand, *Le Populaire*, November 9, 1968, cited in Mitterrand, *Politique*, p. 502.

14. Mitterrand, *Ma Part*, pp. 137–38.

15. Ibid., p. 200–201.

16. Ibid., pp. 201–2.

17. Ibid., pp. 203, 206–7.

18. Ibid., pp. 210, 297.

19. Ibid., p. 304.

20. Ibid., pp. 251, 296.

21. Ibid., pp. 255–60.

22. Mitterrand, *Politique*, p. 518.

23. Ibid., p. 266.

24. Ibid., p. 519.

25. François Mitterrand, *Un Socialisme du possible* (A socialism in the realm of the possible) (Paris: Seuil, 1970), p. 33.

26. Ibid., p. 33.

27. Albert du Roy and Robert Schneider, *Le Roman de la rose d'Epinay à l'Elysée* (The romance of the rose from Epinay to the Elysée) (Paris: Seuil, 1982), p. 23.

28. Ibid., p. 33.

29. Ibid., p. 43.

30. Ibid., p. 58.

31. Ibid., pp. 30–31.

32. Ibid., p. 61.

33. Ibid., p. 63.

34. Ibid., p. 68.

35. Borzeix, *Mitterrand lui-même*, p. 176.

36. The Epinay speech is reprinted in its entirety in Mitterrand, *Politique*, pp. 531–42.

37. Borzeix, *Mitterrand lui-même*, pp. 175–76.

38. Du Roy and Schneider, *Le Roman de la rose*, p. 82.

# 8

# Union with the French
# Communist Party, 1971–1973

"Everywhere the results of Epinay provoked stupor, incomprehension, even consternation, and that kind of haggard bedazzlement which characterizes politicians and journalists when confronted with the extraordinary," observed Pierre Guidoni, one of the founding members of CERES.[1] The PSU was "torn apart," perplexed,[2] while the PC reacted with suspicion. "The Communist leaders see only the men—all those whom they fear, fight, those who inspire worry and mistrust—Mauroy, Defferre, Mitterrand himself. And . . . CERES . . . is in many ways as much an irritant as the PSU."[3]

During his apprenticeship, the new first secretary of the PS avoided posing as the national opposition leader. His business was to consolidate his power within the PS and prepare it for negotiations with the PC. Besides, the relatively popular government of Prime Minister Jacques Chaban-Delmas, which was formed under President Pompidou and included the Mendesist Jacques Delors, did not lend itself well to playing the role of "the enemy" that Mitterrand has always preferred to assign to his opponents on the national political scene. Such a scenario was made all the more difficult by the long, cordial relationship that existed between Mitterrand and the prime minister, a former Resistance fighter who had served with Mitterrand in various governments of the Fourth Republic.

## THE COMMON PROGRAM

The specific purpose of the negotiations with the PC was to conclude a common program of government that would be considered as a legislative agreement binding the two parties together for five years. This was the beginning of the first of four discernible stages of the union of the left spanning the years 1972 to 1976 and was labeled by Branko Lazitch as the complementary stage. (The other three stages he called *convergent, competitive,* and *antagonistic.*)⁴ The term *complementary* hardly describes the abrupt, offensive-defensive moves of the cat-and-mouse game being played by the two large parties of the left at this stage of their relationship.⁵ The PC's approach was, *"Unité, salauds!"* ("Let's get together, you bastards!")⁶ Furthermore, the Communists were condescending, seeing the new PS as nothing more than a supporting force.

Mitterrand, the most fervid exponent of the union of the left, was not in any hurry to sign a common program. According to Philippe Alexandre, "The head of the Socialist Party exhibits patience bordering on insolence."⁷ Mitterrand saw that time was on the side of the PS; as the months went by, the Socialists would have time to spell out their own party program and develop their own language distinct from the wooden language of the PC and purged of the theoretical, technocratic abstractions spewing forth from CERES. Always the rhetorician, Mitterrand wanted dramatic and moving language that would resonate with the public.⁸

Eventually, the pressure exerted by the Communists became, as Mitterrand put it, "frankly intolerable."⁹ They accused the PS of being class collaborators and stalling, and in October 1971 they issued their own party program, which the PS found, not unexpectedly, provocative. It was in the interest of the PC to put pressure on the PS. Their negotiating position was already prepared, and they felt strong with their 21 percent of the vote from 1969 compared to the Socialists' 5 percent. The PC intended to remain the dominant party of the opposition—a situation that gave it the opportunity to protest freely and speak in a loud voice on policy without having to assume any responsibility for results. It much preferred that stance to being the weaker partner in a winning majority (since it realized that it had no serious chance of being the dominant party of a winning majority). Mitterrand fought continuously against this tendency, which led him to emphasize that the PS was a "government party"—in other words, a party prepared to accept the responsibilities of national leadership.

The elaboration of the Socialist program was in itself not a smooth process. The first secretary assigned Jean-Pierre Chevènement, the technocratic head of CERES, the job of proposing a program for the party. The first efforts of Chevènement, who characteristically got carried away, were shot down from all directions: Mitterrand termed them "a lot of blather,"¹⁰ Poperen called them "Ivy League Leninism,"¹¹ and others spoke of them as "anti-American diarrhea" and "incomprehensible." At this point Mitterrand stepped in to assume the dual role of conductor-arranger¹² with the added challenge of having to respect democratic rules—he could not claim the "divine right" of the orchestra conductor. None of the Socialist themes were original to Mitterrand, who in no way resembled a composer. But it was he who decided who played what, when, and how loud. He issued the final interpretation of themes. He rounded the corners and sharpened the edges of the harsh sounds emanating from the party. He was above the fray in order to manage the fray. He harmonized the cacophony and, when that was not possible, organized the dissonance.

Radical differences existed among the players in the essential areas of economics, foreign policy, and the organization of political institutions.[13] Mitterrand reconciled contraries and loosened up rigidities. He resolved the issue of self-management (favored by CERES) versus nationalization (favored by Molletists) by deciding that nationalization would be the short-term goal and self-management the long-term goal. CERES and Molletists came together to force the other factions to accept a provision for worker-initiated nationalizations, which Mitterrand did not favor. In the debate over the Atlantic Alliance, he opted for the Alliance (which was favored by every group except CERES and the Poperenists) as a short-term position and neutrality as a long-term goal, and a conditional one at that. As for the nuclear strike force, the first secretary, who had opposed this Gaullist achievement throughout the 1960s, began to rethink his own position under the influence of Charles Hernu and persuaded the party to call for more debate on the subject and a future national referendum. The issue of European unity, which was stated as a goal in the Socialist program, also successfully united the Molletists and the "majority" of the majority (that is, Mitterrand, Mauroy, and Defferre) against CERES.

On the issue of institutions, the presidentialists opposed the parliamentarians. Mitterrand, now evolving toward a more presidentialist view of the constitution, helped everyone toward a synthesis: He continued to promote the idea of a legislative contract, but he rejected the automatic dissolution of Parliament when one party in a coalition majority decided to withdraw. He insisted that, in order to avoid instability, the president must have a second chance to form a new government and a new majority before dissolution took place and new elections were called.[14]

Mitterrand and his allies, Mauroy and Defferre, had much more in common with the Molletist old guard, which they had deposed, than with their young extremist colleagues in CERES. Nevertheless, it was still Chevènement who was given the job of preparing the revised Socialist program for publication[15] (it was not so much an honor as a way of keeping the rascal busy).

Finally both major parties of the left, the PS and the PC, had published programs, each of which served a dual purpose: (1) to constitute a starting position for negotiations with the other party and (2) to convince the other party that it was a worthy partner, delivered of its "original sin"—totalitarianism in the case of the PC and reformism in the case of the PS.[16] What ensued can best be portrayed as a poker game in which each party had a set of chips—a program—that it was prepared to risk cautiously at the bargaining table with its rival-partner.

As the negotiations of the two parties got underway for the first time in decades, the public was fascinated. The big question was whether current forces conducive to union would outweigh the historical forces dividing the left. The traditional obstacle was still present: The age-old multiparty system had ingrained in politicians the habit of resisting union. But there was now widespread belief that the international and national climate in 1972 was propitious for an agreement in spite of this obstacle. International détente made possible the convergent internal evolution of the two major parties of the left—markedly increased openness and independence from Moscow on the part of the PC and greater "revolutionism" on the part of the PS. Furthermore, the single-member majority electoral system instituted by de Gaulle bestowed an electoral advantage on a large, united front. In short, "the pressure of the majority system combines with economic, social, and international developments."[17]

Mollet had tried for years to negotiate with the PC but had never made any significant progress toward agreement. While the new first secretary of the PS and the Molletists had long understood the electoral advantage of union with the Communists, the moving spirit behind Mitterrand's approach was radically different from Mollet's. In order to establish guarantees for democracy the Molletists always wanted to engage in negotiations on ideology and doctrine before getting into actual policies. Specifically, they expected to persuade the French Communist Party to officially renounce Bolshevism and submission to the Soviet Communist Party.[18] To Mitterrand this was futile, for the French PC's ideology constituted its "theological" essence and loyalty to the Soviet Communist Party was part of its very nature (it was also a practical necessity— the Soviets helped finance the PCF); therefore, such negotiations were doomed to lead nowhere.

Mitterrand found the "existential" level of politics the only productive level at which to operate: "What one says [in a formal agreement], what one does, in the end makes you what you are."[19] For this reason, Mitterrand believed that the best way to encourage the PC's evolution was to create a set of circumstances based on two immediate goals: (1) the negotiation of an agreement based on concrete issues that the two parties had in common (other issues would be ignored) and (2) the restructuring of the left so as to create a new balance of power that would force the PC to respect the agreement.

The path to union between the two parties was so strewn with theoretical and practical hurdles that the only way in which the two parties would be able to reach an agreement was to remove, not surmount, the highest among them; the will to agree was stronger than the adherence to any one point. Oddly, it was the subject on which their differences were greatest, foreign affairs, that caused the least difficulty because the PC was willing to postpone its agenda. Disagreements over social and entitlement programs were also resolved easily since there were no significant differences to start with. When differences proved irreducible, mention of them was either omitted, obscured with euphemisms, or frankly juxtaposed to give the impression of concordance.[20]

Mitterrand's agents, headed by Mauroy, negotiated the easy parts of the Common Program. Their efforts, however, met with only mild approval from the first secretary, who thought that Mauroy had conceded too much at this stage.[21] But only at the very end of the process, on June 26, 1972, did Mitterrand intervene in order to conclude the agreement with the PC. Highly controversial issues that the two delegations had been unable to resolve still remained: the extent of nationalization, forms of self-management, what to do with the nuclear strike force, automatic dissolution of Parliament, and the question of irreversibility.

The self-management versus collectivization disagreement was plastered over with the unspecific phrase "new forms of management," while Marchais continued to loudly denounce self-management as "anarchy," "a rejection of planning," and a "reactionary position."[22] The PS accepted the elimination of the "strategic" but not the "tactical" nuclear force, but the definition of these terms was carefully avoided. The issue of the irreversibility of Socialist rule was one of the most intractable. The PC was not willing to concede. Here, the radical difference was dealt with by juxtaposing two contradictory sentences:

> If the confidence of the country is refused to the majority parties, these would renounce power. . . . But democratic power, whose existence implies the support of a popular majority, . . . will thus be strong with the ever increasing confidence that the popular masses will offer it.[23]

In the end, the PC gave up its demand that the National Assembly be automatically dissolved in case of a breakdown of a given coalition, in exchange for which Mitterrand agreed in vague terms to the requirement that any new government formed have a leftist orientation. This was clearly a sop, since respect for the constitution superseded any legislative agreement.

Nationalization proved to be by far the most thorny of all the issues because of its relatively drastic and immediate practical consequences in case of a leftist victory. It is said that at one point Mitterrand was so annoyed with the PC's unwillingness to make concessions that he packed up his papers and prepared to leave.[24] This little scene had its effect, for Marchais immediately gave up his demand for the nationalization of the whole steel industry. Mitterrand managed to whittle down the list of companies to be nationalized to nine major corporations in key sectors of the economy: banking, finance, natural resources, arms, aeronautical and space industries, nuclear power, pharmaceuticals, electronics, and chemicals; other key sectors—steel, oil, air and sea transport, waterworks, and freeway concessions—were earmarked for future partial participation by the government.

The huge difference between the two parties in the number of companies deemed necessary to nationalize reflects the fact that each party had a different goal in mind. For the Communists, nationalization was to be the means by which the party would take control of whole segments of society; it was a matter of raw power, not economic efficiency. The Communists favored the nationalization of well over a thousand companies, following the Soviet model. For the Socialists, limited nationalization was supposed to end Malthusian capitalism, unleash faster growth, and increase prosperity for all.[25] They felt that the choice of companies should be determined by clear economic criteria and limited to those in which competition and the free market were thought no longer to come into play; where the government was the primary customer (for example, in the arms industry); where modernization, high technology, and future development were at stake (for example, electronics); where the government paid the bills (such as pharmaceuticals); and public utilities of primary necessity (including water, electricity, and public transportation).

After working through the night, at 5:00 A.M. on June 27 the historic agreement was signed by the Socialists and the Communists. A week later, the left-wing Radicals also signed the Common Program. The right-wing Radicals led by Jean-Jacques Servan-Schreiber bucked; they were unwilling to accept any nationalizations. Servan-Schreiber had already proposed to Mitterrand that the Radicals and the Socialists present single candidates in the 1973 legislative elections, an offer that Mitterrand had summarily refused.[26] "There is something of the bourgeois gentleman about this reformer—which does not deny his merits: There is no one like him for breaking down open doors," said Mitterrand of Servan-Schreiber.[27] Maurice Faure and Robert Fabre were the leaders of the new left-wing Radical group that called itself the Movement of the Left Radicals (MRG).

In spite of the extensive treatment given to economic matters, just about everyone (including Mitterrand, Giesbert, Poperen, Alexandre, and Salomon) agreed that the signing of the Common Program had much more political than economic significance; its main function was literally to paper over the parties' differences. After all, implementation of the policies contained in it depended on such things as the balance of power between parties in the National Assembly, the strength of the labor unions, and approval by the Constitutional Council (the body that judges the constitutionality of legislative proposals). Specifically, the signing of this document marked the return of the PC to constructive political life in France (by suggesting its willingness to abide by democratic rules) and the return of the PS to the embrace of the working class.[28]

Although both parties agreed on the political significance of the document, their political purposes continued to diverge. For the PC the positions stated in the document only amounted to a point of departure: "We consider [the Common Program] a step forward, permitting the creation of the most favorable conditions for starting a mass movement based on *our* ideas, *our* solutions, *our* objectives."[29] For the PS the agreement represented a maximum program of traditional socialism; on the other hand, "it did not depart sufficiently from traditional leftist analyses to consider . . . the consequences of a third industrial revolution."[30] All in all, the PS was much more seriously committed to the idea of union; the PC, unbeknownst to the PS (although only the naive could have been surprised), allowed itself an escape hatch in the event that union worked against its interests.

Far from keeping his own intention a secret, Mitterrand declared it to the world at the Congress of the International Socialist Party in Vienna two weeks after the Common Program was signed. To a concerned and skeptical anti-Communist audience he declared,

> When the PS appears to have less power than the PC to defend the workers' legitimate interests, it is indispensable to build a great French Socialist Party. The masses must be convinced of the PS's authenticity. . . . Our fundamental objective is to reconstruct a great Socialist Party on the territory occupied by the PC itself, in order to demonstrate that, of the five million Communist voters, three million can vote Socialist.[31]

The Communist reaction to this proclamation was: Let them try!

Writing from a traditional rightist perspective, Nay called the union of the left "a mortal sin" and asserted that it was the product of something beyond "your ordinary cynicism."[32] But the term cynicism implies that the Common Program was inconsistent with Mitterrand's acts and stated principles, and that is hard to prove. Mitterrand did not make concessions in the Common Program on any of the major policies that he had been calling for since 1969. The specifics to which he agreed might or might not have been wise, but he was of the opinion that they were consistent with his principles and with the national interest and that they were the only positions that could render the union of the left possible at the time. This is pragmatism, not cynicism; the former both pushes and restrains men within limits; the latter pushes only and knows no limits.

The conclusion of this unprecedented accord sent shock waves throughout French politics, and caused ripples to reach Washington and Moscow. The initial reaction of the right was total surprise and disbelief. The center-right Radicals—those under the influence of Servan-Schreiber, Lecanuet, and the writings of Jean-François Revel—were genuinely shocked. For them, the Socialists were by themselves acceptable political allies with legitimate goals, but with the Communists they became untouchable. The moderate liberal (that is, capitalist) right—represented most strongly by Giscard d'Estaing—was publicly shocked but privately rather pleased; the Common Program handed them electoral arguments with which they could clobber a union that, they believed, had no chance at all electorally. The Gaullist right was also publicly scandalized by the agreement, but privately it was a little concerned about this strange political marriage—for the alliance of the PS and the PC threatened to siphon off part of its anti-American working-class constituency that was faithful to the memory of General de Gaulle.

Reactions from the left were generally favorable, but there were also some reservations. Die-hard Social Democrats needed reassuring. CERES thought the program did not go far enough in the direction of the PC. The *gauchistes* (extreme leftists) rejected the union, further marginalizing themselves, although some in their ranks were evolving toward a Mitterrandist viewpoint. The PSU was the most jolted and fragmented by it: Gilles Martinet and his followers went over to the CERES faction of the PS to show their support, while Rocard, now the head of the PSU, remained and called the Common Program "reformist"—a derogatory term in the PSU dictionary. Deep down the PSU knew that this agreement did not bode well for its future as a viable political party. Although Mitterrand may have gone too far to the left for some and not far enough for others (including the PC, CERES, and the PSU), he had found the appropriate point on the left side of the political spectrum to perform the crucial role of *rassembleur* of the left.

In Western Europe, the Soviet Union, and the United States, the accord had predictable diplomatic repercussions. Mitterrand faced explicit disapproval from his continental Socialist brethren (even the Italian Socialists looked askance, for in Italy it was the Christian Democratic Party, not the Socialists, that had made a pact with the Communist devil). In Washington and in Moscow there was concern, but for opposite reasons. Henry Kissinger feared needlessly for the cohesion of the Atlantic Alliance, while the Soviets worried about the loss of a valued fifth column.

In 1973, a new book by Mitterrand, *La Rose au poing* (The rose in the fist, the rose being the party symbol of the new PS), was published to defend and illustrate the Common Program. In substance, this most Marxist-sounding of Mitterrand's books repeated and developed arguments and ideas already presented in *Ma Part de vérité*. Although Mitterrand may not have wanted to be called a Marxist, in this tract he espoused many ideas generally associated with contemporary Marxism, such as the parallel between Soviet military imperialism and American economic imperialism, the irreversibility of socialist progress, the masses unaware of their oppression and in need of "education," and capitalism as inherently unjust but containing the seeds of its own destruction. ("I do not consider capitalism to be a monster eager for human flesh. It is simply satisfying an appetite that is leading it, for want of having enough to satisfy itself, to eat itself. But before reaching that point, it will have devoured everything else.")[33]

Mitterrand is a highly intelligent man, and his memory and his humanistic culture are legendary, but the ease with which he absorbs new knowledge often leads to a fascination with brilliant sounding expositions, hasty or superficial analyses, invalid comparisons, and purely speculative conclusions. In *La Rose au poing* he betrays an astounding degree of intellectual credulity, unquestioningly accepting and ingeniously developing many of the shibboleths of the left. Political expediency, moral and emotional sensibilities, and prejudice all conspire to cloud his brain. In this book he appears to be more a dupe than a cynic (although, in the end, since his words and actions so closely coincide, the question is largely irrelevant).

All in all, Mitterrand's wager on the outcome of the signing of the Common Program of Government had three distinct aspects: electoral, political, and economic. Electorally, he bet that only the strategy of union could make a leftist victory possible; politically, that union with the Communists would not only not stifle civil liberties but not preclude their expansion either; and economically, that the policies spelled out in it would produce enough growth to allow for both progressive prosperity and income redistribution. In sum, he was betting that France would show the world how to have it all through socialism—more freedom, more justice (both legal and economic), and more wealth.

## THE LEGISLATIVE ELECTIONS OF 1973

The first test came with the legislative elections of 1973, although the united left did not really expect to win them so soon after their agreement. Still, it was an important moment to measure the strength of the new PS created in Epinay vis-à-vis the PC, to measure the efficacy of the union-of-the-left strategy in a confrontation with the right, and to influence subsequent policy in the National Assembly. Mitterrand had to perform a delicate balancing act. In order to maintain his national prestige "he must be both part of, and yet distant from—in some ways above—his party."[34] He also needed to strengthen the PS's alliance with the PC without being, or even appearing to be, overwhelmed by it.

"Healthy emulation" in general characterized the two parties' legislative campaigns in spite of concerns on each side: "The Socialists avoided expressing their worries loudly when, during the course of the campaign, they heard that the Communists represented the surest guarantee of faithfulness to the commitments made in the Common Program and its execution."[35] The PC also pushed for more joint public demonstrations, which the PS resisted. The PS wanted to wage a complementary, separate campaign to maintain its distinctness.[36] This, coupled with Mitterrand's extreme discretion concerning the composition of a future government of the left, bothered the PC.[37] The PCF's continued defense of the Soviet invasion of Prague was another shadow cast over the union of the left. The PS openly rejected this position to reassure prospective voters of its concern for civil liberties, a gesture not appreciated by the PC. On top of all this, the union of the left did not receive support from the other factions of the left. To the *gauchistes* it was just too "bourgeois," or square. To the PSU it was both too limited and archaic. To the aging radical left of the 1950s (represented by Sartre and his friends at *Les Temps modernes*) it was a "booby trap"; in his characteristic magisterial fashion Sartre declared: "The Socialist Party does not exist."[38]

President Pompidou played both sides of the Communist issue. He and Leonid Brezhnev met publicly shortly before the election to demonstrate their mutual appreciation. Mikhail Suslov was sent to the PC to express Moscow's displeasure at the prospect of a Socialist-dominated left in power.[39] Pompidou liked to remind Communist voters and others on the left that he continued the Gaullist foreign policy of friendly relations with the Soviet leadership. But he also exploited the traditional themes of the Communist threat to political freedom and economic prosperity. His main strategy was to show voters that the

Common Program implied a "choice of society" and that the right represented the free society. He went so far as to threaten to resign if the voters did not give him "his" majority. Mitterrand called this refusal to respect the principle of the alternation of power "cynical blackmail . . . in the tradition of de Gaulle's 'Me or chaos.'"[40]

For his part, Mitterrand projected an image of the right that conformed to his wishes. The end of Gaullism was at hand, he proclaimed: "Nothing is left of Gaullism, its style, its originality."[41] Of Giscard d'Estaing's party, which claimed to represent the center, Mitterrand said: "We encounter again the ridiculous and apocalyptic language of the old right which hasn't budged for half a century."[42]

Speaking, writing, engaging in numerous interviews and debates, and unabashedly defending the content of the Common Program, the first secretary actively campaigned. "He visited most departmental federations to encourage the friendly, reassure the suspicious, and placate the hostile. From 1971 to 1973 Mitterrand was truly ubiquitous"[43]—not just inside France but outside as well. He turned up in Sweden, the United States, Israel, Chile, Rumania, Yugoslavia, Austria, and Germany, studying the various Socialist experiments and establishing friendly contacts with Socialist leaders throughout the world. Chile was of paramount interest to him because Salvador Allende's program most resembled his own. He blamed the failure of Allende's revolution on International Telephone and Telegraph, the U.S. Central Intelligence Agency, and the Chilean extreme right.[44]

The results of the election offered the principal parties grounds for self-satisfaction. The right was content because it had retained a majority in the legislature, albeit a significantly smaller one than in 1967 or 1968—the Gaullists, in particular, tumbled dramatically. The PC was satisfied because it attained a relatively high percentage of the vote (21 percent) and one that was again greater than the PS's. The PS was encouraged by its respectable showing as compared to the 1969 presidential campaign and the 1968 legislative elections (19 percent versus 15 percent and 11 percent, respectively). The union of the left altogether received over 40 percent of the vote, and the whole left 46.8 percent. This did not quite match the left's performance in 1967 (in 1973 it obtained 171 seats in the National Assembly as compared to 91 in 1968 and 193 in 1967), but it did reinforce the PS's belief that it was proceeding effectively and thus confirmed Mitterrand's hold on the party.

The election brought a flood of young people to the PS, and by the end of 1973 there were approximately 110,000 members. Although the party had lost support in some of its traditional bastions, it had made inroads into groups in which it had previously been weak: blue-collar workers, women, youth, and practicing Catholics. Most important, it was attracting better than all other parties the votes of the fastest-growing sociological group, the white-collar service workers (among whom the percentage of women, youth, and Catholics was steadily increasing).

Michel Rocard, head of the PSU, was one of those who viewed the election as a relative failure for the left and who sharply criticized the economic policies spelled out in the Common Program. He also expressed doubts, although less categorically, about the political concept behind the document. His postmortem (the first of many for which he became famous) constituted a retrospective critique of the Common Program and addressed both its political and technical failings.[45] He believed that it was based on the false premise that the *marais* (marsh), or the poorly defined political center, was centrist in the traditional sense—that is, timid and traditionalist—whereas he felt that the *marais* had evolved into a more dynamic, modern group attracted to innovative positions.[46] He also believed that a simpler, more modest common program would have inspired more confidence because it would have avoided the illusion of a high degree of convergence between the positions of the two parties. Politically, the unified left, through the Common Program, offered the electorate an archaic image of itself:

> It formulated the left's objectives in the most traditional manner that one could imagine. All problems, especially economic ones, are approached from an excessively institutional and quantitative viewpoint, without any truly new ideas and without any serious consideration of the economy's real mechanisms.[47]

Rocard offered some of the most cogent criticisms of the Common Program's economic policies, thereby preempting the rightists but also, from Mitterrand's viewpoint, giving them comfort. The errors he enumerated included failure to recognize that branch offices of multinationals cannot be lumped together with national monopolies, since these groups undergo fierce competition at the international level; an unfair attack on big business, even when it was technologically and socially progressive, and undue support of traditional small businesses that were unproductive and socially repressive; and finally, inflationary policy proposals. The gaps in the program were manifold: it defined no practicable international or European policy; it neglected consumer issues that could help overcome ideological and social divisions; and it did not address the pressing issues of women's and immigrants' rights. For Rocard, an exponent of the self-management school of thought, the failure to grapple with the problem of economic decentralization was a serious omission. While his technical criticisms of the Common Program were both bold and fundamentally correct, his political criticisms—namely, that the Common Program should have been simpler and more limited in scope—revealed that his political strategy was both timid and unrealistic compared to Mitterrand's. Economic and political boldness never seemed more antithetical.

In early 1974, during a time when no major electoral confrontation loomed on the political horizon, it became obvious that President Pompidou was very ill. In April of that year he died of cancer. Although Mitterrand had always been respectful of the man Pompidou, after his death he issued a politically merciless "anti-eulogy." Of the statesman with whom he had never exchanged a word face to face, he opined,

> What will he leave as a memorial of his times? Nothing or very little. Therein lies the cruelty of the destiny that confronts him . . . : so much power, and no power, and History has escaped him. He loved the State, and enjoyed wearing its mantel, but, after five years of a solidly unified presidency, nothing was yet underway.[48]

The death of Georges Pompidou brought about the first truly unpredictable presidential election of the Fifth Republic, an election that "forced Gaullism to descend into politics, [and] dragged the left to the threshold of presidentialism."[49]

## NOTES

1. Pierre Guidoni, *Histoire du nouveau Parti socialiste* (History of the new Socialist Party) (Paris: Téma-Editions, 1973), pp. 206–7.

2. Ibid., p. 228.

3. Ibid., p. 207.

4. Branko Lazitch, *L'Echec permanent* (The permanent failure) (Paris: Editions Robert Laffont, 1978), p. 87.

5. Catherine Nay, *Le Noir et le rouge* (The black and the red) (Paris: Grasset, 1984), p. 358.

6. Guidoni, *Histoire de nouveau PS*, pp. 228–29.

7. Philippe Alexandre, *Le Roman de la gauche* (The story of the left) (Paris: Plon, 1977), pp. 280–81.

8. Ibid.

9. Ibid., p. 282.

10. Albert du Roy and Robert Schneider, *Le Roman de la rose d'Epinay à l'Elysée* (The romance of the rose from Epinay to the Elysée) (Paris: Seuil, 1982), p. 87.

11. Ibid., p. 88.

12. Jean–François Bizot, *Au Parti des Socialistes* (How it goes with the Socialist Party) (Paris: Grasset, 1975), p. 16.

13. Du Roy and Schneider, *Le Roman de la rose*, pp. 89–93.

14. François Mitterrand, *La Paille et le grain* (The wheat and the chaff) (Paris: Flammarion, 1975), p. 69. See also Guidoni, *Histoire du nouveau PS*, pp. 242–43, 252; Jean Poperen, *L'Unité de la gauche* (Unity of the left) (Paris: Fayard, 1975), pp. 368–77; André Jeanson and Gérard Fuchs, "A Propos du programme du Parti socialiste," *Projet*, 64 (April 1972): 426–32.

15. Parti socialiste, *Changer la vie: Programme de gouvernement du Parti socialiste* (Changing life: the program of the Socialist Party) (Paris: Flammarion, 1972).

16. Alexandre, *Le Roman de la gauche*, p. 283.

17. Olivier Duhamel, *La Gauche et la Cinquième République* (The left and the Fifth Republic) (Paris: Presses Universitaires de France, 1980), p. 332. See also Lazitch, *L'Echec permanent*, p. 86, on the "electoral, political, and ideological necessity" of union.

18. Duhamel, *La Gauche*, p. 326.

19. François Mitterrand, cited in Jean–Marie Borzeix, *Mitterrand lui-même* (Mitterrand himself) (Paris: Stock, 1973), p. 197.

20. Lazitch, *L'Echec permanent*, p. 93.

21. Franz-Olivier Giesbert, *François Mitterrand ou la tentation de l'histoire* (François Mitterrand or the temptation of history) (Paris: Seuil, 1977), pp. 271–76.

22. Poperen, *L'Unité de la gauche*, p. 419.

23. *Le Programme commun de gouvernement du Parti communiste et du Parti socialiste* (The Communist Party and Socialist Party's common program of government) (Paris: Editions sociales, 1972), p. 149.

24. Alexandre, *Le Roman de la gauche*, p. 292.

25. Lazitch, *L'Echec permanent*, p. 137.

26. Guidoni, *Histoire du nouveau PS*, p. 232.

27. Mitterrand, *La Paille*, p. 138.

28. Alexandre, *Le Roman de la gauche*, p. 294.

29. Georges Marchais, cited in Robert Verdier, *PS/PC: Une Lutte pour l'entente*, p. 276.

30. François Mitterrand, *La Rose au poing* (The rose in the fist) (Paris: Flammarion, 1973), p. 34.

31. Mitterrand, cited in du Roy and Schneider, *Le Roman de la rose*, p. 111.

32. Nay, *Le Noir et le rouge*, p. 357.

33. Mitterrand, *La Rose au poing*, p. 212.

34. Vincent Wright and Howard Machin, "The French Socialist Party in 1973: Performance and Prospects," *Government and Opposition*, no. 9 (Spring 1974): 124.

35. Verdier, *PS/PC: Une Lutte pour l'entente*, p. 278.

36. Du Roy and Schneider, *Le Roman de la rose*, p. 119.

37. Poperen, *L'Unité de la gauche*, pp. 424–25.

38. Guidoni, *Histoire du nouveau PS*, p. 323.

39. Du Roy and Schneider, *Le Roman de la rose*, p. 119.

40. Ibid., p. 118.

41. François Mitterrand, "La Fin du gaullisme," *Le Monde*, March 10, 1973, p. 1.

42. Ibid.

43. Wright and Machin, "The French Socialist Party in 1973," p. 126.

44. Mitterrand, *La Paille*, pp. 187–92.

45. Michel Rocard, "Perspectives de la gauche," *Preuves*, no. 3 (1973): 55–78.

46. Ibid., p. 62.

47. Ibid., p. 61.

48. Mitterrand, *La Paille*, pp. 263, 265.

49. Duhamel, *La Gauche*, p. 310.

# 9

## The Presidential Election of 1974

By the time of Pompidou's death the farsighted first secretary of the Socialist Party was no doubt already looking forward to the presidential election scheduled for 1976. Because he realized that this campaign would be radically different from any that had preceded it, he had sent Claude Perdriel of the *Nouvel Observateur* to the United States in 1972 to observe the George McGovern campaign (managed by Gary Hart). Suddenly, there was no time for calm observation; the acceleration of political events brought on by Pompidou's death caused anguish in a man used to planning ahead and setting his own tempo. The 57-year-old first secretary felt as if he were being forced to jump off the edge of a cliff.[1]

One lesson learned from the study of American presidential politics was that public nomination by a major party conferred a legitimacy and prestige on a candidate that self-declaration, designation by a party boss, or enlistment by an elite could not. It did not matter that there were no American-style caucuses or primaries preceding the first ballot. (In France the first ballot functions somewhat like a national primary, eliminating all but the two strongest candidates.) And it did not seem to matter that the nomination was determined by a handful of leftist leaders rather than by the grassroots; according to tradition, if the leaders agree, the rank and file usually fall into line.

Many prominent organizations quickly called for Mitterrand to run: the MRG, the PC, two labor unions—the Communist-dominated General Confederation of Labor (CGT) and the Christian-dominated French Democratic Confederation of Labor (CFDT)—plus Rocard. (At some point after the 1973 legislative elections, in spite of his strong objections to the Common Program, Rocard had decided to support Mitterrand for president—no doubt as part of his own ambitious plan to play a more prominent role in national politics and to prepare the way for an eventual Rocard presidency.) In the end, Mitterrand had the support of 63 percent of the PSU and all the major national labor unions—the CGT, CFDT, Work Force (FO), the National Union of French Students (UNEF), and the National Education Federation (FEN). A less and less active Mendès France endorsed his candidacy, too. Although most of the major press supported Giscard d'Estaing, several notable exceptions favored Mitterrand: *Le Monde, L'Humanité, Le Nouvel Observateur, Témoignage Chrétien, Le Provençal* (Defferre's Marseilles daily), *Le Canard enchaîné,* and *La Dépêche du Midi.* Sartre and his intellectual group at *Les Temps modernes* never rallied behind Mitterrand because, in their opinion, "the union of the left [was] a joke."²

The newly nominated candidate again had to resist intense pressure from the PC to negotiate a presidential program and dealt very bluntly with Marchais.³ After one terse conversation, the Socialist candidate refused to receive any further personal visits or even any written messages from Marchais and other PC members.⁴ Once the PC had publicly announced its support for Mitterrand, there were both private and public meetings with Marchais, but it had been essential for the PC first to support Mitterrand unconditionally so that he could enjoy the utmost freedom of movement.

That freedom was nowhere more important than in the area of foreign policy. There was virtually no common ground with the PC regarding Israel, Czechoslovakia, or the crisis in Portugal that had pitted the Portuguese Communists and Socialists against each other. At the same time, France was coming to grips with Aleksandr Solzhenitsyn's work and, in particular, with the *Gulag Archipelago,* which was on display in every bookstore in France. The Socialists did not miss this opportunity to condemn Soviet totalitarianism and the PCF's unquestioning support of it; collaboration with the Communists necessitated even open criticism of the PC's "errors" in order to hold on to the chance of attracting center-left votes. The PC accused the PS of fanning the fires of anti-Communism. Mitterrand replied in doublespeak: "Even though anti-Communism is incompatible with the union of the left, criticism of the theoretical and practical positions of the PCF cannot be forbidden."⁵

Mitterrand deemed it essential that he keep his distance not only from the PC but also from his own party. He immediately resigned his secretaryship and did not set foot in the Cité Malesherbes during the whole campaign.⁶ There was a certain irony about his having worked to take control of the party only to push it aside. The PS leadership was perturbed about being excluded from the inner workings of the campaign; although it was called upon to operate as a supporting organization, it had little say regarding campaign strategy. The candidate explained that it was the constitutional nature of the office he was seeking that required this distance from the parties and the Common Program:

> As a candidate for the presidency . . . it is not my responsibility to propose a program. That is up to the government, named by the head of state. Furthermore,

it is not up to me to propose a legislative contract. That is a matter for the deputies. I will campaign on general options which I alone will establish, without negotiating with anyone.[7]

While not disowning the Common Program, Mitterrand acted as if it had never existed.

The savvy Mitterrand knew that the logic of a presidential election was radically different from that of a legislative election and, hence, required a different strategy. Legislative elections demand partisan commitment both to specific policies and allies, the goal being control of the National Assembly by a prime minister who is a member of its majority and is responsible to that legislative majority. At this level the logic of the Fourth Republic still prevails—ideas are more important than the individuals who represent them. On the other hand, a successful presidential candidate has to find a happy medium not between the precise program of his own party and that of an allied party, but between the dual roles that a president of the Fifth Republic is expected to play. He needs to simultaneously respect the tradition of president-arbiter inherited from the Fourth Republic and descend at least part way into partisan politics. Certain "orientations" or "options" must be proposed and defended, but without too much specificity. Elaboration would be the job of the Cabinet issuing from a new legislative majority. Mitterrand understood the implications of the Gaullist constitution better than the Gaullists themselves.

In addition to Mitterrand, who represented the union of the PC and the PS, there were initially five other leftist or centrist candidates representing marginal groups: an independent workers' party, *gauchisme*, the ecology movement, European federalism, and submerged ethnic minorities.

The right also presented a plethora of candidates: Giscard d'Estaing of the center-right Independent Republicans (RI), the Gaullist Chaban-Delmas, the extreme right-wing Jean-Marie Le Pen, plus two other marginal far-right candidates. Many on the right wanted to know who Pompidou had considered his dauphin. Some insiders felt it might be Giscard d'Estaing, but Pompidou's attitude had been, "It's up to [the contenders] to work it out."[8]

The rightist camp presented the most disorder and the fiercest rivalries, causing Lucien Neuwirth, the Gaullist, to quip, "It's Mitterrand or chaos!"[9] Giscard d'Estaing, as head of the center right, was personally challenging Chaban-Delmas. Although Chaban-Delmas was supported by such founding Gaullists as Michel Debré and Alexandre Sanguinetti, who were, however, both wasting assets,[10] the younger Pompidolian Gaullists, such as Jacques Chirac, Pierre Juillet, and Marie-France Garaud, strongly opposed him. To them, Chaban-Delmas's "New Society," elaborated in association with Jacques Delors, was heresy. Although Chirac was still not experienced enough to run for president, he was already powerful enough to obstruct Chaban-Delmas. Chirac's plan was to get Pompidou's lackluster prime minister, Pierre Messmer, elected to carry the Gaullist torch until he himself was ready. At first Chirac managed to persuade Giscard d'Estaing not to run on the condition that Chaban-Delmas would not; Giscard d'Estaing would defer to Messmer. But upon hearing of Chaban-Delmas's declaration, Giscard d'Estaing was determined to enter the race no matter what Messmer did. Messmer hesitated several days and then declined to declare himself. Chirac decided to subvert the campaign of the Gaullist heretic and become Giscard d'Estaing's "objective ally."

The center was, as usual, narrow and divided. Lecanuet declared for Giscard d'Estaing, while Servan-Schreiber remained uncommitted. The MRG naturally supported Mitterrand, and a few centrists even favored Chaban-Delmas.

The joint candidate Mitterrand thus enjoyed at least one major advantage over his opponents: He had no serious rivals on his own territory. Given the fact that there were only forty days between his declaration and the beginning of the official campaign, this placed him ahead of all the other candidates in terms of personal support. His army stood poised and ready.

Mitterrand's campaign staff was composed of both longtime friends and associates and younger, newly acquainted professionals: Georges Dayan, Georges Beauchamp, André Rousselet, François de Grossouvre, Louis Mermaz, Charles Hernu, Pierre Joxe, Robert Badinter (Mitterrand's lawyer and future minister of justice), Jacques-Antoine Gau (a former Savaryst), Joseph Franceschi, Paul Legatte (a former Mendesist), Georges Fillioud, and François Luchaire. Generally, the seasoned politicians played the more prominent public roles while the younger ones contributed their technical expertise. However, Georges Dayan, Mitterrand's oldest and perhaps closest friend (their friendship began in the army in the late 1930s), and one of the very few individuals outside Mitterrand's family with whom he used the familiar *tu* form of address, played a special role in this campaign as he had throughout Mitterrand's career.

Dayan was Mitterrand's most dedicated and loyal political worker. Although his official profession was that of magistrate on the prestigious *Conseil d'Etat* (a judicial review body dating back to the monarchy), during the 1974 campaign, as in earlier campaigns, he played the subtle but crucial role of scout for his friend. According to André Laurens, Dayan was "attentive, ironic, discreet when need be, . . . a man of personal contacts, who dines in town with all those whose viewpoints the deputy from the Nièvre wishes to know but with whom he cannot personally meet because of the rigidity of the rules of the French political game."[11] Also, he was Jewish and helped Mitterrand maintain close ties to the Jewish community. Georges Dayan died in 1979, two years before Mitterrand became president.

On economic affairs Mitterrand's key advisors were Christian Goux, Michel Rocard, and Jacques Attali, who said of Mitterrand, "His ignorance of economics is encyclopedic, but he asks the right questions."[12] By 1974, economics had become the central focus of the national political debate. Knowing that his reputation for incompetence in this area was a major handicap, Mitterrand surrounded himself with economic experts. They provided him with a vocabulary and a fresh image, but their recommendations were always subordinated to political considerations; with Mitterrand, politics governed economics, never the reverse.

To outside observers Mitterrand's campaign apparatus appeared disorganized. Colliard described it as "excessively personal." This was the

> result of the fact that [Mitterrand] neither is accustomed to nor likes to delegate power. He excels in the art of assigning the same task to three different people, in giving the impression that he is granting each one of them an exceptional privilege; the result is a certain confusion about who is responsible for what and jealousies worthy of a little "court."[13]

But this method also offered the advantage of providing Mitterrand with differing perspectives on a single problem while at the same time preventing any one person from obtaining a monopoly over an issue or from dominating him on it.

At first, the PC was disturbed by Mitterrand's economic plan, which they knew was elaborated in consultation with Rocard and Mendès France. In order to resolve the contradictions inherent in the Common Program, the candidate's plan called for a greatly extended timetable. The PC also did not like Mitterrand's idea of dissolving Parliament as soon as he took office, fearing that too strong a Mitterrandist majority would be returned.[14] In spite of all this, the Communists eventually were surprisingly cooperative. The PS and the PC managed to present a perfectly united front though their respective campaign events remained completely separate. Between the first and second ballots, Mitterrand was backed up by the Communists' continued efforts, and their support remained solid and thoughtfully discreet even in places such as Lille and Marseilles, where local PS-PC rivalries were particularly intense.

The Communists appeared to believe that the left could really win this time around, and they naturally wanted to be able to demand a large share of credit for the victory, since this would enhance their status within an eventual presidential majority and would position them well for the legislative election that would inevitably follow a Mitterrand victory.[15] Mitterrand had made it clear publicly that although a Communist prime minister was out of the question, a handful of technical posts would be reserved for the Communists, depending on the level of their support. They did not demand more than this.

Polls, which played a crucial role throughout the campaign, showed the inexorable rise of Giscard d'Estaing and the corresponding decline of Chaban-Delmas, the "rapid early increase of support for Mitterrand, which gradually slowed down," and the electoral insignificance of the marginal candidates.[16] Polls also strongly indicated electorate "fluidity," or frequent switching of sides,[17] and, as the date of the election grew closer, greater unpredictability of its outcome. The left's candidate felt strongly that he needed to win at least 45 percent of the vote on the first ballot to assure victory on the second.

Chaban-Delmas's free fall in the polls added some drama to the first part of the campaign. It puzzled many and called for explanation, for initially he appeared to be the best organized candidate and the one most favored to win. But he also had possessed a number of major handicaps, which he and others had underestimated or not foreseen. First, he had committed a serious political faux pas by announcing his candidacy the very day of Pompidou's funeral; both Mitterrand and Giscard d'Estaing had the decency to wait a week. Second, once in public view Giscard d'Estaing developed a much better public image than Chaban-Delmas; both exuded an aura of competence and experience, but Giscard d'Estaing also had youth and charm in excess. Third, there were several "character factors" that worked against the Gaullist candidate: He was tainted by a tax scandal dating from 1971, which showed that this wealthy man had managed legally to avoid paying income tax (a scandal possibly instigated by Giscard d'Estaing, who was then minister of finance), and Catholics and other traditionalists found it offensive that he had been married three times. Last but not least, his campaign strategy turned out to be incoherent; he changed direction three times—first he was against the left, then he was against Giscard d'Estaing, and then he tried to rise above the right-left division.[18]

## THE FIRST GISCARD D'ESTAING–MITTERRAND DUEL

It soon became clear that the campaign was mainly a contest between Giscard d'Estaing and Mitterrand. Mitterrand must have been relieved, for he much preferred to have the young aristocrat-technocrat as his major opponent rather than a former colleague and Resistance fighter. Although Chaban-Delmas was a political adversary, Mitterrand considered him to be a good man. It was much easier to go into battle against someone who could be portrayed as an heir to Vichy.[19] Giscard d'Estaing was only sixteen years old in 1942, the year Mitterrand wrote propaganda for Marshal Pétain's government. But Giscard d'Estaing's family background and ideological imprecision lent themselves to a rough association with the spirit of Vichy, which Mitterrand was not above exploiting. (It is odd that Giscard d'Estaing did not return the compliment.)

Tactically, it was also much easier on a second ballot to attract significant numbers of Resistance-generation Gaullist voters and Chabanist "New Society" adepts than disciples of Pompidou's former finance minister. However, Mitterrand was not very successful at replacing Giscard d'Estaing's public image as a man of technical expertise, moderation, and youthful dynamism with his own portrait of Giscard d'Estaing as a retrograde, disgraceful Vichyite.

There was indeed a wide gulf between Giscard d'Estaing and Mitterrand. The center right's candidate, much more willing than the left's candidate to exploit the electorate's susceptibility to image, discussed policy little. It was up to the electorate to trust him.[20] He assumed the role of monarch rather than partisan or arbiter.

One has no contract with one's electors. The electors designate you, they choose you, you do not enter into any binding agreement with them; whereas Mitterrand [intends] to be faithful to the obligations subscribed to in speaking to the country.[21]

Mitterrand, on the other hand, tried with partial success to minimize image making and to apply a strategy similar to the one he had adopted in 1965—that is, to represent certain "options"; he played more subtly on the presidentialist-parliamentarian ambiguities of the constitution.

The candidate of the left downplayed the Common Program without disavowing it, emphasizing the "consensual" and "quality of life" issues—inflation, unemployment, economic growth, education, transportation, housing, and so on—while incorporating some feminist and ecological issues into his "platform." But Giscard d'Estaing did not settle for the terms of the conflict offered by Mitterrand's camp. Giscard d'Estaing persistently criticized the precise economic weaknesses of the Common Program, which the center-right candidate refused to allow Mitterrand to shelve. He presented statistics, which Mitterrand called "imaginary," to demonstrate that the program would lead to inflation, stagnation, and financial instability, and because he was considered knowledgeable about financial matters, his credibility in this area was much greater than Mitterrand's.

Giscard d'Estaing also exploited traditional fears of Communism, but it is hard to tell what proportion of the voters still believed that a Castro-like coup was possible in France. In the political sphere the Common Program attempted to reassure voters that Communist participation in government in no way threatened the right of private property, civil liberties, or the democratic process. By the same token, the Common Program did not go anywhere near as far as Soviet-style collectivization and explicitly forbade confiscation of property. But public opinion was still wary. After all, past behavior on the part of the PCF and other Communist parties lent credibility to Giscard d'Estaing's warnings of the threat that the PC's presence would pose to the democratic process and the economic system. Neither the Common Program, Mitterrand nor the PS could offer absolute guarantees to the contrary.

While Mitterrand was striving to doff his image of incompetence in the sphere of economics, Giscard d'Estaing was attempting to don one of a leader sensitive to the need for "social justice." He refused to grant a monopoly of heart to his Socialist rival. This did not constitute any real reversal of roles, but merely reflected an effort on both sides to increase their support at the center. The two men also held significantly different views on foreign policy, defense, and civil liberties, but their approach to economic issues most concerned voters.

Although Mitterrand's performances on television improved somewhat during the course of the campaign, he was always most at ease and effective before live audiences, and the larger the audience the more inspired he became. He had sharpened his oratorical weapons over the years during the rowdy and frequently hostile sessions of the National Assembly, and he clearly enjoyed brandishing them before the friendly audiences of mass rallies.

> Brilliant, sarcastic, ironic, humorous, even lyrical, frequently demagogic and always didactic, he raised to fever pitch the enthusiasm of his vast audiences: 10,000 at Montpellier and Dijon, 15,000 at Lyons, La Rochelle, and Lille, 20,000 at Nice, 25,000 at Nantes, 40,000 at his final rally at Toulouse.[22]

Voter turnout was exceedingly high on the first ballot: 84 percent of the eligible population went to the polls. Mitterrand obtained 43.36 percent of the vote; Giscard d'Estaing, 32.76 percent; and Chaban-Delmas, 14.76 percent. On the right, the humiliation of Chaban-Delmas was profound, while the triumph of Giscard d'Estaing was exhilarating.[23] "Giscard was . . . the man who the most skillfully and the most effectively projected the image of being a reformer."[24] The marginal candidates together received less than 10 percent of the vote.

At first, extreme discouragement gripped Mitterrand's camp, for he had not reached the crucial 45 percent mark that he felt would have assured him victory on the second ballot. The painful truth, as Defferre unhappily pointed out, was that the PS had failed to fully mobilize the leftist electorate in precisely those districts where Mauroy, Defferre, Mollet, Savary, and Mitterrand were most powerful.[25] By setting the party aside, Mitterrand and his cohorts had demotivated it. It was also obvious that at the national level the Common Program represented at best a questionable asset and at worst a major liability. Between the first and second ballots the candidate of the left would try harder than ever to sound "consensual."[26]

After some reflection, hope reappeared in Mitterrand's camp. After all, these election results could also be interpreted as a relative success compared to those of 1965, when the single candidate of the left received only 32 percent of the vote on the first ballot, to those of 1969, when the left together collected a mere 31 percent, and to those of 1973, when the unified left received 41 percent. In addition, Mitterrand had come in first in over three-quarters of the departments (there are ninety-five in metropolitan France), had won an absolute majority in eleven (whereas he had captured only two in 1965), and had showed strength in areas where the left was traditionally weak. So, after a closer look at the results and the polls, the contest still appeared wide open.[27]

Since Chaban-Delmas was now out, one of the keys to victory lay with the Gaullists. Chaban-Delmas offered grudging support to Giscard d'Estaing, knowing that the vast majority of his Gaullist followers would vote for him anyway. A few Gaullist old-timers, essentially those of the Resistance generation, saw Giscard d'Estaing in the same way that Mitterrand did—that is, as a descendant of "aristocratic" Vichy France—and some of them, such as Edgar Pisani and the writer Romain Gary, went over to Mitterrand. A small committee of "Gaullists for Mitterrand" was even formed.

Antoine Pinay and Jean-Jacques Servan-Schreiber went over to Giscard d'Estaing at the last minute, but their support was not very significant in terms of the number of votes that each could bring to the candidate. (Servan-Schreiber stated that he would have supported Mitterrand had the latter not given in on the issue of nationalizations.)

The only significant political event to occur between ballots was the much awaited presidential debate between the two run-off candidates; it was the first such debate in French history. The televised debate was held on May 10, nine days before the second ballot.[28] It was not the kind of situation that Mitterrand relished, for televised proceedings, which reminded him of oral examinations during his schooldays, made him uneasy.[29]

Giscard d'Estaing went on the offensive immediately and maintained that position throughout the debate. He was aggressive, forceful, and intense. Mitterrand, on the other hand, never stopped being defensive. Even when attacking, he seemed to miss the mark; his attacks were more personal than pertinent, and he appeared less energetic in his assertions, less well prepared than Giscard d'Estaing, and too detached. When Giscard d'Estaing identified his opponent with the past, and himself with the future, Mitterrand responded, "When you speak of change, I always want to say: well, what is change? It's doing what you have not done!"[30]

Mitterrand portrayed Giscard d'Estaing as a patricide before the French viewers. Reminding his opponent that in 1969 Giscard d'Estaing had called for a no vote on de Gaulle's referendum on regional participation, he concluded his accusation by stating: "Politically you stabbed him since you determined his downfall."[31] According to Michel Bassi and André Campana, Giscard d'Estaing "had the embarrassed look of a son who has been reproached for killing his father."[32] Thus, Mitterrand succeeded in shaming Giscard d'Estaing in the eyes of the most loyal Gaullists. But in the end, the vast majority of the Gaullist electorate still voted for Giscard d'Estaing.

Most commentators on both the left and the right (including this author) felt that Giscard d'Estaing had won the debate. Mitterrand attributed his poor performance to pity for a "suffering" opponent: "It would have been more exciting to strike a steeled, smooth Giscard. His weakness was so obvious that it became a strength in this subtle relationship established between adversaries at a moment when anything goes."[33] To the contrary, the text of the debate suggests more the presence of a "steeled, smooth Giscard" and a blood-stained, sniping Mitterrand. In the end, the effect of the television debate on voters was not at all clear. For a couple of days it seemed to have benefited Giscard d'Estaing, but by the eve of the second ballot, the polls showed a virtual draw.

Again, there was an extraordinarily high (87 percent) voter turnout: Giscard d'Estaing won by only 342,000 votes out of over 26 million cast. He received 50.81 percent of the vote; Mitterrand, 49.19 percent. Giscard won in 51 departments; Mitterrand, in 44. Surveys showed that Giscard d'Estaing was favored by women, rural people, older citizens, the self-employed, members of the managerial class, and practicing Catholics; Mitterrand tended to be favored more by men, the young, salaried workers, and the secularly oriented.[34] Giscard d'Estaing won in twelve regions; Mitterrand, in ten.

This was by no means a stunning victory for Giscard d'Estaing. Not only was the race close between the right and the left, but also the rival Gaullist party was stronger than the Giscardians in the National Assembly. Instead of dissolving that chamber and challenging the Gaullists in the legislative domain, the new president chose to accommodate them by naming Chirac as his prime minister—a big mistake. Mitterrand foresaw the problem right away: "There is no longer a true majority. It will soon become apparent."[35] While the former finance minister was very knowledgeable about economics, he had neglected to establish a broad political base. His claim to a clear victory was further tainted by serious evidence of widespread election fraud in the overseas territories.

In hindsight, the reasons for Mitterrand's defeat are obvious. The Common Program, which had enabled him to maximize the leftist turnout, kept too many centrists away. The recent legislative elections were still fresh in the minds of voters, and it was impossible for Mitterrand to wish the program away or defend its contents convincingly. It is highly improbable that Mitterrand could have won without the Common Program either; he probably would not have fared as well on the left. Giscard d'Estaing made a strong, appealing candidate, representing enough change to excite and enough continuity to reassure, whereas Mitterrand and his associates represented too much radical policy change combined with a personal image that was old hat, more Fourth than Fifth Republic. In short, it was too late for the old Mitterrand and too early for the new one.

Although after this defeat Mitterrand did not imagine that he would ever run for president again, he did not intend to retreat from the front lines of politics. The political warrior's postelection statement echoed many of his earlier speeches: "I felt ready to lead the country. This loss is not serious, however. Soon the left will win. But I will not be the one to lead it to power. It will be you. We are taking up the fight again as of today."[36]

## NOTES

1. François Mitterrand, cited in Franz-Olivier Giesbert, *François Mitterrand ou la tentation de l'histoire* (François Mitterrand or the temptation of history) (Paris: Seuil, 1977), p. 279.

2. Michel Cardoze and Jean Le Lagadec, *Quarante-neuf pourcent: Naissance d'une majorité* (Forty-nine percent: Birth of a majority) (Paris: Editions sociales, 1974), pp. 62-63.

3. Mitterrand, cited in Giesbert, *François Mitterrand*, p. 278.

4. Philippe Alexandre, *Le Roman de la gauche* (The story of the left) (Paris: Plon, 1977), p. 316.

5. Mitterrand, cited in Robert Verdier, *PS/PC: Une Lutte pour l'entente* (PS/PC: A struggle for agreement) (Paris: Seghers, 1976), p. 282.

6. Albert du Roy and Robert Schneider, *Le Roman de la rose d'Epinay à l'Elysée* (The romance of the rose from Epinay to the Elyséé) (Paris: Seuil, 1982), p. 140.

7. Alexandre, *Le Roman de la gauche*, p. 315.

8. Michel Bassi and André Campana, *Le Grand Tournoi: Naissance de la Sixième République* (The great tournament: Birth of the Sixth Republic) (Paris: Grasset, 1974), pp. 61-62.

9. Du Roy and Schneider, *Le Roman de la rose*, p. 136.

10. Jack Hayward and Vincent Wright, "'Les Deux France' and the French Presidential Election of May 1974," *Parliamentary Affairs*, no. 27 (Summer 1974): 218.

11. André Laurens, *D'une France à l'autre* (From one France to another) (Paris: Gallimard, 1974), p. 121.

12. Jacques Attali, cited in Bassi and Campana, *Le Grand Tournoi*, p. 166.

13. Sylvie Colliard, *La Campagne présidentielle de François Mitterrand en 1974* (The 1974 presidential campaign of François Mitterrand) (Paris: Presses Universitaires de France, 1979), pp. 39, 61.

14. Alexandre, *Le Roman de la gauche*, pp. 320-21.

15. Colliard, *La Campagne présidentielle*, p. 110.

16. Hayward and Wright, "'Les Deux France,'" p. 220.

17. Ibid.

18. Michèle Cotta, *La VIᵉ République* (The Sixth Republic) (Paris: Flammarion, 1974), pp. 172-77.

19. Bassi and Campana, *Le Grand Tournoi*, p. 176.

20. Colliard, *La Campagne présidentielle*, p. 6.

21. Debate on Radio-Télévision Luxembourg, May 2, 1974, cited in Olivier Duhamel, *La Gauche et la Cinquième République* (The left and the Fifth Republic) (Paris: Presses Universitaires de France, 1980), p. 281.

22. Hayward and Wright, "'Les Deux France,'" p. 219.

23. Ibid., p. 223.

24. Ibid., p. 221.

25. Du Roy and Schneider, *Le Roman de la rose*, p. 145.

26. Alexandre, *Le Roman de la gauche*, p. 325.

27. Hayward and Wright, "'Les Deux France,'" p. 223.

28. The debate is reproduced in its entirety in Jean-Marie Cotteret, Claude Eméri, Jean Gerstlé, and René Moreau, *Giscard d'Estaing–Mitterrand: 54,774 mots pour convaincre* (Giscard d'Estaing–Mitterrand: 54,774 words in which to convince) (Paris: Presses Universitaires de France, 1976).

29. François Mitterrand, *La Paille et le grain* (The wheat and the chaff) (Paris: Flammarion, 1975), p. 83.

30. Cotteret et al., *Giscard d'Estaing–Mitterrand*, p. 107.

31. Ibid., p. 113.

32. Bassi and Campana, *Le Grand Tournoi*, p. 136.

33. Mitterrand, *La Paille*, pp. 270-71.

34. Hayward and Wright, "'Les Deux France,'" p. 208.

35. François Mitterrand, "Un 'statut' pour l'opposition? Parlons-en! . . . ," *Le Nouvel Observateur*, no. 498 (May 27, 1974): 29.

36. Mitterrand at the first postelection meeting of the PS, cited in du Roy, *Le Roman de la rose*, p. 151.

# 10

## Political Ascendancy and the Breakup of the Union of the Left, 1974–1978

By the end of 1974, after sixteen years of finding his way through the maze of leftist French politics, François Mitterrand was the undisputed prince regent of the "people of the left"—the ruler of a country within a country. At Socialist Party headquarters, membership forms kept flowing in, including from such eminent public figures as de Gaulle's and Pompidou's former minister of agriculture Edgar Pisani and Chaban-Delmas's recent economic adviser Jacques Delors. Mitterrand's control of the PS was complete; the PS was clearly the gravitational force on the left, and the left itself was at the threshold of becoming an absolute majority in the nation. Although it was misinterpreted by some foes within the party as a decline, the second hair's-breadth presidential defeat actually confirmed Mitterrand's dominance over his people.

Mitterrand had the power to mobilize the party cadres at meetings of the *comité directeur* and raise the emotions of Socialist delegates to fever pitch at party congresses. Since the presidential campaign of 1965, the Socialist leader had perfected his ability to arouse a crowd:

> To wax historical, he resurrects the ancestors of socialism. To be social-minded, he gets the earth's downtrodden moving. To be technical, he explains once more the mechanics of value added and the accumulation of capital. To be poetic, he evokes the fields and the forests. To be political, he stigmatizes the heedlessness of governmental leaders. To be insolent, he upbraids the party's minority. To be ironic, he pokes fun at the thickheadedness of the Communist ally. To be prophetic, he promises the Socialist myth.[1]

There would be challenges ahead, including intraparty friction and criticism, sniping from a PC now obviously past its peak, and electoral battles with the right—all routine matters—but the long march was over. Once again

Mitterrand assumed the unofficial role of counterpresident with total self-confidence, absolute certainty about the appropriateness of his positions, and an aura of historical legitimacy. The fact that he maintained his old habits of rarely carrying much money or wearing a watch, which naturally resulted in chronic mooching and tardiness, further symbolized his scorn for the petty, bourgeois details of life.

## THE COUNTERPRESIDENT

Although still a deputy from the Nièvre and a small-town mayor, Mitterrand himself offered fewer long-winded oratorical offensives and entered into fewer skirmishes in the National Assembly, for his lieutenants, under the leadership of Gaston Defferre, were holding this front for him much of the time. Leaving Mauroy to take care of the day-to-day administration of the party, Mitterrand fought his battles from Mount Olympus. He traveled much, met with world leaders, wrote enough articles to compile into two more books, gave press conferences, appeared on radio and television news programs regularly, and spun his web of relations across party and professional lines, throughout France, and increasingly outside the country's borders.

Not only did Mitterrand fight his battles from Mount Olympus, but he preferred to cross swords only with other Olympians—Giscard d'Estaing was worthy of his attention only as the agent of the capitalist system that he was now combating. Mitterrand understood Giscard d'Estaing's fundamental weakness as a leader: He was held hostage by Gaullist Prime Minister Jacques Chirac, whose party was much stronger than Giscard d'Estaing's. As for Chirac, a man of "energy" and "appetite," Mitterrand declared that he may try to "imitate . . . the accent of the man of June 18 [the defiant de Gaulle of 1940], whom he knew only during the period of self-parody, that is after May 13 [1958] . . . [but] the sound does not come from the same depths."[2] (After de Gaulle's death in 1970 Mitterrand's references to him became much more respectful—there were orphaned Resistance-generation Gaullists to gather in.)

Mitterrand had no national army or economy with which to wield power on his own, but he undertook in his travels at least to match wits with the superpowerful men of the day, including Henry Kissinger (who, in the post-Watergate United States presided over by Gerald Ford, appeared to be the most prestigious American) and Leonid Brezhnev (Mitterrand actually spent only one hour in conversation with Brezhnev himself but *nine* in intense dialogue with Mikhail Suslov, the seventy-three-year-old guardian of Communist ideology). Mitterrand's portraits of Brezhnev and Kissinger reveal as much about the portraitist as they do about his subjects. The political philosopher–moralist took pleasure in observing the powerful, caricaturing them and demonstrating his ability to see through them.

To Mitterrand, Brezhnev belonged to the "Khrushchev family" of Russians, those who are

lively, spontaneous, passing from laughter to anger, from anger to laughter, suddenly hitting the table or their belly, obeying sudden impulses; one notices after
the fact that their variations do not stray from the rules of the dialectic.[3]

He described Brezhnev as being particularly concerned about convincing him of
the Russian hatred of war and the "German menace"[4]—a rather obvious
attempt to establish common ground and trust with his Western guest. Mitterrand was not taken in; he knew his history and had been properly briefed on the
Soviet buildup of offensive nuclear weapons aimed directly at Western Europe.
Rather, he was prematurely optimistic in his assessment that the Soviet regime
would soon collapse under internal pressure alone. He overestimated by about
ten years the "end of the revolution," explaining that Brezhnev was a "figure of
transition" and expressing doubt "that the gulag is still a system, in a system that
doubts itself."[5]

Mitterrand's portrait of Kissinger offers a sharp contrast to that of Brezhnev. While the latter personified art*ful*ness, it was the art*less*ness of the former
that stood out:

> I . . . thought that in spite of all his voluntary changes in mood and tone, my
> interlocutor had only one way of being himself. . . . He is depicted as hurried,
> agitated, always ready to leave for the opposite end of the world for a fifteen-
> minute discussion. I believe rather that he finds his faithfulness to his character
> a way of gaining time. There is nothing less duplicitous than his diplomacy. He
> seduces or he strikes. Certainly, it is easier for the Prince than for any other to
> disdain false maneuvers. By always suspecting that he is tricking you, you have
> already lost. Cleverness cannot begin to explain the destinies of great men.[6]

Mitterrand's occasional references to the "Prince" reveal his conscious reflections on the theory and practice of power from a Machiavellian perspective.
Interestingly, here he slips into flattering self-portraiture, veiled by the use of
the third person.

Mitterrand's feelings of political superiority over the Soviet and American
world leaders was not justified on intellectual grounds. Predictably, Kissinger
appears much more knowledgeable and intelligent than Mitterrand about foreign affairs; and it is even doubtful that after nine hours of heroic ideological
combat with Mikhail Suslov Mitterrand got the better of him. What distinguished him from his interlocutors was that his power and prestige derived from
being regularly and freely chosen by voters.

## UPDATING THE COMMON PROGRAM

Mitterrand had the most solid power base of any political figure in France,
with the possible exception of Giscard d'Estaing (who, although elected president by universal direct suffrage, was institutionally handicapped by having a
slim presidential majority and a weak party in the National Assembly). The

manner in which Mitterrand managed potential challenges to his authority within the party—that is, the integration of the Rocardian PSUs into the PS and the progressively bullying, Leninist behavior of the CERES faction—demonstrated further his mastery of partisan politics.

The PS announced the Socialist Assizes for October 1974, at which time the members of the PSU and the CFDT were to be formally admitted into the PS, a move highly desired by Mauroy and Defferre but not by Mitterrand, who saw the pitfalls of admitting the fractious PSU and Christian union militants into the PS ranks. Mitterrand was also wary of Rocard, whose previous strong criticism of the Common Program, preoccupation with self-management, and *gauchiste* aura left over from the events of 1968 made him particularly suspect to Mitterrand, who was also concerned about the fact that the Communists detested him. This new element could easily upset the delicate balance of power on the left.

The entry of the PSU Rocardians would make not only the strategy of the union of the left trickier to maintain, but also Socialist unity. It was not at all clear what position Rocard would occupy on the Socialist ideological spectrum. His outspoken respect for and defense of market forces put him to the right, but his faith in the future of a version of self-management even more radical than that of CERES put this sympathizer of the *gauchistes* to the far left of the party. All the strongest advocates of the union-of-the-left strategy (CERES, the Poperenists, the Molletists) were unenthusiastic about these new adherents, too. To CERES, the Rocardians represented an "American [read 'detestable'] left" within the PS. Also, the extremely intense internal divisions within the PSU between the technocratic Rocardians and the more spontaneous *gauchistes* aggravated the Socialists' apprehensions. Naturally, all these doctrinal and personal misgivings masked much nervousness about the future pecking order of the party leaders. No one, least of all Mitterrand, was about to tolerate a takeover of the PS by the PSU comparable to Mitterrand's takeover in 1971. The party was no longer up for grabs.

Therefore, precautions were necessary. Mitterrand set three conditions to PSU and CFDT entrance. First, he rejected the anarchistic, *gauchiste* idea of the necessity of the mobilization of the masses. Second, knowing that it would alienate social strata that could go over to his side, Mitterrand objected to the PSU proposal to eliminate most small and medium-size companies from the private sector. In both instances, Mitterrand used his authority to reject extremist demands. Third, the first secretary required that the admission of new, somewhat "foreign" elements depended on their willingness to adhere to the Common Program—to reassure the Communist partner, no doubt. Mitterrand knew that the Communists were getting ready to press for more nationalizations and that it would be difficult to get the Rocardian faction of the PSU to swallow even the original, relatively conservative Common Program.

Nonetheless, the Rocardian wing of the PSU was absorbed fairly smoothly. Rocard had lost control of the majority of his party, which was demanding fusion (admission as an entity) into the PS, a move that would have created yet another rival faction in the PS. Over a third of the PSU members, including Rocard, accepted the Socialists' conditions and joined the PS by absorption (as individuals), as did large numbers from the CFDT, including its head, Edmond Maire. The others refused to join, and a much reduced PSU maintained a separate existence. The newcomers dispersed among the existing factions, but Rocard and many of his followers were prepared to join Mitterrand's majority if allowed in. This eagerness to join the governing ranks testified to their belief in the political future of the PS. Although some Rocardians would be accepted into the governing majority, Rocard, whose "erudite and moralizing speeches" irritated Mitterrand,[7] would be left dangling until the Socialist Party congress held in Pau in January 1975; members of a party that had deemed Mitterrand unworthy of their own group in the 1960s could not immediately expect positions of leadership.

The ejection of Chevènement and CERES from the governing majority of the party coincided with the entry of Rocard himself at the time of the Pau congress. The CERES current was more trouble than it was worth, and Mitterrand could afford to do without it, at least for the time being. He still had Defferre, Mauroy, and his faithful CIRs behind him. The Poperenists and Savarysts had come around. (Poperen obtained a deputy seat in 1973.) The diehards of the SFIO (Jules Moch, Max Lejeune, and others) had left the party, and the remaining Molletists were reduced to a minuscule minority. Virtually all the Rocardians now supported the first secretary. Mitterrand controlled about 70 percent of the party, which stood at about 30 percent of the electorate at large.

Only one cloud loomed on the horizon during this period. It was the Common Program, or more precisely, the problem of updating this document that symbolized the union of the left. The conclusion of the first agreement had been miraculous, and a second miracle seemed almost too much to hope for. New negotiations would require the first-time participation of the MRGs (who had signed the first Common Program a posteriori) and the Rocardians (who had openly criticized it), plus a PC feeling more and more threatened by the political momentum of the PS.

The Communists were already recoiling. They strongly resented the competition in the workplace for worker sections that came from the Socialists (thanks to the zeal of CERES). Even more serious was the fact that in several off-year elections (viewed by most as larger-than-life public opinion polls) the Socialists had significantly outperformed the Communists. The trend was even more pronounced in the 1975 cantonal elections.[8] The left obtained 53 percent of the vote, and the right 47 percent. The PS and MRG together obtained 30 percent; the PC, 21 percent; and the remnant of the PSU, 2 percent. This boded well for the left in general and for the PS in particular. The cantonal elections tend to prefigure the municipal elections, which forecast the legislative elections.

For months the Communists condemned Mitterrand personally and the PS in general as faithless partners, accusing them of being accomplices of Giscard d'Estaing, *le grand capital,* and the bourgeoisie. At the twenty-first congress of the PC they turned the volume up several decibels, with Marchais calling for a new nationalization (of the French oil company Elf-Aquitaine), the total liquidation of the nuclear strike force, and an enlarged "union of the French people" (a concept implying the drowning of the PS in a broad, amorphous alliance that would include nearly everyone except the PS and the 200 richest families). At their twenty-second congress the Communists formally sacrificed one of Communism's most sacred dogmas, the dictatorship of the proletariat, and temporarily disassociated themselves from Moscow in order to prepare the way for this ploy. Their aim was to draw Mitterrand into battle, discredit him, and divide the PS.

Mitterrand ordered his ranks to be silent and to stay calm; he did not want to give the Communists any excuse to pursue the barrage. Such lack of polemical cooperation no doubt frustrated the Communists. Mitterrand spoke publicly only to express his "understanding" of the PC's anxiety and reaffirm his adherence to the Common Program. He felt confident that the PC would not risk a break with the Socialists and that the attacks would only last until the 1976 municipals, when it would be clearly in the PC's interest to be united with the PS.

This request for patience was very upsetting to Mitterrand's colleagues and supporters, who were eager to respond to the Communists. But the first secretary refused to allow the Socialists to play the Communists' game; the PS was to be "unitary for two"—Mitterrand was not about to allow the PS to release the PC from its hard-won, clutching embrace. He was intent on driving a wedge between the PC and its traditional electorate, betting that a large share of Communist voters, if forced to choose between the Socialists, who preached the union of the left, and the Communists, who attacked the Socialists, would choose the former because the Socialists could actually win power and enact social reforms. For the Socialist leader, the union of the left was not simply a game of power politics between party leaders; it was a "profound popular reality."[9]

If the PS was to have any hope of winning power in the 1978 legislative elections, three goals had to be achieved: (1) the left had to win a majority in the municipal elections, (2) the PS had to continue to increase its power in relation to the PC, and (3) the PC itself had to continue to make gains. The third goal was the most problematic, for polls showed that the PC was beginning to stagnate. Indeed, it was difficult to see how the PC could continue to grow in a postindustrial society since the PS was continually chipping away at the PC's electoral base and Soviet actions (not to mention those of other Communist governments) during this period, such as the harsh treatment of dissidents, posed special problems for the PC. However, these were of less concern on the local level, where the PC has often profited from a nonideological protest vote.

The negotiations over what type of common approach to adopt for the municipal elections, where substantial political and financial control over cities and towns was at stake, foreshadowed the difficulties ahead in renegotiating the Common Program and demonstrated beyond a shadow of a doubt that the union of the left, at least at the top, was truly a "battle."[10] Charges and counter-charges flew back and forth between the two leaders of the left. Marchais accused Mitterrand and the PS of "ambiguity" concerning a future government of the left (the legislative elections were already on everyone's mind), betrayal of the workers, and so on. Mitterrand, in turn, accused the PC of attacking his and his party's integrity, and especially of undermining the partnership with an out-spoken defense of the Portuguese Communist leader Alvaro Cunhal, who had not respected the results of democratic elections in Portugal in which Mario Soarès, the Socialist leader, had triumphed. If the Communists wanted to gain the trust of the French people on issues concerning civil liberties, it was essential for them to condemn the Stalinist behavior of Cunhal and the Communist Party of Portugal. In spite of these differences, the PCF still demanded that the PS include them on joint lists for the municipals (in which Communists and Socialists would run together) rather than present on the first ballot two sepa-rate homogeneous lists (in which the two parties would measure their strength separately). Mitterrand tried unsuccessfully to link the PS's acceptance of joint lists on the first ballot to the PC's cessation of its defense of the antidemocratic Cunhal.

While these interparty squabbles were being negotiated on the left, an important change had taken place on the right: Raymond Barre, whom Giscard d'Estaing called the "best economist in France," had replaced Jacques Chirac as prime minister. Barre, a professor with economic expertise, had no political party in tow and seemed at the time to have no ambitions other than doing well the job that Giscard d'Estaing had assigned him. Giscard d'Estaing and Chirac, essentially political rivals (as Mitterrand had pointed out many times), had dis-agreed on almost everything. For example, Giscard d'Estaing had wanted to dedramatize the problem of inflation, whereas Chirac had wanted to attack it by means of executive ordinances. In exploiting every constitutional prerogative allowed to him, Prime Minister Chirac, who issued from the "presidentialist" party, was behaving remarkably like a parliamentarian.

These two leaders of the right also differed characteristically on how to fight the left. Giscard d'Estaing, a centrist, wanted to use conciliation to recuperate part of the PS and MRG electorate, thereby weakening it and strengthening his own base vis-à-vis the Gaullists; Chirac, known as the "steamroller," thought it best to oppose the PS head on. Chirac believed that Giscard d'Estaing was wasting his time trying to do to the PS what the PS was doing to the PC. On the other hand, it was not in Chirac's personal interest to give the president the best advice either. This would have meant encouraging Giscard d'Estaing to adopt a strategy that was the mirror image of Mitterrand's—that is, to develop policies capable of chipping away at the Gaullist electorate, thereby weakening Chirac. But with Chirac out, the president was free to pursue his "soft" approach to the municipal campaign.

Eventually the PS and PC reached an agreement on an approach to the municipal elections. Each municipality was to negotiate its own accord in order to compose a joint list or separate lists, depending on which alternative had the greatest chance of increasing the left's overall representation on the city councils. In the case of joint lists, the proportion of Communists and Socialists would be based on the average of the results of the 1973 legislative elections (favorable to the PC) and those of the 1976 cantonal elections (favorable to the PS). Mitterrand persuaded the Communists to agree to "municipal solidarity"— that is, Communist support for city government budgets prepared by predominately Socialist city councils. At the local level, where enthusiasm for union was not counterbalanced by the astute toughness of the national leaders, the Socialists too frequently gave in to Communist demands for joint lists. The predictable result was that the Communists did much better in these elections than what would have been expected from the historical trend.

Although the union-of-the-left strategy worked disproportionately to the benefit of the Communists in the municipal elections, its advantages were confirmed. The municipals of 1977 were the most important elections in years in which the left won a significant national majority of votes (52.1 percent to 47.9 percent) and obtained a majority of the seats in a group of legislative bodies. The PS gained the mayoralties of thirty-five cities with populations of 30,000 or more; the PC, twenty-two cities. The Communists sailed into approximately eighty new mayoralties in all, bringing their number of mayors to approximately 150, and 28,000 Communists were now seated on municipal councils throughout France. This gave the PC control of immense resources and also an exaggerated sense of its national strength, which would make cooperation in the 1978 legislative elections particularly difficult.

Mitterrand immediately began preparing for the imminent renegotiation of the Common Program with the Communists. The precondition for success was a solidly unified Socialist majority. The more probable the conquest of power in 1978 appeared, the more concerned Mitterrand became about the weaknesses of his party—its factionalism, amateurism, dogmatism, and "angelism," as well as the complacency of the SFIO old-timers and the inexperience of the newcomers. A new generation of young, energetic, and idealistic post-Epinay Socialists came on the scene in large numbers at this time. They impressed Mitterrand but worried him, too, for they were naive and knew nothing about the difficulties of standing up to the Communists. The Socialist congress held in Nantes in 1977 was the occasion for shoring up the majority that would have to confront the Communists in negotiations later that year.

Mitterrand was not looking forward to updating the Common Program, although he knew that it had to be done. It was understood by all that the document, being a legislative program, would not apply beyond the five-year term of the legislature for which it was drafted. Times had changed since 1972. The major factor unforeseen at that time was the 1973 Arab oil embargo and the ensuing energy crisis that drastically affected France's potential for future growth, which the Common Program had assumed to be 6 percent—an even less realistic estimate in 1977. But renegotiating the program meant a very bloody polemical battle with a high risk of failure. Mitterrand knew that the PC, feeling inordinately strong since the municipals, would take every opportunity to outbid the PS on the left by demanding more nationalizations and airing all its old grievances against the PS, from land use policy to foreign affairs. To complicate matters further, the MRG was now eager to participate actively in negotiations, but it wanted to pull the Common Program of 1972, which it had signed but not negotiated, in the opposite direction. The MRG's natural constituency was small business, and it wanted to delete several clauses that it believed impeded free enterprise.

The Socialist first secretary's position was no deletions and no additions, except for items not specifically addressed in 1972, such as the rights of ethnic minorities, a wealth tax, environmental policy, and a reduction of the work week to thirty-six hours. On the crucial issues of European policy, the Atlantic Alliance, and nationalizations, no changes would be considered.

Mitterrand was never overly optimistic about the possibility of concluding an agreement. By May he had already written in his chronicle:

Everything points to the fact that the Communist Party is trying to free itself from the constraints of an alliance that serves as a launching pad for [the PS] and makes [it] the major force in the country. The difficulty for [the PC] is that it cannot commit the crime without bringing down on itself the people's anger and causing lengthy confusion in its ranks. The difficulty for us is to appreciate the exact point at which the updating-outbidding process takes precedence over the reasonable revision required by the passing of time.[11]

A joint committee composed of five representatives each from the MRG, PS, and PC reached agreement on many points of domestic policy, but none of the truly crucial issues—the wealth tax, the salary spread, the minimum wage, retirement pensions, land use, electoral reform, ministerial reorganization, nuclear policy, and most important, nationalizations—could be resolved at this level. All of these problems were left for the September summit, during which Mitterrand, Fabre, and Marchais were expected to hammer out the final agreement.

Miraculously, European policy and the Atlantic Alliance were not explicit issues by themselves, although they were closely connected to the contentious issue of nuclear policy, an area in which the Communists had made a 180-degree turn since 1972. The "Kanapa Report," published by the PC in 1977, called not only for acceptance of a nuclear strike force but even for its modernization. The catch was that the force was to be "independent of detection and surveillance"; in other words, information about it would be withheld from the Atlantic Alliance, which meant theoretically that it could be used against the Alliance. In addition, the PC demanded a "no first use" guarantee, renunciation of civilian targets, and, in the event of an attack by a foreign power, a collegial decision to unleash the strike force, all of which provisions bore the stamp of the Soviet government and would have entirely negated France's nuclear deterrent credibility. The PS was still sharply divided on the issue of a nuclear strike force, and even Mitterrand, long an opponent of it, was unsure of what policy to pursue other than the maintenance of the status quo and, after the expected legislative victory, a national referendum. But the Communist position was clearly unacceptable.

The Communists' ideas concerning institutional reform at the level of the ministries were also revealing. They wanted to split up two key ministries, Finance and Interior. Finance would be divided into two separate ministries: one that would elaborate the government's economic plan, prepare the budget, and spend the money (for all of which the Communists had a natural predilection), and another that would devise tax policy and collect taxes (which the Socialists could do). The Ministry of the Interior would also be divided in two, with one ministry managing the departmental prefectures and another running the police force. The PC clearly wanted to control some functions and avoid others within these two key ministries. These demands were entirely consistent with a French Communist pattern of behavior—maximize power, minimize responsibility. In addition, the PC called for interministerial committees to be empowered to set policy without consulting either the president or his prime minister. Thus, the PC sought maximum autonomy and control of the ministries by means of a Balkanization of the government.[12]

On September 14, 1977, at the first of two summit meetings at which Mitterrand, Rocard, Mauroy, Fabre, and other leaders of the Socialist majority and MRG met with their Communist counterparts, an atmosphere of intense political drama and high expectations prevailed. The stakes were perceived to be enormous. The equation in the mind of many in the political world, on the right, on the left, and in the press, was: Success in achieving an updated Common Program equaled a legislative victory in 1978, which equaled a left coalition government that would include Communists, which equaled the resignation of President Giscard d'Estaing (all the while the president maintaining that in the event of a left victory, although he could not legitimately prevent the implementation of the Common Program, he would remain in office his full term), which equaled an early presidential election, which equaled a probable Socialist presidential victory, which equaled, if not real revolution, at least the radical disruption of political and economic life in France. Immediately, it was obvious that each party leader had arrived in a different mood and with different aims, although they all proclaimed that their goal was to achieve agreement.[13]

Still, Fabre stunned everyone when he abruptly broke off negotiations early on over the issue of nationalizations, about which the MRG was naturally skittish. Not only was there no progress on this issue in 1977, but the parties involved could not even agree on what they had approved in 1972. The Communists claimed that the Socialists had agreed to nationalize totally any subsidiary even partially owned by a nationalized corporation, which would have resulted in over 1,400 new nationalizations. The Socialists did not seem to remember what they had agreed to, but they could not believe that they had agreed to that. And Marchais would not budge. Hence, the precipitous departure of the MRG.

One thing that Mitterrand and Marchais could agree on: that this featherweight party had torpedoed their plans to blame each other for the breakdown of negotiations. Momentarily, the two men had lost both the "firmness" card to the MRG and the opportunity to accuse each other of betrayal of the union of the left.[14]

It took a week for the PC to lure the MRG back to the table to complete the aborted process of the PC-PS breakup. The debate over what had been agreed to in 1972 resumed. For Mitterrand it had always been clear. The wording and intent of the 1972 version was such that ownership of the portion of the subsidiary that was owned by the nationalized parent company would be transferred to the state, while ownership of the rest would remain in the private sector. Marchais, not satisfied with this clarification of the Socialist position, demanded further clarification, at which point Mitterrand mused: "There is nothing more difficult than explaining something to someone who has already perfectly understood."[15]

Still no one budged. As a last ditch effort to save the alliance, Mitterrand had his Socialist team draw up a set of final proposals on the nationalization of subsidiaries. It included the future nationalization of the steel industry, an eventual majority state ownership of three more large corporations, acceptance of the idea of extending the status of workers at companies with 50 percent or more state ownership to that of "public servant" with all the benefits that this entailed, and it listed the 227 subsidiaries or companies whose nationalization they foresaw based on the criteria that they had developed in the past. The Socialists stretched to the limit Mitterrand's guideline: retain all of and add nothing to the Common Program of 1972.

The Communist verdict was immediate and uncompromising: "This is insufficient . . . less than timid," said Philippe Herzog, the principal Communist economist.[16] And, of course, the Radicals objected to this new proposal for exactly the opposite reasons.[17] No updated agreement was signed. Marchais left the meeting the happiest. The PC wanted to get out of a relationship that benefited the PS more than itself; a victory for the left was not desirable if the PC could not sufficiently manipulate the coalition. The MRG and Rocardians were relieved, too, since they would not have to swallow policies that went against their principles. Mitterrand was no doubt the most disappointed. The union of the left was going to be more difficult to sell without the PC leadership behind it.

## THE LEGISLATIVE ELECTIONS OF 1978

Any other party leader would have been ready to throw up his hands and begin making new political arrangements. Not Mitterrand. While CERES urged more concessions toward the PC in order to conclude a fully updated agreement at all cost and the Rocardians preached renunciation of the union-of-the-left strategy altogether, Mitterrand continued to resist adamantly both of these pressures. If the Communists refused union, the Socialists would continue to be "unitary for two."[18] The first secretary refused to consider turning toward the center, and he still regarded the union of the left as a "profound popular reality."

Thus, Mitterrand was determined to follow through with the union-of-the-left strategy whether or not the Communists cooperated. He demanded of his party: (1) complete fidelity to the spirit of the 1972 Common Program to the point of requiring that the Socialists desist in favor of well-placed Communists even if the Communists refused to do the same for top Socialists, and (2) abstention from engaging in polemics with the PC. He emphasized that one had to be prepared for the worst. A relative majority on the first ballot could lead to defeat on the second ballot, meaning loss of deputy seats, if the Communists did not desist in favor of well-placed Socialists. In this eventuality, the sacrifice of deputy seats would have to be accepted because the election as a whole would (1) demonstrate the real political strength inherent in the PS and, most important, (2) cast historical shame on the PC for torpedoing a victory of the left. The PC and PS had entered a new phase of combat, life-or-death struggle. As no other European leader had done before, Mitterrand was calling the PC's decades-long bluff, questioning its claim to lead the political struggle on behalf of the French working man. (The PC never recognized the special needs of the working woman.) His approach was disciplined, implacable, and consistent with socialist and democratic principles.

During the winter of 1978 the PS campaigned independently on the original Socialist Project (the PS's starting positions going into the renegotiation of the Common Program). Between ballots, it intended to go ahead as planned and campaign on the partially updated Common Program that the PC had refused to sign. (This is another example of Mitterrand's legalistic reliance on contractual documents, even incomplete, unsigned ones.) All the while the Communists were attacking the Socialists as class collaborators yet still demanding ministerial portfolios in the event of a victory of the left. As du Roy and Schneider put it,

By quarreling over portfolios, the Communists kill two birds with one stone. They gain the confidence of their troops, who were doubting their will to obtain a share of the power, and they frighten away moderate voters, apparently more and more numerous, who dream about a homogeneous Socialist government.[19]

In response to the latter point, the first secretary asserted that "that would be counting the chickens before they hatch. Especially considering where we are now! But if the Communists affirm that they will not share power with us, it will be difficult for us to say that we, too, will refuse to govern."[20] At this point governing without the Communists was not a serious possibility.

The election results in March greatly disappointed the Socialists, who only months earlier had believed that, after the steady progress made in the various national elections from 1973 to 1976, victory was finally at hand. On the first ballot, on March 11, the PS obtained 23.03 percent of the vote; the PC, 21.25 percent; the MRG, 2.3 percent; and the extreme left, 3.3 percent; for a total of just under 50 percent—not enough to give hope for a victory. The right was relieved after feeling seriously threatened. Marchais was not unhappy. His party was still a major force, not as far behind the Socialists as he had feared, and the complications of attaining power had been averted.

But now, *"Il faut sauver les meubles!"* (The furniture must be saved!), particularly incumbent deputy seats. Within twenty-four hours, Mitterrand, Marchais, and Fabre signed an electoral agreement based on the partially updated Common Program. No one on any side showed the slightest desire to haggle; the PC did not even bring up the issue that had been the major stumbling block the previous September, the nationalizations. Policy and tactical zigzagging were routine behavior on the part of the PC. For the PS, on the other hand, there was no satisfaction in making this last-minute agreement. "We have to swallow our pride," commented an uncomfortable Mitterrand. No one mistook this for union, but consistency required signing an agreement.

The second ballot held no surprises. The left managed to win 49.26 percent of the vote and gained seventeen seats, while the right lost ten. But because of the majority list electoral system in force, the right still won a large majority of the deputy seats—290 to the left's 201. (The Giscardians, having switched strategies themselves since the municipals, had gained some strength in relation to Chirac's Gaullist party, but the latter maintained its predominance on the right in the National Assembly.) The PS won a respectable 28.3 percent of the vote, the PC only 18.6 percent; but the former had gained only nine seats while the PC had gained twelve.[21] The balance of power between the PS and the PC had tilted in favor of the PS, but not as far as the Socialists had hoped. (Throughout the years of the Fourth Republic and the Fifth up until this election the PC had always outperformed the Socialist Party.) Shortsighted, impatient Socialists viewed these mixed results as evidence that the union-of-the-left strategy had reached the limits of its effectiveness in terms of (1) the compromises it could extract from the PC leadership, (2) the votes it could attract from the Communist electorate, and (3) the votes it could hold on to in the center left. The Rocardian and MRG pressures to scuttle the Common Program and the union strategy mounted as a movement within the party to dump Mitterrand got underway.

After the election, at the first meeting of the Socialist *comité directeur* in July 1978, the first secretary, in an atmosphere of disappointment and contestation, directed his party's attention toward the future—a future, however, that maintained complete continuity with the recent past. The temptations of both the "neo-Leninists" (Chevènement and CERES) and the "modernists" (Rocard and his followers) had to be resisted. According to Mitterrand, the party's program had to be elaborated democratically, by way of party congresses (which he was expert at manipulating), not imposed from the top. Once a decision was reached, the party as a whole would have to support publicly the whole program: The militants' choice "would be the law of the party."[22] There was no viable alternative to the union-of-the-left strategy. The nationalization of monopolies and of corporations on which national security and public service depended would remain a primary policy as a means of social transformation. Economic planning would play a large role in controlling the undesirable effects of the free market. Newer concerns would be addressed: feminism, ecology, decentralization, and so on. In the international field, Europe—a Europe that had to confront the "imperialism of the multinationals"—would be given priority. In sum, the first secretary demanded the clarification of principles, the union of the left, and most of all party unity. Unperturbed, Mitterrand continued his slow steady walk across an ever tighter tightrope in spite of partners who were attempting to push him forward, pull him back, or even shove him off.

## THE MAN OF CULTURE

Up until this point this biography has been largely a linear examination of Mitterrand's development as a man of action, focusing on how, from a practical viewpoint, this successful democratic politician went about accumulating power and prestige. Now that a fully mature and accomplished politician has come into view, it is time to look more at Mitterrand as a man of culture and what inspires him.

We have already noted that Mitterrand's early cultural, especially literary, experiences, his independent nature, and his fervent youthful Catholicism formed the basis for his later actions. Cultural knowledge must be contrasted here not only with technical and scientific knowledge, of which Mitterrand seems largely deprived, but also with systematic logical thinking about abstract concepts such as truth, justice, and freedom. With the exception of his rational grasp of democratic rules and a certain body of law, Mitterrand's culture consists of knowledge and sensitivities resulting primarily from subjective perceptions—

his own and his absorption of those of others through their writings. All new knowledge is filtered through a set of sincerely held but unquestioned biases. This does not mean that cultural knowledge can never be rational or objective; it is just that in Mitterrand's case it is not. More precisely, culture refers here to the humanistic knowledge acquired by Mitterrand through reading or contemplating works of mainly ancient Western and modern French literature and history in which heroic characters, in both senses of the word, are central features; poetry is also an important part of that culture. To educated French people such as Mitterrand, lifelong self-cultivation is a way of life, a reason for living going beyond professional goals; French culture for some is a national religion.

Mitterrand's cultural perspective is not amoral, but its morality, resting on the bedrock of his Catholic upbringing, is governed more by the heart and its noble intentions than by pure reason. His concept of justice is infused with a sentimentalism that automatically endows physical suffering and struggle with inherent moral nobility. By the same token, moral righteousness is easily conferred on the politically and economically weak. This perspective both limits the depth of Mitterrand's thinking about the concept of justice and, by virtue of its traditional focus on the individual, also safeguards him from being able to accept certain abuses. For example, it keeps him respectful of individual freedom in general and artistic freedom in particular and makes him wary, if not totally invulnerable, to "socialist realism" and the *littérature d'engagement.*

The question of whether, in the political sphere, Mitterrand's cultural background "saved" him morally or caused some of his errors and weaknesses naturally arises. A high degree of cultural refinement did not prevent Mitterrand from overlooking or turning his back on serious moral violations in the political sphere (for example, the treatment of Jews in Vichy France, torture in Algeria in the mid-1950s, and, at the international level, organized communist criminalism, especially in the Soviet Union and China). Neither did his breadth of cultural knowledge allow for an appreciation of the complex economic mechanisms on which a modern, prosperous democracy depends; on the contrary, it tended to exclude economic reality as a subject unworthy of serious thought.

In spite of all of the above, the cultural products assimilated by Mitterrand, on balance, enabled him to do more good than harm and were not the cause of his moral missteps. While it is true that certain elements of that heritage, for example, the romanticism of Maurice Barrès, were ideologically linked to the nationalism of Charles Maurras and Pétainism, they were checked by other influences (the French seventeenth century moralists, the eighteenth century philosophers, and the nineteenth century poets) which encouraged adherence to universal values (while frequently not sounding them very deeply). Also, the kind of liberal ideas that Mitterrand progressively absorbed reinforced the precedence he gave, throughout his postwar political career, to civil liberties and the democratic process over any particular policy, and his humanistic moral principles supported him in effectively restraining the radical elements of the left, inside and outside his party. His colleagues could think and write all the Leninist nonsense they wanted, which gave the impression that he approved of it (made all the worse by the fact that he did tolerate it, "cover" for it, or rationalize it); but in the end, the official, binding programs of the party and its allies and the more personalized political platforms of the presidential campaigns were purged, if not of leftist errors, at least of leftist excesses. As an embodiment of subjective cultural knowledge, Mitterrand demonstrates, in addition to the limits of such knowledge, its undeniable yet unquantifiable value. In Mitterrand self-cultivation did not produce either a fanatical man of passion or a rigorously rational man but rather a man of extraordinary rhetorical skill, of unabashed feeling, and of deep practical wisdom.

Although Mitterrand never discourses speculatively on political philosophy in his writings, his works bristle with political aphorisms reminiscent of the wise sayings of the ancient philosophers and the seventeenth century moralists. For every political "story" he offers there is a political moral—for example: "A people forgives everything, even failure, if it keeps in its heart of hearts its reasons for living and hoping,"[23] or "I have often found that the proper management of an error is worth more than certain kinds of successes."[24] These two nuggets highlight the importance Mitterrand attributes to capturing the "heart" of his people and to subjective, collective perception (the goal of "proper management" being to transform a negative perception of offending facts into a positive, or at least indifferent, perception of them).

The two chronicles that Mitterrand published in the 1970s, *L'Abeille et l'architecte* and *La Paille et le grain*,[25] offer extended glimpses into the cultural sphere of the Socialist leader's life while still maintaining the veil of discretion with which he covers most of his private life.[26] Originally, most entries were published in the weekly Socialist publication *L'Unité*, edited by Claude Estier. Each one consists of his reactions to a particular current event, issue, government pronouncement, book or article read, landscape viewed, author, friend, prince, or dialogue with a prince. For the most part, they bypass the larger political events, treated elsewhere, and give a more personal view of Mitterrand. The whole is seasoned with allusions to a vast array of authors read (from Thucydides, St. Augustine, Pascal, Voltaire and Leo Tolstoy to Julien Benda, Thomas Mann, Boris Pasternak, and Gabriel García Márquez, to name just a few) and with comparisons of the present with past historical events, revealing extraordinary cultural breadth.

Mitterrand's preoccupation with "nature" is one of the most striking features of his "culture," which one would suppose to be almost totally centered around politics and history. Mitterrand's love of nature, which is connected to his political concerns by an almost equal interest in geography, is of a special kind and tightly bound up with his family past, his literary background, and French and European history. Mitterrand is neither a fanatical lover of wild nature (governed by the "law of the jungle"), a rustic outdoorsman like certain ecologists, nor a doctrinaire worshipper of French soil à la Maurice Barrès (although Mitterrand appreciates Barrès's high lyricism)—his love of the French countryside does not preclude a similar appreciation of foreign landscapes. While something of an amateur naturalist, he can best be described as an admirer of the aesthetic qualities of nature, a nature domesticated by those who know how to live in harmony with it, a nature which, according to the classical ideal, encompasses both formal, pleasing aspects and edifying or beneficial ones—that is, the lessons it teaches man about life, growth, fruition, and death (in addition to its strictly immediate practical value). Organized nature, such as gardens, orchards, farmland, represents the ideal.

Connoisseurship of landscapes and geography is a tradition with cultivated Frenchmen. Mitterrand signifies his intimacy with and even cultural mastery over nature and geography by referring to a wide variety of animals, plants, and geographic formations and locations by their common or proper names. Rivers represent, simultaneously, very powerful phenomena, signs, and symbols. They are providers of a fundamental ingredient of life, sources of raw power, metaphors of life itself—its fall, its origins, its relentless flow, its dissolution, its ascent. As natural geographical borders, barriers, and communication links, rivers are also signs of monumental historical and political evolution. The "unchanging" Loire, Rhine, Danube, and Oder have all changed the course of history. Although some places seem to have escaped the flow of history altogether, even in France, others have a special story of their own to tell, making pages out of the history books come alive. The ancient Romanesque church at Vézelay, a favorite place of pilgrimage for Mitterrand and his entourage on Pentecost, symbolizes the convergence of the manifold dimensions of all being: nature (the stone substance), art (its Romanesque style), history (for centuries it was the inauguration site of French kings, and Mitterrand visited it just before he was sworn in as President in 1981), and the divine.

One of the most important lessons that Mitterrand has learned from his intimacy with nature is that "natural" or prolonged time (as opposed to unnatural speed) is crucial in all meaningful human endeavors. The naturally slow rhythms of nature provide him with the standard against which human time, and human progress, can be measured: The more synchrony that exists between the two, the more beneficial the progress. The slower the rhythm of a process, the more "natural" and fruitful will be the result. Going one step further, the ideal moments of life are those in which time seems to stop altogether for a few minutes, a few hours, allowing for a full flowering of experience, an exquisite Epicurean stimulation of the senses, or a "fraternal" communion with the "other" (a book, mistress, friends, or landscape), in short, an experience of total feeling, where a pleasing harmony (which includes managed discord or contradiction) exists between the self and the other or the self and a group. Wearing a watch would spoil all this.

Patience is not only a virtue, but properly timed, a force. Hurrying leads naturally to failure, error, or worse yet, disaster. Mitterrand establishes his own natural rhythms. A combination of mule and tortoise, he never allows himself to be hurried. . . or held back:

> Politically, I am incapable of taking one step without having assembled all the resources of my [practical] reason and equally incapable of stopping without having exhausted all the force of my will. I offer up only the minimum to chance.[27]

One of the destructive aspects of capitalism for Mitterrand is its tendency to accelerate time or progress to an "unnatural," inhuman degree; instead of progressing, time is actually spinning out of control and represents the return of human civilization to the primitive laws of the jungle. One of the functions of Mitterrandian socialism is to regulate the "unnatural," constantly accelerating rate of change associated with capitalism, to domesticate what he sees as its wild, destructive energy.

For Mitterrand nature, geography, and history are closely linked concepts. On the one hand, man's natural surroundings predetermine up to a point his existence, and on the other, historical events are the result of the combined effects of collective and individual human nature—part of eternal nature. But History is another matter. For Mitterrand there are two kinds of history: history with a small h is made up of year-to-year events and small changes determined by the minor actors; the major players and the monumental shifts they exact from history constitute History. Mitterrand acknowledges the importance of the former but attributes real significance only to the latter. The role of great princes is to do what de Gaulle did in 1940, to "lie in the path of fate, take it by the horns, force it to change course and create by virtue of his intuition and his will a new chain of events."[28] History, as fate, is accidental, ephemeral, close to primitive nature, and essentially tragic, but History, driven by some eternal, providential force mainly through "chosen" political heros, is cumulative and progressive.

Mitterrand enjoys thumbing through historical atlases, telescoping centuries of tumultuous History into seconds, an act that typifies perfectly his princely view of it. He "animates" the maps by flipping the pages, making squiggly worms out of the static borderlines drawn on individual pages. Nothing highlights better than a historical atlas the constant organic growth and deterioration of states and empires and their submission to the eternal "laws" of History, which Mitterrand constantly alludes to but never elucidates systematically. One can infer two fundamental, inexorable laws in dynamic tension with one another that drive History at both the domestic and international levels: (1) man's continuous will to power over others and (2) man's equally strong love of justice and freedom from the power of others. Both laws have a foundation in nature, and both can lift man out of a purely natural state. This is the History that

Mitterrand considers himself a part of; these are the forces that he is up against. Here is the vision that puts the significance, or lack thereof, of a lost election, a slanderous attack, or a dreary poll response into perspective.

Thus, Mitterrand, as a man of action who views History as a series of heroic acts, believes that the greatest strides toward justice and freedom are achieved through political, military, or even diplomatic "conquests," as opposed to the more prosaic processes that occur in the course of voluntary exchanges. Mitterrand "militarizes" democracy itself. The vocabulary of combat permeates his discourse; between 1958 and 1981 he was at war with the right, the "enemy." From a practical viewpoint, his political wars are cold-blooded affairs, but to rally the troops he launches romanticized crusades in which he demonizes the adversary in the abstract by positing "straw" oppressions such as dictatorship (in de Gaulle) or capitalism (in the post-Gaullists).

In the course of the 1970s he carefully prepared for his entry into the *"club des princes"* by establishing personal relationships with the principal Socialist and Communist leaders of the day, including those both in and out of power: Leonid Brezhnev of the Soviet Union, Mao Tse-tung of China (whom he could already count among his relations), Olof Palme of Sweden, Helmut Schmidt (and Willy Brandt) of Germany, Bruno Kreisky of Austria, Janos Kadar of Hungary, George Papandreou of Greece, Bettino Craxi of Italy, Felipe Gonzalez of Spain, Mario Soarès of Portugal, Golda Meir of Israel, Salvador Allende of Chile, and Fidel Castro of Cuba. The U.S. political figure with whom he came into the closest contact was Henry Kissinger. In spite of the objective, conflicting interests separating the international "princes," Mitterrand demonstrates a deep feeling of subjective complicity with those he perceives as the greatest, whether they be allies or adversaries either politically or ideologically.

That there is a kind of "brotherhood" of princes transcending national boundaries, ideological divisions, and cultural barriers becomes obvious as one reads Mitterrand's portrayals of these various leaders. What all the members of this fraternity have in common, in Mitterrand's view, is character—that is, strength of political will. He most admires those who have demonstrated persistent resistance to foreign invasion, encroachment, or influence, and loyalty to their convictions (or stubbornness).[29] This ability to resist foreign pressures takes precedence over the fact that several of these figures—for example, Brezhnev, Castro, and Mao, were not adverse to directly or indirectly invading or subverting other nations. From his subjective viewpoint, Mitterrand can admire both a Castro, seen as an underdog vis-à-vis the United States, and a Kissinger.

In the end, Mitterrand's moral subjectivism leads him to prize loyalty and fraternal solidarity more than anything else. Mitterrand has never burned a bridge. The list of his close and long-standing friendships include sharp contrasts, the most astounding being between, on the one hand, Jews known to have helped him formulate his economic, constitutional, judicial, and foreign policies, such as Dayan, Beauchamp, Robert Badinter, and later Laurent Fabius and Attali, and on the other, individuals with flagrant anti-Semitic pasts such as André Bettencourt, Jean Bouvyer, and René Bousquet. His personal loyalty toward a compromised Vichy official such as Bousquet and such corrupt associates as Roger Pelat, his prolonged solidarity with the weak Mollet Cabinet in 1956, his continued reverence for Marshal Pétain, his willingness to offer clemency to the OAS rebels (whom he viewed as faithful to their convictions), and his continued admiration for Mao Tse-tung and Fidel Castro are evidence that for Mitterrand fraternal loyalty, fidelity to one's convictions, forgiveness, and national reconciliation are the highest of his moral ideals.

One can explain, though not justify, Mitterrand's sense of loyalty in two ways. First, vestiges of Christian sentimentality (even though he now claims to doubt the existence of God), or an a priori spiritual love, allow him to forgive or offer clemency without "humiliating" preconditions (such as atonement, reparations, or commensurate punishment). Charity of the heart comes before rational justice (hence, his absolute opposition to the death penalty). Second, Mitterrand has always identified with large, close "families," which prize solidarity. Though independent-minded and occasionally "orphaned," Mitterrand has never been disconnected for long. A lengthy list of affiliations delineate his political career; these range from the large Mitterrand family itself to such "fraternal" groupings as the Conférence Saint-Vincent-de-Paul, the Volontaires nationaux, the MNPGD, UDSR, CIR, FGDS, PS, the *"club des princes,"* and ultimately the French nation itself. (This is why one must forgive a Frenchman, who has added national betrayal to other crimes, for actions for which a German cannot be forgiven.) Although Mitterrand's record has improved somewhat over the years, he tends to react strongly to injustices inflicted by outside forces on members within the fraternal circle as well as to readily forgive those within the circle who have victimized outsiders; the intensity of the reaction has more to do with the degree of subjective sympathy and identity, or lack thereof, that he feels with the perpetrators and victims than with the actual severity or magnitude of the injustice.

In sum, to Mitterrand culture (and cultivated nature), Mitterrandian socialism, and History are an order superior to raw nature, capitalism and history. The former are typically achieved through "conquest" or heroic struggle. Mitterrand emphasizes that raw nature, capitalism, and history tend to be accompanied by such flaws as inequality, injustice, and the survival of the fittest, and he ignores their association with such positive forces as creativity and freedom. The art, science, technology, wealth, and human well-being that have resulted from these positive aspects are either depreciated by Mitterrand or appropriated for his side. He overestimates the benefits and underestimates the failings and limits of his culture-socialism-History trinity.

Those who respect nature still must recognize that it is morally neutral and needs disciplining; rational adherents of capitalism know that it does not produce equality and requires control; serious students of history acknowledge that it is a messy process based primarily on amoral motives of self- or collective interest, some legitimate, some not. But Mitterrand claims for culture, socialism, and History a set of inherent and distinct superiorities—moral refinement, greater well-being for all, and justice—that history, with a large or small h, has disproved time and time again.

## NOTES

1. Thierry Pfister, *Les Socialistes: Les Secrets de familles, les rites, le code et les hommes du premier parti de France* (The Socialists: The family secrets, the rites, the code, and the men of the premier party of France) (Paris: Albin Michel, 1977), p. 40. Pfister, a Socialist and former journalist with *Le Monde* and *Le Nouvel Observateur*, is closely linked to Pierre Mauroy.

2. François Mitterrand, *L'Abeille et l'architecte* (The bee and the architect) (Paris: Flammarion, 1978), p. 54.

3. Ibid., pp. 28–29.

4. Ibid., pp. 27, 30.

5. Ibid., p. 30.

6. Ibid., pp. 116–17.

7. Philippe Alexandre, *Le Roman de la gauche* (The story of the left) (Paris: Plon, 1977), p. 345.

8. In France, a canton is a regional voting district that is larger than a municipality but smaller than a departmental *arrondissement*. The winners of cantonal elections sit on the regional *Conseils généraux* (General Councils) and the members of these *Conseils*, together with the municipal councilmen, elect the national Senators.

9. Albert du Roy and Robert Schneider, *Le Roman de la rose d'Epinay à l'Elysée* (The romance of the rose from Epinay to the Elysée) (Paris: Seuil, 1982), p. 220.

10. Etienne Fajon, *L'Union est un combat* (Union is a battle) (Paris: Editions Sociales, 1975). In this Communist publication a report written by Marchais shortly after the conclusion of the Common Program in 1972 was published for the first time. It offered incontrovertible proof that Marchais and the Communist leadership had never ceased considering the Socialists as "class collaborators," traitors to the workers incapable of change, and therefore potential enemies; contingency plans for withdrawal had been devised accordingly.

11. Mitterrand, *L'Abeille*, p. 301.

12. Olivier Duhamel, *La Gauche et la Cinquième République* (The left and the Fifth Republic) (Paris: Presses Universitaires de France, 1980), p. 402.

13. There are several good accounts of the two summit meetings held in September 1977. The most informative are two articles by Franz–Olivier Giesbert and Bernard Guetta, "Les Dessous de la négotiation," *Le Nouvel Observateur*, no. 671 (September 19, 1977): 39–42, and "La Gauche 'déprogrammée'?" *Le Nouvel Observateur*, no. 672 (September 26, 1977): 41–43; Robert Fabre, *Toute Vérité est bonne à dire* (The whole truth is worth telling) (Paris: Fayard, 1978); François Loncle, *Autopsie d'une rupture* (Autopsie of a breakup) (Paris: Editions Jean-Claude Simoën, 1979); and du Roy and Schneider, *Le Roman de la rose*.

14. Giesbert and Guetta, "Les Dessous de la négotiation," p. 42.

15. Giesbert and Guetta, "La Gauche 'déprogrammée'?" p. 42.

16. Ibid., p. 43.

17. Fabre, *Toute Vérité est bonne à dire*, p. 96.

18. Du Roy and Schneider, *Le Roman de la rose*, p. 220.

19. Ibid., p. 222.

20. Franz-Olivier Giesbert, "Le Défi de François Mitterrand," *Le Nouvel Observateur*, no. 675 (October 17, 1977): 40.

21. Raymond Barrillon, "La Majorité l'emporte avec 290 sièges (–10) contre 201 (+17)," *Le Monde*, March 21, 1978, pp. 1, 6.

22. François Mitterrand, *Politique 2* (Paris: Fayard, 1981), p. 208.

23. Mitterrand, *L'Abeille*, p. 366.

24. Ibid., p. 263.

25. François Mitterrand, *La Paille et le grain* (Paris: Flammarion, 1975).

26. By the end of 1974 Mitterrand was the father of an illegitimate baby daughter. The mother Anne Pingeot, whom he met in 1973, and their child became virtually a second family whose existence was well known in Paris, but the relationship was publicized only recently. (*People*, November 21, 1994, p. 139.)

27. Mitterrand, *L'Abeille*, p. 12.

28. Mitterrand, *La Paille*, p. 16.

29. François Mitterrand, "Interview," *Le Nouvel Observateur*, no. 1542 (May 26, 1994): 51.

# 11

## Challenge and Victory

"Yes, I said 'archaism.'"

These words were spoken by Michel Rocard in a television interview in the fall of 1978. He was purposely vague about *whose* archaism. He later claimed that he was referring to the PC, but Mitterrandists took immediate offense—the shoe seemed to fit. Thus began the debate that would propel the evolution of the PS for the next three years.

Mitterrand was convinced that the defeat in the 1978 legislative elections represented only a setback—not a debacle—that was due largely to the PC's lack of cooperation in a war that the left was sure to win eventually. But while he continued to press ahead with the same strategy that he had been following, the more market-oriented, libertarian Rocard persisted in launching an "agonizing reappraisal" of Socialist policy and strategy as part of an attempt to rescue the party from its fatal errors in economic policy and to set it on the path to victory in the 1981 presidential election, with himself as its candidate. Again, a struggle for power within the party coincided with a battle of ideas:

> In 1978 we lost. Everyone here agrees with the fact that the PC politburo's desire to divide, indeed to fail, constitutes the main reason for this defeat. But it would be serious to forget another reason for it: for public opinion as well as for our own candidates, the darkest mystery reigned concerning the way in which we would produce the enormous quantity of wealth that we generously promised to boldly redistribute. . . . There is a profound archaism in the way in which we have approached these problems and notably that of nationalizations.[1]

Here the term *archaism* refers to the Mitterrandist PS. Rocard could not have been more blatantly and provocatively heretical.

Furthermore, he appeared to be winning the public opinion game. He was "more attractive to the youngest socialist voters, [who were] the most active in economic life."[2] As Rocard's public opinion ratings rose, Mitterrand's stagnated, but they both hovered around 30 percent. Although Rocard showed more momentum in these polls and enjoyed much wider support beyond the confines of the Socialist Party in addition to being highly respected as an economist, Mitterrand was bolstered by party support and confidence. Rocard made the mistake of confusing popularity ratings with political strength. In fact, too much popularity outside the party increased distrust within the party. Mitterrand himself did not take the polls too seriously: "Polls confuse popularity with credibility. Now, one can be popular and not appear to be in a position to govern."[3]

Rocard was always a man in a hurry politically and had the habit of jumping the gun in campaign races and skipping important steps in the political process. His economic policies were innovative, but his political actions were rash, and his strategy was timid. Mitterrand's economic proposals often appeared unwise, while his political maneuvers were bold (his opposition to de Gaulle and the established powers), prudent (his reliance on popular, traditional ideas and existing documents and his resisting the radical demands of the PC leadership), and innovative (his willingness to deal with the PC in the first place). Having chosen the left, he never rushed ahead of public opinion on that side of the spectrum.

## THE METZ CONGRESS OF 1979

A party crisis was brewing. In 1977 Rocard had spoken dramatically at the Socialist congress in Nantes about the two "cultures" that were splitting the party: the Jacobin tradition of *dirigisme* (the belief that the national government should intervene actively and directly in the economic life of the nation) and the libertarian tradition, which emphasized the decentralization, where possible, of collective life. Rocard favored the latter, considering it to be more dynamic, progressive, and conducive to greater freedom and prosperity; he implicitly classified Mitterrand and his supporters in the former category.

While admitting the rivalry between these two traditions, Mitterrand claimed to represent their synthesis.

> These two histories have produced two different and, one must admit, rival cultures. I would prefer that they complement each other in order to fuse together rather than compete in order to destroy each other. Socialism needs all those who reject the power of the dominant class and who refuse [to accept] the alienation of man.[4]

The cantonal elections of 1979 served as a kind of pre-presidential campaign. Mitterrand attended three or four campaign meetings a day, covering

224 cantons in 51 different departments. Because he wanted to get his people elected at the grassroots level, he campaigned assiduously with them and for them. Support gathered here would constitute the basis for his later presidential bid.[5] In the 1979 cantonals the left topped 50 percent, which showed that the PS and the left in general were holding steady under Mitterrand's guidance in spite of the recent legislative defeat.

The Socialist party congress held in Metz in April 1979, the last congress before the 1981 presidential election, amounted to a showdown with Rocard. The existing party majority was under great strain—Mauroy and Rocard wanted the party to change direction, and neither wanted anything to do with CERES. But the overall party configuration looked fuzzy—no one had a clear majority. Mitterrand took control of the congress by speaking first and presenting himself as the *rassembleur* of the two cultures. He won the hall over from the start. Rocard spoke next but with less success; he gave the appearance of a disrupter of unity.[6]

During meetings the existing majority fell apart over the issues of the market (favored by Mauroy and Rocard) versus the plan, the union of the left, and the internal workings of the party (the Rocardians and Mauroyists wanted more "collegiality"). And for the first time, a note of personal resentment was heard:

> In all the factions, there were men who hoped for a synthesis. On the plan and the market, we could have come to an agreement. On the union of the left, it's impossible. And then, there is the text against the first secretary. I was insulted. If you tolerate the authority of a high priest without protesting for eight years— What servility![7]

Mitterrand was able to form a majority coalition, which he dominated, but only with the help of a somewhat chastened CERES (down 10 points to only 15 percent of the party) and the old Molletists, in addition to his usual support from Defferrists and Poperenists. The final motion, which obtained the majority of congress votes and was signed by Mitterrand, bore the strong stamp of Marxist CERES rhetoric (and Chevènement):

> The supposed "economic laws" of the right are only the old recipes of the exploitation of man by man in industrial society. Let's avoid calling "economic rigor" what is only social rigor. . . . It is normal . . . that the social measures of our program contradict the economic laws foisted upon us.[8]

Considering the history of the PS since the Epinay congress, these were very strange alliances indeed. It was particularly odd to see Mitterrand in league with the Molletists against Mauroy. Mauroy, Rocard, and their followers now found themselves on the right wing of the party and in the minority. The split of the old majority was particularly traumatic for the Mauroyists, who had been in the majority both before and after the Epinay congress. The Rocardians, on the other hand, were probably quite comfortable in the "opposition" of the party, a position that they felt gave them more freedom to state their distinct views. In an awkward attempt to belie the accusations made against him of being disruptive, Rocard vowed before thousands of party delegates and the press (even addressing Mitterrand directly across the immense hall) that he would never be a presidential candidate against Mitterrand.

The more dominant Mitterrand became, the more criticism he drew from both old party veterans and more recent Rocardian arrivals for his personal power and "authoritarianism." (Outsiders, such as Nay, love to exploit this insider critique.) Many felt that his hour had passed and that it was time to hand the torch gracefully to a new leader. The fact that Mitterrand was not ready to do this caused bitter resentment and intensified criticism of his leadership. The prominent Socialist André Salomon (himself an SFIO veteran converted to Rocardianism) summed up the various currents of discontent by labeling Mitterrand "domineering and sure of [him]self"[9] (this was the notoriously ambiguous expression that de Gaulle had chosen to describe Israel right after the Six-Day War in 1967). Usually the negative terms applied to Mitterrand were the very ones he had used against de Gaulle, adding piquancy to the criticism.

It is true that Mitterrand almost always ended up getting his way by using his most powerful weapon, the threat of resigning as first secretary of the PS. On the other hand, in every instance on record in which he coerced the party to vote against the wishes of its majority, it was in order to force the party to moderate an extremely radical position; for example, he demanded a more even-handed Socialist policy on the Arab-Israeli conflict, more openness to the idea of European unity, and, preceding the legislative campaign of 1973, the inclusion of moderate Radicals on Socialist electoral tickets.

What Salomon and Nay call *authoritarianism* Roger Gérard Schwartzenberg more aptly terms *moral constraint*. Exercised by an individual leader, moral constraint constitutes a safety valve when the majority errs; assuming it is not a bluff, it is also a means of saving personal honor if the group cannot be saved (for example, Mendès France saved his political honor by resigning from the incompetent Mollet Cabinet, and Mitterrand lost some of his by not doing so). Furthermore, resignation or its threat is consistent with the European (especially the Latin) political tradition. De Gaulle used the same weapon when he presented a referendum. And it is not paradoxical that, several years earlier when Pompidou had "warned" that he would resign in the event of a leftist legislative victory, Mitterrand denied Pompidou the right to practice at the national level what he himself did at the party level. For Pompidou was playing fast and loose with the rules of the constitution—a document that Mitterrand has always understood better and taken more seriously than any of the Gaullists—while Mittterrand was merely exploiting his personal prestige within his party.

## THE PRESIDENTIAL ELECTION OF 1981

On the threshold of a new decade and a crucial presidential election, the objective situations of neither the right nor the left looked very propitious. After seven years in power, the liabilities of the right were more obvious than its assets. Any incumbent at the end of a seven-year term is in an inherently defensive position. The aura of charm and competence surrounding Giscard d'Estaing had faded in the light of various scandals, his personal arrogance, economic disappointment (though the budget was balanced, unemployment was steadily increasing and growth seemed too slow), and an inability to demonstrate effective leadership both domestically and internationally. Whereas de Gaulle's distance from the Atlantic Alliance was based on an obsession with national independence, Giscard d'Estaing's "soft" approach led him into accommodationist positions vis-à-vis the Soviets and the Arab world (it was during his presidency and the prime ministership of Chirac that France sold Iraq the Osirak nuclear reactor that the Israelis later destroyed). This type of policymaking, coupled with his weak responses to renewed outbreaks of anti-Semitic violence in France, had disaffected Jews and many others. For example, in October 1980, when the synogague on rue Copernic in Paris was attacked, Giscard d'Estaing took several days to make a statement, and Prime Minister Barre made an inept reference to the non-Jewish victims as "innocent Frenchmen"; by contrast, Mitterrand went immediately to the scene of the crime (committed by Moslem terrorists). While Giscard d'Estaing thought he was more sophisticated and clever than others, he was actually more naive and simplistic. His intelligence, his sincere struggle to liberalize French society both socially and economically, his concern for sound economic management of public finances, and his efforts to work toward a more unified Europe could not compensate for his deficiencies.

The liabilities of the left, where party and doctrine are supposed to take precedence over individuals, were also considerable but characteristically less associated with any one person than were the liabilities of the right. By 1980 the grand ideas of the left had been largely demystified. Their contestation by the New Philosophers—a group composed mainly of former student Maoists and Trotskyists such as André Glucksmann, Bernard-Henri Lévy, and other bona fide *gauchistes*—had been fueled by the works of Solzhenitsyn and was given further impetus by the Soviets' harsh treatment of Solzhenitsyn and other dissidents. The New Philosophers were progressively supplanting the old "master thinkers," who were dying off (Sartre) or creating their own personal scandals (Louis Althusser, who murdered his wife). But the New Philosophers were largely negative political thinkers. They did not adopt any of the particular ideas promoted by the established political parties, right or left; rather, they devoted themselves to taking on the sacred cows of the left. Mitterrand was not favorably impressed by Lévy's *La Barbarie à visage humain.*[10]

It is, in the image of its author, a superb and naive book. Superb by virtue of the
language, the inner rhythm, the bitter certainty that there is only uncertainty.
Naive by virtue of the object of its quest, which flees it as soon as it approaches
it.[11]

Mitterrand seized upon the obvious weakness of the argument. The New
Philosophers were disillusioned with the phenomena of power in general and
seemingly all political processes. However, they stopped short of proposing the
abolition of the existing political process. They were wise enough to know that
there was nothing better with which to replace it. In turn, this implied an
acceptance, no doubt not lost on Mitterrand, which served the right more than
the left. The New Philosophers, while highlighting evils, offered nothing in the
way of concrete choices or political alternatives. These young intellectuals gave
the impression that the discussion of particular policies was beneath them—they
had mastered and would make liberal use of the brilliant, abstract language of
the *grandes écoles* (the highly elitist state professional schools). But it was the
egregious violations of human rights taking place in the world in 1979 that most
concerned them, and the best known of these were committed by leftist governments. Unlike so many of their leftist elders and contemporaries, including
Mitterrand, they did not try to explain away the evils perpetrated in the name of
leftist doctrine.

Thus, the sustaining walls of the traditional left were being blown in by the
dissident winds coming from both the heartland of socialism, the Soviet
Union,[12] and from the soul of the French left, its young post-Marxist intellectuals. These did more damage than any rightist politician or rigorous thinker such
as Raymond Aron could have hoped to do in a lifetime, and further complicated
Mitterrand's task of reaching the 50 percent mark. Now that the historical
process of disaffection had begun, it was not just a matter of persuading a few
more waverers to come over to his side but also of retarding the process of dis-
enchantment among the educated elite, who were quickly moving beyond simplistic Marxist categories.

While many within the traditional audience of the left were paying close
attention to the leftist dissidents, the established left remained faithful to the
fundamental myths of their tradition, and Mitterrand was no exception.
Because the (now) revered Jean Jaurès and Léon Blum had also subscribed to
Marxist theory, he labeled the connection between Marxism and the gulag a
"Parisian syllogism."[13] However, it was not just in the Parisian salons that the
connection between Marx and the gulag was being made, and syllogism or not,
it signaled that the leaders of the left could not take for granted the leftward
trend of the rising generation of French voters. Mitterrand managed these shifting tendencies by playing them both ways. His Marxist rhetoric attracted those
catching up to Marxism; his assertions that he was not a Marxist appealed to
those who were going beyond it as well as to those who had never embraced it.[14]
There were also those who supported or opposed Mitterrand precisely because

they believed that he was not a real Socialist. Michel Jobert, a Gaullist who supported Mitterrand momentarily, commented on Mitterrand's capacity to project different images of himself: "Mitterrand is $H_2O$, water one minute, mist the next, [then] rain or snow. It flows, and if a barrier stops it, it seeks to go around the obstacle. . . . It is a force that moves but whose contours are difficult to discern."[15]

To many younger, more educated Socialists, Rocard looked like an appealing alternative to Mitterrand as a presidential candidate. He was in a position similar to Giscard d'Estaing's in 1974—he projected the image of an attractive, dynamic, intelligent, professionally well trained expert on his way up. (CERES alternately referred to him as "Rocard d'Estaing" and "the left's American.") But he had little control over the party, and the Communists disliked him intensely. The votes he could pick up for the Socialists in the center would never compensate for the massive rejection of the Communist voters that was sure to occur if he ran for president. A Rocard candidacy threatened to result in a Third Force–style failure à la Defferre or Poher.

Mitterrand also had his liabilities. Even though he had performed better than any other political figure of the left, he had tried and failed over a period of thirteen years to lead a left majority to victory in two presidential and four legislative elections; loyal followers such as Mauroy were beginning to lose patience. Although these defeats had occurred in admittedly unfavorable, even impossible, circumstances and gave evidence of overall progress, they had taken a toll on Mitterrand's image, and it showed in the polls. Nonetheless, Mitterrand's power base was more solid than ever. Despite the criticism, his control of the party was firm, and his credibility among Socialists and Communists was still the highest of any other candidate of the left.

The lack of party unity was also a liability for Mitterrand. The parties of the right and the left all had internal divisions, but the PS was the only major party with an obvious rift at the top. The first secretary was determined to eliminate this drawback by completely fusing his own political identity with that of the Socialist Party. He disingenuously claimed not to have brought any "troops" with him to the Metz congress, and he lamented the existence of factions within the party, overlooking the fact that these same factions had served him well in the past and that they were the logical result of the proportional system for which he had voted at the Epinay congress.[16] To bolster unity he continually insisted that once debate ended on an issue, all must submit to the party line (and the first secretary set the example). Rather than implying, "*Le Parti, c'est moi!*" (I am the party)—for this would have indicated an authoritarian attitude—he implied, "*Moi, c'est le Parti*" (I best represent the party).

Rocard's challenge caused turmoil within the party but in no way disturbed Mitterrand's tortoise-like march to the Elysée. His plan for the first hundred days of the presidency was fully developed in his book *Ici et maintenant* (Here and now), a series of quasi interview/conversations published shortly after the Metz congress. The plan was presented as what any winning Socialist candidate would logically have to do—namely, dissolve the National Assembly immediately, call for national legislative elections, and ask the voters to send deputies to the National Assembly who would enact the president's program (to avoid the as yet unprecedented situation of opposing presidential and legislative majorities). This would in turn lead to the creation of a new government, whose composition would reflect the balance of the majority parties' forces in the National Assembly. There would be no negotiations with the Communists on their participation in the new government prior to the new legislative elections.

In addition to being Mitterrand's action plan for a Socialist president, *Ici et maintenant* was also the Socialist first secretary's summation on a wide range of issues. The views expressed adhered faithfully to the spirit of the Epinay congress, the Common Program, and the Socialist Project and revealed no new direction in Mitterrand's thinking, strategy to capture the presidency, or policy considerations, save his ideas on defense policy. He now favored the maintenance of the nuclear strike force and the installation of American Pershing missiles in Europe to counterbalance the Soviets' SS-20s. However, the old parallel between Soviet military imperialism and American economic imperialism still obtained, and Mitterrand even extended it to include American military imperialism, comparing the Soviet invasion of Afghanistan to the American "aggression" in Vietnam and Cambodia.[17]

Mitterrand elaborated further on international affairs in *Ici et maintenant*, since this domain takes on more importance in a presidential election. With the realization of the threat to France's security posed by the Soviet SS-20s, Mitterrand's East-West foreign policy continued to be centered on the Atlantic Alliance. It was in the area of Third World relations that he asserted his left-wing credentials, and where he felt that the United States was demonstrating military as well as economic imperialism. Whereas the United States tended to view civil wars in the Third World as proxy conflicts between itself and the Soviet Union, Mitterrand viewed them as revolutionary movements wherein the oppressed masses were fighting for social justice and only resorted to Soviet Communist assistance because the West was unsympathetic to their cause; he believed that more sympathy in the form of material aid would pull them away from the Soviet sphere of influence (which would, of course, benefit France's defense industry, too).

The dictators of Latin America were adversaries sent from heaven for Mitterrand and the French Socialists. (Franco, who died in 1975, was the last true dictator worthy of epic opposition in Western Europe.) Unlike the dictatorships of Eastern Europe, Africa, and Asia, the old European-style Latin American dictatorships fit relatively easily into the right-left framework of European politics. Despite the failures of Soviet and Oriental-style socialism, Mitterrand still saw hope in Latin America for the development of a new model of socialism that would combine public control of economic life and civil liberties. Cuba had proved a disappointment; Chile's failure was a tragedy blamed publicly on the United States (which Henry Kissinger refuted);[18] but in

Nicaragua, the Sandinista movement led by Daniel Ortega still appeared to be a possibility for success.

The Socialists thought that the underdeveloped countries were to the West what the exploited working class was to the ruling class. Whereas in the 1950s Mitterrand had been deeply suspicious and critical of national liberation movements and had believed that the colonizers (France in particular) had contributed to the betterment of the lives of the colonized, he now embraced the orthodox leftist, quasi-Marxist viewpoint that the West's export of its capitalism—its investment funds, jobs, technology, and ideas—was largely exploitative and detrimental to the developing nations. Third World peoples were victims of the international division of labor, the imperialism of the (American) multinationals, and the repression of national liberation movements. He also believed that because the industrialized West was exploiting the resources of the Third World it should compensate these countries with massive transfers of aid.

Mitterrand enumerated various other socialist reforms concerning the Atlantic Alliance, the European Community, the International Monetary Fund, arms control, and trade talks that any Socialist president would have to propose to France's allies at the earliest negotiating opportunities. However, given the well-known unpopularity of many of the French Socialist ideas (particularly those related to the Third World, trade, and the international financial system) with the governments of France's major partners (in particular, Helmut Schmidt's West Germany, Ronald Reagan's United States, and Margaret Thatcher's Great Britain) and the relatively weak political and economic leverage France possessed, Mitterrand's claims to more effective leadership at the international level lacked credibility. Mitterrand was always confident of his powers of persuasion, but it is still difficult to see how a Socialist French president could go beyond the role of witness or conscience of the world in this realm. Such were the ideas with which Mitterrand entered the 1981 presidential race.

Mitterrand had no trouble in obtaining the PS's nomination for the presidency, which Rocard supported as promised. Never was Mitterrand more serenely confident. "*La force tranquille*," which became the slogan of his campaign, was very much in evidence. Even after obtaining the nomination, he resisted public campaigning. This would not start until his only serious opponent, Giscard d'Estaing, declared himself on March 2, less than two months before the first ballot: "I do not intend to get started actively before Giscard is a candidate. Everything that I would say would be lost in the sand."[19] Mitterrand understood the importance of timing. While he appreciated certain aspects of American political life, he eschewed the endlessness, as well as the exhibitionism, of American campaigns.

Mitterrand's campaign was based on his 110 Propositions, an encyclopedic list of policy proposals, purged for the most part of jargon and ideologically charged terms, but still closely related to the positions developed throughout the 1970s in the Common Program, the Socialist Project, and *Ici et maintenant*. The key features of the program were the nationalizations and several demagogic proposals: (1) to reduce the forty-hour work week to thirty-five (without a decrease in salary), (2) to increase the four-week paid vacation to five, (3) to allow retirement at age sixty, and (4) to increase the minimum wage. Mitterrand and his economic advisors still sought to achieve economic growth and egalitarianism by stimulating domestic consumption through income redistribution, more government regulation, public borrowing, and protectionism. Critics saw this as producing nothing but "stagflation"—a combination of economic stagnation, more unemployment, and inflation. The 110-item list demonstrated that Mitterrand had come to accept, no matter what the constitution stated, that the president of the Fifth Republic was steeped in politics and that the arbiter role was no longer predominant; Mitterrand was behaving like a good "presidentialist."

From his first official campaign meeting on February 18 to the second ballot on May 10, the Socialist candidate's goals and strategy remained constant, clear, and precise. The goals: (1) obtain at least 25 percent of the vote on the first ballot (this in itself would be a feat, since the Socialists had never done better than 23 percent) and (2) obtain 70 percent of the Communist vote and 15 percent of Chirac's Gaullist votes on the second ballot (the center right was logically sacrificed to Giscard d'Estaing). The strategy: aim to the left. There would be no second ballot for him if he did not collect all of the traditional Socialist votes and a good number of Communist votes, including all the Communists who would vote productively on the first ballot.

Although many substantive issues separated the two parties of the left—the Polish Solidarity movement, the Soviet invasion of Afghanistan, the Soviet SS-20s, domestic immigration policy, and the extent of nationalization—none of them would have precluded Communist-Socialist cooperation if the Communists had not decided to run their own candidate, for Mitterrand's desire for union superseded any disagreement: "What unites us [basically a handful of nationalizations, redistribution of wealth, and social reforms] is more important than what separates us." But in the 1980 Senate elections the PC had refused to desist in a number of cases, causing the rightist candidate to win, which showed the PS what to expect in 1981.[20] Nevertheless, Mitterrand continued to campaign in the name of the union of the left, while the PC worked against it.

There was no doubt about it now: "One of the main goals of [the Marchais candidacy] was to show that the PS could not dominate the left."[21] Any president was considered better than a Socialist one. It was highly desired also that Mitterrand be toppled from his pedestal. Preferring to ignore the signs of internal disgust and frustration with the PC's general secretary and central committee, Marchais and his supporters persisted in denouncing the Socialists as collaborators of the right, in outbidding the PS on every social issue, in attacking Mitterrand personally, and in pandering to the xenophobic, far-right protest vote. Yet they still badgered the Socialists about the necessity of including Communists in a government of the left (as in the 1978 legislatives, this served both to scare the center and reassure the rank and file). Despite the barrage, the PS continued to call out to the Communist voters.

As the campaign progressed, however, it became obvious that the Communists would not do well, and their decline in the polls was accompanied by a decline in their rhetoric. The question for the PC had become how a defeatist Marchais could torpedo his erstwhile ally's juggernaut without appearing to do so. By merely refusing to exclude the possibility of strikes, demonstrations, and other social disturbances, Marchais hoped to scare some middle-class voters away from Mitterrand.[22] Meanwhile, it appeared that the campaign of invective was backfiring in that it highlighted Mitterrand's independence vis-à-vis the Communists and weakened Giscard d'Estaing's argument that the Socialist candidate was hostage to them.[23]

As usual, the Socialist candidate managed to turn the accusation against the accuser, noting that although Giscard d'Estaing was free of the Communists, he was not free of the Gaullists, who were continually working against him. By the same token, the fact that on the international level, Reagan, Schmidt, and Brezhnev all openly preferred Giscard d'Estaing only went to show that they found him more accommodating, unlike Mitterrand, whom the superpowers thought so troublesome:

> If they all want him it is because he is too convenient for everyone. It is the French who are voting. And with the French I have no problems. I am a free man vis-à-vis the superpowers, the money establishment. No one will weigh on my decision-making. That is why I bother some people.[24]

By March 2, when Giscard d'Estaing finally declared his candidacy, there was a fourth serious candidate, the Gaullist Chirac. Michel Crépeau, the new president of the MRG, also ran, a fact that Mitterrand did not appreciate. (Robert Fabre had resigned the presidency of the MRG after the 1978 legislative elections and had accepted an appointment from Giscard d'Estaing.) In addition, there were several splinter candidates: Arlette Laguillère, a leftist labor candidate; Brice Lalonde, the ecology candidate; Huguette Bouchardeau of the PSU; and two other Gaullists, Marie-France Garaud and the still active Michel Debré.

Mitterrand gathered wide and deep support among the vast national cohort of teachers and professors working in the highly centralized public education system. As unionized state employees, they expected much from a Socialist presidency. In addition, an articulate, self-conscious Marxism permeated their ranks, and Mitterrand came the closest to their ideological viewpoint. Many were active members of both the PS and the Fédération de l'Education Nationale (the National Teacher's Association) that together enjoyed a satisfying symbiotic relationship. The educators constituted a valuable part of the campaign and propaganda machine.

Many among the intellectual elite also endorsed Mitterrand. They included

Françoise Giroud, Simone de Beauvoir, Jacques Derrida, Félix Guatarri, Gilles Deleuze, Jean-Pierre Faye, François Lyotard, Michel Butor, Pierre Bourdieu, Françoise Sagan, and Régis Debray. The last, Debray, whom Henry Kissinger deemed "an idolatrous chronicler of revolutions,"[25] had gained his activist, leftist credentials fighting alongside Che Guevara and getting imprisoned in Bolivia in the 1960s. He actively campaigned for the Socialist candidate, became a close advisor, and was the principal architect of Mitterrand's Third World policy.

Keith Reader, a British scholar and student of French thought, analyzed the intellectual elite's peculiar reticence toward Mitterrand in *Intellectuals and the Left in France since 1968* and noted that support from the intellectuals, with the exception of Debray, was relatively lukewarm and blasé—the result of a process of elimination rather than a clear preference for Mitterrand. Although it is probable that the majority of the intellectual elite indeed voted for Mitterrand,[26]

> the link between the left-wing intellectual activity and the Socialist triumph was not a self-evident one, and it may have been difficult for intellectuals to think of the Mitterrand regime as "theirs," particularly given the problems into which the new government almost immediately ran.[27]

Debray thought that they "feared being subjected to the organs of power and deprived of their individual autonomy or corporate power."[28] Reader himself described the phenomenon in terms of natural rivalries on one hand between the intellectual and political lefts, which overlap but do not coincide, and on the other between the intellectual left and the powers that be, whether of the left or right:

> They were more prolific and self-confident in opposition, not merely because it is always easier . . . to criticize than administer, but also because they were the dominant source and repository of symbolic power on the left. Once the Socialist government had come to power, a host of other discourses—now the voices of the State rather than the mere opposition—were able to deprive the intelligentsia of their previous effective monopoly.[29]

Yet there could be no doubt that the intellectual elite, in spite of their indifference to day-to-day politics and halfhearted personal support of Mitterrand, had greatly helped prepare the way for a Socialist presidential triumph. For so many years these academic stars and their vast network of disciples at both the secondary and university levels had preached their leftist ideas to several generations of students plowing their way through the highly centralized French education system. The prestige they enjoyed in French society gave a weight to their political opinions that was totally out of proportion with their actual knowledge of politics or political responsibilities.

Though the intellectual stars sowed the seeds and Mitterrand reaped the political fruits, there was no love between them. While Mitterrand claimed many friends, supporters, and workers among them—especially among novelists, poets, and historians, he did not particularly admire the lionized master thinkers who had polished Marx for French consumption. Mitterrand had his own term for them—the *monstres sacrés:*

> Cultural births are prepared in the shadows, often unnoticed or unsuspected by the most seasoned observers, while fashion indiscriminately glorifies all the products of the mind, runs out of breath carrying anything and everythng to the altar of immortality, then, worn out by its frivolity, suddenly wonders, "So where are the sacred monsters?" Without noticing that the discourse about things has replaced the things themselves.[30]

It was their penchant for explaining the whole world and all of history in an abstract, magisterial manner coupled with their obsession with language as the ultimate reference that annoyed him. He was not above borrowing their ideas when they served his purpose, but he was not willing to sacrifice his own freedom of thought and action to any of their systems.

France's feminists also endorsed Mitterrand, even though traditionally women had generally supported conservative candidates (a fact that he took pleasure in recalling before feminist audiences). Politically and intellectually Mitterrand was one of the first leaders to recognize the importance of legitimate feminist concerns such as equal pay for equal work, day care, legalized birth control, and legalized abortion (for which he nevertheless rejected state subsidies). He realized that the needs and demands of women did not fall neatly into the simplistic right versus left, socialism versus capitalism dichotomies. Also, while claiming not to like quota systems, he approved the use of one within his own party to promote more active participation by women militants. Increasingly one saw women experts surrounding him and advising him on a wide range of issues (not just on women's issues), while Giscard d'Estaing paid little attention to the feminists.

Mendès France spoke out from his retirement to publicly and firmly support Mitterrand. He agreed with the basic premises of the Socialist's campaign: that both equality and growth must be addressed, and that the former must precede the latter in order to gain the cooperation of the nation as a whole. Uncharacteristically, Mendès France was willing to approve a slight loosening of the economic reins: "We can tolerate a limited deficit, on the condition that foreign borrowing serves to finance investments that will later be productive and not to cover current consumption."[31] (It was precisely consumption, however, that the Socialists were determined to stimulate, thinking that it would, in turn, promote productivity.)

# THE SECOND GISCARD D'ESTAING–MITTERRAND DUEL

Polls increasingly pointed toward only two serious candidates, Giscard d'Estaing and Mitterrand, and toward a closing of the gap between them; going into the first ballot they were virtually neck and neck. Marchais's campaign tactics proved counterproductive—the long months of invective had only served to hurt his own party and help his rival on the left. In contrast, Chirac's campaign revealed real but insufficient strength in relation to Giscard d'Estaing. His fuzzy public image was his main problem; he had sent too many mixed signals to the voters. His flirtatious glances toward the Socialist electorate had no effect, since he was running on an explicitly Reaganomic platform. Yet he was suspect among pure liberals, too, because of his *dirigiste* background. Other voters on the right still closely associated him with Giscard d'Estaing because he and his party had voted for most of Giscard d'Estaing's policies for seven years.

Sensing that he was losing ground, Giscard d'Estaing turned pugnacious and aggressive. His strategy and arguments remained essentially the same traditional, largely negative ones, but they now lacked either credibility or force. He imprudently pulled out the well-known Gaullist disdain for political parties in general, accusing them of undermining political institutions. He exploited the constitutional issue by claiming that his prime minister, Raymond Barre, would not be forced to resign in the event of a left victory, an ineffectual statement in view of Mitterrand's well-publicized assertion that, in the event of a left victory, he would immediately dissolve the National Assembly. At the same time, Giscard d'Estaing allowed himself to be much more distracted by Chirac's rearguard campaign than Mitterrand was by Marchais's.

In the past one of France's most sincere political defenders of continental liberalism (in France, polls show that the French by and large favor "liberalism" but dislike "capitalism"), Giscard d'Estaing was weak and ineffective in promoting it as president. Instead of directly attacking Mitterrand's greatest weaknesses (his economic and financial policies and "Third Worldism"), he tried to outbid him by proposing alternative state-supported programs. A statist employment program for the young was the centerpiece of his program. Mitterrand accused Giscard d'Estaing of stealing five of his seven anti-unemployment proposals.[32]

The election results of the first ballot reinforced the left's hope for victory; Mitterrand passed the 25 percent mark, receiving 25.8 percent of the vote. Giscard d'Estaing won 28 percent; Chirac, 18 percent (an unexpectedly strong showing, offering promise for the future); and Marchais, 15.3 percent (a humiliating defeat considering the PC's traditional strength of 20–22 percent). Going against party orders, approximately a quarter of the Communist electorate went over to Mitterrand on the first ballot. None of the marginal candidates surpassed 4 percent, although Lalonde, the ecology candidate, received 3.9 percent of the vote.

It was unclear at this point whether this Communist debacle signaled a historical decline or was merely a blip. In retrospect, it appears to have been part of a worldwide historical decline that Mitterrand exploited well at the domestic level. His national political strategy both contributed to and restrained the PCF's decline. For while Mitterrand stole large numbers of votes from the PCF, he also gave it new respectability by recognizing it as a viable partner. His vocal advocacy of the installation of American cruise missiles in Europe, however, did work in the direction of Soviet Communist decline.

Prior to the second ballot another dramatic televised debate between Giscard d'Estaing and Mitterrand took place. Since the 1974 debate, the two candidates had switched roles. This time it was Giscard d'Estaing who was too relaxed, too courteous, and too defensive; Mitterrand accused, attacked, condemned, offended. Giscard d'Estaing's remarks, generally interrogatory and focused on technical details, were directed at Mitterrand himself, not the journalists, and conspicuously defeatist in tone. He persisted in using the future tense in asking his questions. For example, "Will this [Socialist] government come before the National Assembly?"[33] (will it try to work with the existing rightist majority?) and "What conditions will the Communist Party demand in order to conclude an electoral agreement?"[34] In contrast, Mitterrand generally disdained to address his opponent, preferring to pursue an interview format with the journalists. However, as the debate progressed, he directly and relentlessly condemned Giscard d'Estaing's record: "You have always been mistaken."[35] "You didn't act against [unemployment]. You accepted it." "My program will never cost the French as much as what you have cost them: 135 billion [francs] this year."[36] "You have failed [regarding European affairs], you lacked firmness. That happens to you often."[37] "You stand for bureaucracy. You created it."[38] Mitterrand was well rehearsed this time around. He also made good and safe use of Chirac, citing every instance in which the former prime minister had criticized the president. Without having to concede anything to Chirac, he turned him into his objective ally.

Showing much greater energy, Mitterrand was the clear winner of this debate. It was not so much what the Socialist candidate had said (he was unconvincing on a number of points), but how he had said it. In 1981 Giscard d'Estaing, despite his twenty-five years of political experience, came across as a buzzing fly, more of a nuisance than a threat, and seemed tired, while Mitterrand had the air of a supremely confident statesman already enthroned in history by virtue of his past activities. The linguist Dominique Labbé summed it up well:

> While Giscard d'Estaing [is treated by Mitterrand as someone who has merely passed through the political world], fleeting and ephemeral, [Mitterrand] presents himself as though he were carved in marble, inscribed in history, the archetype of the statesman whose superior legitimacy escapes the accidents of events. Universal suffrage is not the source of this legitimacy but its logical result; the former only ratifies the latter.[39]

In the end, the voters had a clear choice. Although both candidates advocated a prosperous, "progressive" society within a democratic system, each represented a highly distinct pattern of political thought—with Giscard d'Estaing emphasizing the values of a state-tempered free enterprise system and Mitterrand favoring an aggressive state-interventionist approach. Giscard d'Estaing presented the conflict in terms of freedom versus collectivism and productivity versus impoverishment, while Mitterrand framed it in terms of right versus left, conservative versus progressive, personal power versus republicanism. Giscard d'Estaing's ideas were closer to Thatcher's and Reagan's, but he chose a conciliatory, accommodationist style—a "soft" approach—for dealing with the opposition. Mitterrand's ideological approach was fundamentally conciliatory and compromising with his allies and even rivals on the left, but he was firm, disciplined, and frankly aggressive with his major opponent.

Reality confirmed prophecy on the second ballot; Mitterrrand won with 51.8 percent of the vote to Giscard d'Estaing's 48.2 percent; this was significantly better than Giscard d'Estaing's 1974 victory. Several phenomena had benefited Mitterrand. First, most of the left's fringe and splinter candidates' votes predictably went to him on the second ballot. Second, Chirac's personal support of Giscard d'Estaing on the second ballot was so backhanded that fully 16 percent of his first-ballot supporters, or almost 3 percent of the total electorate, went over to Mitterrand, and 11 percent of it, or almost 2 percent of the electorate, abstained. The crossover vote of the Communists to Giscard d'Estaing was less—only 4 percent. Third, Mitterrand picked up a crucial 1 percent in the center—those voters whose desire for change was greater than their fear of the Communists. But the decisive factor was the million and a half Communist votes (or 70 percent of the Communist electorate) that Mitterrand reaped. The union-of-the-left strategy had paid off handsomely in spite of, and in the some instances because of, the lack of cooperation on the part of the Communist leadership.[40]

According to a Sofres poll, (1) the young had shunned the election but acclaimed the Socialist's victory (Giscard d'Estaing had lowered the voting age to eighteen); (2) the vote for Mitterrand was above all a vote for change; (3) the unemployment problem had cost Giscard d'Estaing more than the diamond scandal (Giscard d'Estaing had accepted a diamond as a gift from the retired president of Central African Republic Eddine Ahmed Bokassa); (4) the upper middle class, not the self-employed middle class, let go of Giscard d'Estaing for Chirac on the first ballot (most still voted for Giscard d'Estaing on the second ballot); (5) for the first time, the Socialists had received more votes from the working class than had the Communists; (6) the salaried middle class had slid to the left; (7) the left was not the domain of the poor but that of salaried working people; and (8) the rate of satisfaction with the election outcome, even among those who did not vote for Mitterrand, was exceptionally high.[41]

Chirac's and Marchais's showings revealed that the strongest and most immediate challenge to Mitterrand's power would come from Chirac and the

Gaullists. Even though Chirac received many fewer votes on the first ballot than Giscard d'Estaing and was therefore eliminated from the race, he immediately became the recognized leader of the new opposition. This was because, having completely knocked out Debré and Garaud as rivals, he was now the undisputed leader of the largest and best organized party of the new opposition and because Giscard d'Estaing, by losing the presidency, had fallen the farthest. Chirac was on the way up, Giscard d'Estaing on the way down.

Marchais, with his respectable but relatively low 15 percent, still appeared to be hanging on to his compact and highly organized party at least for the time being; furthermore, since the PC was in effect a part of the presidential majority, he had gained the opportunity to exert some influence on domestic policy. Yet, as a serious candidate for national office, the Communist leader failed totally; he was quickly becoming a caricature of himself.

## VICTORY AT LAST

Without a parliamentary majority to coincide with the presidential majority, Mitterrand's victory would not have been complete. The "third ballot"—the election of a new National Assembly—was yet to come. As promised, Mitterrand immediately dissolved the National Assembly that had been elected in 1978. While waiting out the three months set aside for this campaign, the new president appointed his longtime colleague Pierre Mauroy as prime minister, and together they assembled an all-Socialist interim government.

Chirac took the lead of the opposition, garnering support from the various elements of the UDF (the French Democratic Union), Giscard d'Estaing's center-right coalition. He rejected the old Gaullist argument—routinely propounded by the right while it was in power—that a constitutional crisis, even chaos, would ensue if a legislative majority conflicted with a presidential one. Now Chirac was telling the voters not to put all their eggs in one Socialist basket. Using the traditional scare tactics, he was trying to recapture the Gaullist defectors and abstentionists. It was unlikely that an economic crisis worried him any more than did a constitutional one. He simply judged that a dynamic power struggle in Parliament would better serve his future bid for the presidency than would a situation in which Gaullists appeared to be relatively weak; political principle yielded again to perceived political interest.

The landslide legislative election results surpassed the Socialists' wildest dreams. On the first ballot the Socialists and MRGs together obtained 37.5 percent of the vote. By the end of the second ballot, the left occupied 70 percent of the deputy seats, the Socialists having 269 seats, the PC 44, and the MRG 14. The French were clearly in a mood for change.

The moment of truth vis-à-vis the Communists had come; it was time to negotiate Communist participation in the new government. Many commentators, such as Raymond Aron, wondered why Mitterrand, with such a strong, homogeneous majority, brought Communists into the government at all since he did not need them. Though there was no longer any credible threat of a Leninist-type Communist takeover by this exceptionally domesticated Communist Party, there was fear that the Communists would prove obstructionist and might take control of certain agencies. But Mitterrand had a memory of the past, the whole past, and an eye to the future. By giving Communists token representation in the government, he recognized the extent of the electoral support that traditional Communist voters had accorded him. Their inclusion also precluded, at least for the time that they remained in solidarity with his government, Communist-led strikes and social agitation; he would never be the one to release the PC from his clutching embrace. Thus, the new president offered them four of the thirty ministerial posts available—Health, Civil Service, Transportation, and Professional Development.

The Communists were forced by Mitterrand into a situation they had dreaded, being a support force for a presidential majority based on the left. Although they would have liked to, they could not refuse the perches held out by the new president—they would have totally lost face with traditional Communist voters. The ministries handed to them were a far cry from the prestigious Ministries of Finance and Interior that they had demanded in 1978, but they had no power with which to bargain for something better.

While polls in France showed that many of those who had not voted for Mitterrand on the first or even the second ballot were not disappointed by the outcome, the president and his government faced skepticism from the strongest of their international allies and, not surprisingly, a profound lack of faith from the world financial community. Mitterrand's campaign proposals ran counter to what was happening in the economies of France's major trading partners, where the economic processes of "wringing out" were well under way (this refers to efforts to lower inflation and cool an overheated economy by raising interest rates; the short-term effect is recession, the long-term effect lower but sustainable growth and relatively low inflation and unemployment rates). Schmidt was probably the least worried. He and Mitterrand had their international Socialist credentials in common, they had a working relationship, and Germany was in a very strong position vis-à-vis France economically (although Schmidt liked Giscard d'Estaing better, and Mitterrand was personally and ideologically linked to Willy Brandt). Reagan's Washington was wary. Mitterrand's acceptance of the Pershing missiles for NATO and his criticism of Soviet defense and foreign policy were reassuring, but his economic policies, his inclusion of Communists in his government, and his approach to Third World issues were cause for concern. It remained to be seen how Margaret Thatcher and Mitterrand would get along. Britain's thorny presence in the Common Market combined with Thatcher's political ideology and economic policy plus her pugnacious style suggested interesting days ahead.

Even with the Commmunists' participation, Mitterrand and the Socialist Party were firmly in control of the new government, the National Assembly, and the future course of France. Together they constituted a new and independent-minded force to be reckoned with in the European Community and Atlantic Alliance. The principal ministers were all veteran politicians (in contrast to a typical American Cabinet), several of whom had been (or even continued to be) party rivals: Pierre Mauroy, prime minister; Charles Hernu, Defense; Jacques Delors, Finance; Alain Savary, Education; Pierre Joxe, Industry; Gaston Defferre, Interior and Decentralization; Michel Rocard, Planning and Regional Development; Jean-Pierre Chevènement, Research and Technology; Michel Crépeau of the MRG, Environment; Robert Badinter, Justice; and Claude Cheysson, Foreign Affairs. Pierre Bérégovoy was Mitterrand's first chief of staff. "Mitterrand does not hesitate to pardon offenses in order to mobilize competence . . . [his old maxim being] rancor must [not] exist, simply memory."[42] For the first time in French history, a Socialist president proceeded to lead a united government of the left (Léon Blum's Popular Front government of 1936 was supported by but did not include Communists), marking the beginning of a new Socialist experiment in the West—one more attempt to reconcile democracy, socialism, and prosperity.

## NOTES

1. Speech before the PS National Convention, April 29, 1978, cited in Michel Rocard, *Parler vrai* (Speaking the truth) (Paris: Seuil, 1979), p. 86.

2. Hervé Hamon and Patrick Rotman, *L'Effet Rocard* (The Rocard effect) (Paris: Stock, 1980), pp. 268–69. Hamon is a Rocardian.

3. François Mitterrand, *Ici et maintenant* (Here and now) (Paris: Fayard, 1980), p. 25.

4. Ibid., pp. 20–22.

5. David S. Bell and Byron Criddle, *The French Socialist Party: Resurgence and Victory* (Oxford: Clarendon Press, 1984), p. 104.

6. Hamon and Rotman, *L'Effet Rocard*, p. 276.

7. Ibid., pp. 278–79.

8. Jacques Kergoat, *Le Parti socialiste* (The Socialist Party) (Paris: Le Sycomore, 1983), p. 250.

9. André Salomon, *PS: La Mise à nu* (PS: Laying it bare) (Paris: Laffont, 1980), p. 121.

10. Bernard-Henri Lévy, *La Barbarie à visage humain* (Barbarism with a human face) (Paris: Grasset, 1977).

11. François Mitterrand, *L'Abeille et l'architecte* (The bee and the architect) (Paris: Flammarion, 1978), p. 329.

12. In a private conversation in 1988, Georgette Elgey told the author that the revelations of the gulag had little impact in France in the 1970s. The author was studying in France at the time, and her impression was exactly the opposite.

13. Mitterrand, *Ici et maintenant*, p. 21.

14. Catherine Nay remarks, "Everything he says always corresponds to a part of himself," meaning Mitterrand is sincere about all the contradictory things he says [Nay, *Le Noir et le rouge* (Paris: Grasset, 1984), p. 344].

15. Michel Jobert, cited in ibid., p. 344.

16. Mitterrand, *Ici et maintenant*, pp. 16–17.

17. Ibid., pp. 229, 239.

18. Henry Kissinger, *The White House Years* (Boston: Little, Brown, 1979), p. 683.

19. Claude Estier, *Mitterrand Président: Journal d'une victoire* (President Mitterrand: Diary of a victory) (Paris: Stock, 1981), p. 98.

20. Bell and Criddle, *The French Socialist Party*, pp. 110–11.

21. Jacques Chapsal, *La Vie politique sous la Cinquième République* (Political life under the Fifth Republic) (Paris: Presses Universitaires de France, 1981), p. 683.

22. Estier, *Mitterrand*, p. 140.

23. Ibid., p. xix.

24. Ibid., p. 167.

25. Kissinger, *The White House Years*, p. 655.

26. Keith Reader, *Intellectuals and the Left in France since 1968* (New York: St. Martin's Press, 1987), p. 136.

27. Ibid., p. 22.

28. Régis Debray, cited in ibid., p. 139.

29. Reader, *Intellectuals*, p. 139.

30. Mitterrand, *Ici et maintenant*, p. 164.

31. "Pierre Mendès France," *Le Nouvel Observateur*, no. 857 (April 13, 1981): 37.

32. Estier, *Mitterrand*, p. 146.

33. François Mitterrand and Valéry Giscard d'Estaing, "Le Débat radio-télévisé entre les deux candidats," *Le Monde*, May 7, 1982, pp. 8–14.

34. Ibid., p. 9.

35. Ibid., p. 10.

36. Ibid., p. 12.

37. Ibid., p. 13.

38. Ibid., p. 12.

39. Dominique Labbé, *François Mitterrand: Essai sur le discours* (François Mitterrand: Essay on discourse) (Grenoble: La Pensée Sauvage, 1983), p. 35.

40. For an excellent overview of this election see Vincent Wright and Howard Machin, "Why Mitterrand Won: The French Presidential Elections of April–May 1981," *West European Politics*, 5, no. 1 (January 1982): 5–35.

41. Jacques Juillard, "Comment la France a basculé" (How France has tilted), *Le Nouvel Observateur*, no. 864 (June 22, 1981): 37.

42. Thierry Pfister, "L'Equipe du troisième tour" (The third-ballot team), *Le Nouvel Observateur*, no. 862 (June 8, 1981): 26.

# Conclusion

In 1988 François Mitterrand went on to win an unprecedented second seven-year presidential term. His margin—55 percent to Chirac's 45 percent—equaled de Gaulle's victory over Mitterrand in 1965. At the end of his second seven-year term the inevitable "lame duck" phenomenon has come into play in addition to the strains of another "cohabitation," numerous scandals, revelations of an impure past, and terminal cancer. But Mitterrand remains an active if discreet political force and his disciples remain in control of the PS.

This marked change in his political status was accompanied by a significant shift in his public image. As he gradually won over the majority of the French electorate, he also went from being one of the most ridiculed and reviled personages in French politics (his image resembled that of a Richard Nixon of the left), to being a respected, if enigmatic, European leader. Up until his first presidential victory, he was viewed predominantly as a Machiavellian in the most pejorative sense of the word, but recently terms such as *enigma, mystery, puzzle,* and *sphinx* have become prevalent in commentary about him.[1] This stems in part from the discretion with which he conducts the French presidency and from his insistence on always retaining room to maneuver. The perception of complexity, contradiction, and mystery also results from a failure to discern simple patterns in Mitterrand's behavior and thinking. Indeed, few French statesmen have been more clear and open about their principles, positions, and goals throughout their career than Mitterrand; he was never more honest and less disingenuous than when he stated in a now famous French television special on him that he had a "simple mind." As Mitterrand said of Kissinger, "It is easier for the Prince than for any other individual to disdain false maneuvers. By always suspecting that he is tricking you, you have already lost."[2] Mitterrand's whole career is based on consistent adherence to three principles: (1) the scorn of money and a profound distrust of the business and financial communities, (2) the love of justice (as he perceives it), and (3) the belief in his own vocation of national and world leader.

Mitterrand's ability to acquire, consolidate, and hold on to power has depended on a Machiavellianism that goes beyond a simple ability to connive successfully (although this has been required on occasion); rather it amounts to a complete understanding of politics as art. The first and most fundamental element of this art is an unshakable belief in one's princely vocation or worthiness to lead. For Mitterrand this resulted in supreme self-confidence and unswerving perseverance against all odds. This is more than mere opportunism or ambition, more than simply a will to, or lust for, power. It is as if one has been chosen to pursue a preordained destiny that one cannot elude. In Mitterrand's case, there was a responsibility to fulfill, a "debt" to pay.

In addition, his Machiavellianism requires a profound understanding in three important areas—human nature, history, and the extant political system— as well as the ability to apply this knowledge. Mitterrand's ability to attract, motivate, and bring together individuals, many of whom might normally have despised one another, is evidence of his knowledge of the first area. This skill was necessary for him to persuade others of his princely vocation and to form an effective organizational network. Virtually the only tools at Mitterrand's disposal were what one would today call *communication skills*, although this term inadequately describes Mitterrand's rhetorical prowess, which had been sparked by the French belletristic tradition and energized by parliamentary oratory. While Giscard d'Estaing tried to work both his physical and statistical charms, Mitterrand incessantly plied his verbal skill—in books and articles, in dinner table conversations, at meetings and rallies, and in Parliament. He was by turns poetic, sarcastic, debonair, arrogant, pugnacious, authoritarian—whatever the situation required. Not just Socialist ideology but also economics and history became subjects of rhetorical discourse on Mitterrand's tongue. Playing on the many levels of human experience, he went from offering demagogic promises to defending the right to human dignity, thereby appealing to both the baser and nobler instincts of his audiences.

Mitterrand's extensive knowledge of European history enabled him to read events and circumstances, to understand their potential for disaster or opportunity, and to act, or rather, react accordingly. No one knew better than he how to milk opportunity out of the most inauspicious events and circumstances—from war, captivity, colonization, and opposition to defamation and defeat. Mitterrand managed better than any other French politician to stay one step ahead of events, to alter circumstances, to initiate a bold stroke from time to time, or by contrast to hold events, time, even history itself at bay until he was ready to act.

But nothing was more crucial to Mitterrand's ultimate success than his quick and complete mastery of the existing democratic structures under the Fourth and Fifth Republics. He understood well the interrelationships among the local, regional, and national levels of politics. He caught on quickly to the specific nature of the balance of power and hence of the struggle for power that existed between and within the legislative and executive branches under the two republics. And he positioned himself advantageously from both an ideological and partisan viewpoint in order to reap the maximum benefit from whatever system and structures were currently in force.

Finally, and most important, what Mitterrand mastered better than any other French politician of the postwar era were the various electoral systems used at the national and party levels. Whether majority, semimajority, semiproportional, or purely proportional, whether by direct or indirect suffrage, he discerned immediately the implications, drew the proper conclusions, and forged the necessary alliances. (As president, he has continued to play with electoral laws in order to contain the opposition.) Paradoxically, his relative distance from the large parties (even after his takeover of the PS) and his public stance as a "loner" for most of his career gave him the greatest flexibility and maneuverability in this area. He did not win every election, nor was every victory a landslide. On the contrary. But he read election results the way a successful investor reads earnings reports, spotting recent trends while others saw only the profits and the losses, the victory or the defeat; he knew when a defeat meant progress and when victory indicated a decline.

Mitterrand has his share of flaws. In spite of his intelligence, amazing memory, articulateness, extensive knowledge of history, and mastery of power and partisan politics, he suffers greatly from intellectual susceptibility, or vulnerability; this is coupled with the successful politician's need to exorcise all forms of self-doubt and self-criticism. The combination of his moral and religious background, his fascination with intellectual brilliance and his corresponding lack of intellectual discipline, often aggravated by large doses of wishful thinking, have predisposed Mitterrand to noble errors. Diverted by ideals that, in the end, proved impractical or unattainable, Mitterrand was, by his own admission, on the wrong side of history on several major issues: Pétain versus de Gaulle, colonialism versus national independence, parliamentarianism versus presidentialism, and socialist economics versus capitalist economics, to name the most glaring. His lack of rigor was most evident in the economic domain. The only important issue on which he appears to have been ahead of his time is European unity.

But Mitterrand is no diehard. He is smart enough to know when to give up on a hopeless idea—although he has remained loyal to his ideas to the last possible moment. When one examines his career closely, a stark pattern of political behavior emerges: Characteristically, Mitterrand would adopt a cause and then elaborate policies to serve it. Upon encountering opposition, he would strongly and even boldly resist, taking the lead in fighting for his cause. He supported Pétain until the latter's political demise; he fought for Algerian reform until the bitter end, and for the Fourth Republic even after its death. But once it became obvious that events were moving irreversibly in a direction different from the one he had chosen, Mitterrand recognized the fact, reflected on it a while, and then accepted it, making any necessary turnaround and adapting perfectly to the new situation. He may have moved from one erroneous noble cause to another, but as he mastered each new set of givens, whether brand new democratic rules or changed circumstances, his leadership grew, his level of political control rose, and his constituency broadened. Although he does not easily recognize looming historical forces, he is excellent at spotting a developing consensus or recent trend. In politics he learned that it is much better to be a little bit behind history than too far ahead of it.

Although the amount of "glory" that Mitterrand has achieved as France's Socialist "redeemer" has yet to be determined, it is already apparent that his contributions in this area will prove to have been less revolutionary than he had claimed they would be, as well as less catastrophic than opponents had predicted. And while Mitterrand possesses his share of weaknesses, many of the faults charged against him have been the very sources of his strengths. All of the elements of his Machiavellianism, including his ideological impurity, his acquired cynicism, and his authoritarianism at the party level—in and of themselves morally neutral—were necessary attributes for effective and durable leadership. For Mitterrand domesticated the Communist Party, moderated the radicalized Socialists, reestablished a certain balance on the left itself by bringing the center left back into the fold, harmonized all of these discordant political voices, and then won the presidency for the left twice. Even if Mitterrand had never won the presidency, these other achievements would have assured him of a place in French history, for they contributed enormously to the reestablishment of democratic equilibrium in the young and heavily Gaullist Fifth Republic.

## NOTES

1. One of the most recent manifestations of this perspective is Wayne Northcutt's *Mitterrand: A Political Biography* (New York: Holmes and Meier, 1992).

2. François Mitterrand, *L'Abeille et l'architecte* (The bee and the architect) (Paris: Flammarion, 1978), p. 116.

# Acronyms

CDS        Centre des Démocrates Sociaux. Center-right coalition led by Jean
           Lecanuet consisting of the old MRP and CNI.

CERES      Centre d'Etudes, de Recherches et d'Education Socialistes. A left-
           wing faction of the PS led by Jean-Pierre Chevènement.

CFDT       Confédération Française Démocratique du Travail. A non-Commu-
           nist Christian-oriented labor union.

CGT        Confédération Générale du Travail. The Communist-dominated labor
           union.

CIR        Convention des Institutions Républicaines. A center-left political
           organization founded by François Mitterrand and Charles
           Hernu in the mid-1960s.

CNI        Centre National des Indépendants. A Fourth Republic conservative
           political party to which Antoine Pinay and the young Valéry
           Giscard d'Estaing belonged.

FEN        Fédération de l'Education Nationale. A teachers union.

FGDS       Fédération de la Gauche Démocratique et Socialiste. The coalition of
           non-Communist leftist groups led by Mitterrand from 1965 to
           1968.

FLN        Front de Libération Nationale. The Algerian rebel movement.

FO         Force Ouvrière. A non-Communist labor union.

GPRA       Gouvernement Provisoire de la République Algérienne. The national-
           ist Arab Algerian party created by the FLN.

| | |
|---|---|
| MNPGD | Mouvement National des Prisonniers de Guerre et des Déportés. The prisoner-of-war and deportee movement that Mitterrand helped organize during World War II. |
| MRG | Mouvement des Radicaux de Gauche. The left wing of the centrist Radical Party that signed the Common Program. |
| MRP | Mouvement Républicain Populaire. The Fourth Republic Christian Democratic party led by Georges Bidault. |
| MTLD | Mouvement pour le Triomphe des Libertés Démocratiques. A reformist Algerian political movement. |
| OAS | Organisation de l'Armée Secrète. The organization of French military officers who tried in 1962 to prevent the implementation of the Evian Accords. |
| ORA | Organisation de la Résistance Armée. The Resistance military organization, led by Henri Giraud, that originated in the French Armistice Army and was long faithful to Marshal Philippe Pétain. |
| PC or PCF | Parti Communiste Français. The French Communist Party. |
| PS or PSF | Parti Socialiste Français. The name given to the French Socialist Party in 1971. |
| PSA | Parti Socialiste Autonome. A socialist party formed by defectors from the SFIO soon after the return of Charles de Gaulle to power in 1958. |
| PSU | Parti Socialiste Unifié. The new name given to the PSA in the early 1960s. |
| RDA | Rassemblement Démocratique Africain. A Central African political party led by Felix Houphouët-Boigny and allied with Mitterrand's UDSR during the 1950s. |
| RI | Républicains Indépendants. The name in the 1970s of the center-right political party led by Valéry Giscard d'Estaing. |
| RPF | Rassemblement du Peuple Français. The postwar Gaullist movement. |
| SFIO | Section Française de l'Internationale Ouvrière. The name of the French Socialist Party before 1969. |
| UDF | Union pour la Démocratie Française. A coalition of the center-right parties in the 1970s. |
| UDMA | Union Démocratique du Manifeste Algérien. A moderate Algerian political movement of the 1950s. |
| UDSR | Union Démocratique et Socialiste de la Résistance. A small centrist swing party to which Mitterrand belonged throughout the years of the Fourth Republic. |
| UNEF | Union Nationale des Etudiants Français. A university student organization. |

# Selected Bibliography

## BOOKS BY FRANÇOIS MITTERRAND

*L'Abeille et l'architecte*. Paris: Flammarion, 1978. Available in English together with *La Paille et le grain* as *The Wheat and the Chaff/The Bee and the Architect*. New York: Seaver Books, 1982.

*La Chine au défi*. Paris: Julliard, 1961.

*Le Coup d'état permanent*. Paris: Plon, 1964.

*Aux Frontières de l'Union Française*. Paris: Julliard, 1953.

*Ici et maintenant*. Paris: Fayard, 1980.

*La Paille et le grain*. Paris: Flammarion, 1975. Available in English; see *L'Abeille et l'architecte*.

*Ma Part de vérité*. Paris: Fayard, 1969.

*Politique*. Paris: Fayard, 1977.

*Politique 2 (1977-1981)*. Paris: Fayard, 1981.

*Présence française et abandon*. Paris: Plon, 1957.

*Les Prisonniers de guerre devant la politique*. Paris: Editions Rond-Point, 1945.

*Réflexions sur la politique extérieure de la France*. Paris: Fayard, 1986.

*La Rose au poing*. Paris: Flammarion, 1973.

*Un Socialisme du possible*. Paris: Seuil, 1970.

## BOOKS BY OTHER AUTHORS

Alexandre, Philippe. *Exécution d'un homme politique*. Paris: Grasset, 1973.

———. *Le Roman de la gauche*. Paris: Plon, 1977.

Bassi, Michel, and André Campana. *Le Grand Tournoi: Naissance de la Sixième République*. Paris: Grasset, 1974.

Bell, David S., and Byron Criddle. *The French Socialist Party: Resurgence and Victory*. Oxford: Clarendon Press, 1984.

Bizot, Jean-François. *Au Parti des socialistes*. Paris: Grasset, 1975.

Borzeix, Jean-Marie. *Mitterrand lui-même*. Paris: Stock, 1973.

Cardoze, Michel, and Jean Le Lagadec. *Quarante-neuf pourcent: Naissance d'une majorité*. Paris: Editions Sociales, 1974.

Cayrol, Roland. *François Mitterrand 1945-1967*. Paris: Fondation Nationale des Sciences Politiques, 1967.

Chapsal, Jacques. *La Vie politique sous la Cinquième République*. Paris: Presses Universitaires de France, 1984.

————. *La Vie politique en France de 1940 à 1958*. Paris: Presses Universitaires de France, 1984.

Cole, Alistair. *François Mitterrand: A Study in Political Leadership*. London: Routledge, 1994.

Colliard, Sylvie. *La Campagne présidentielle de François Mitterrand en 1974*. Paris: Presses Universitaires de France, 1979.

Cotteret, Jean-Marie, Claude Eméri, Jean Gerstlé, and René Moreau. *Giscard d'Estaing–Mitterrand: 54,774 Mots pour convaincre*. Paris: Presses Universitaires de France, 1976.

Derogy, Jacques, and Jean-François Kahn. *Les Secrets du ballottage*. Paris: Fayard, 1966.

Desjardins, Thierry. *François Mitterrand: Un Socialiste gaullien*. Paris: Hachette, 1978.

Dreyfus, François. *Histoire des gauches en France (1940–1974)*. Paris: Grasset, 1975.

Duhamel, Olivier. *La Gauche et la Cinquième République*. Paris: Presses Universitaires de France, 1980.

Du Roy, Albert, and Robert Schneider, *Le Roman de la rose d'Epinay à l'Elysée: L'Aventure socialiste*. Paris: Seuil, 1982.

Fabre, Robert. *Toute Vérité est bonne à dire*. Paris: Fayard, 1978.

Faucher, Jean-André. *L'Agonie d'un régime (1952–1958)*. Paris: Editions Atlantic, 1959.

Fauvet, Jacques. *La Quatrième République*. Paris: Fayard, 1959.

Giesbert, Franz-Olivier. *François Mitterrand ou la tentation de l'histoire*. Paris: Seuil, 1977.

Goguel, François. *France under the Fourth Republic*. Ithaca: Cornell University Press, 1952.

Goguel, François, and Alfred Grosser. *La Politique en France*. Paris: Armand Colin, 1975.

Griffith, William. ed. *The European Left: Italy, France, and Spain*. Lexington, Mass.: Lexington Books, 1979.

Guidoni, Pierre. *Histoire du nouveau Parti socialiste*. Paris: Téma-Editions, 1973.

Hamon, Hervé, and Patrick Rotman. *L'Effet Rocard*. Paris: Stock, 1980.

Johnson, R. W. *The Long March of the French Left*. New York: St. Martin's Press, 1981.

Kergoat, Jacques. *Le Parti socialiste*. Paris: Le Sycomore, 1983.

Labbé, Dominique. *François Mitterrand: Essai sur le discours*. Grenoble: La Pensée Sauvage, 1983.

Laurens, André. *D'une France à l'autre*. Paris: Gallimard, 1974.

Lazitch, Branko. *L'Echec permanent*. Paris: Editions Robert Laffont, 1978.

Loncle, François. *Autopsie d'une rupture: La Désunion de la gauche*. Paris: Editions Jean-Claude Simoën, 1979.

MacShane, Denis. *François Mitterrand: A Political Odyssey*. New York: Universe Books, 1982.

Manceron, Claude. *Cent Mille Voix par jour*. Paris: Laffont, 1966.

Manceron, Claude, and Bernard Pingaud. *François Mitterrand: L'Homme, les idées, et le programme.* Paris: Flammarion, 1981.

Moulin, Charles. *Mitterrand intime.* Paris: Albin Michel, 1982.

Nay, Catherine. *Le Noir et le rouge ou l'histoire d'une ambition.* Paris: Grasset, 1984.

Northcutt, Wayne. *François Mitterrand: A Political Biography.* New York: Holmes and Meier, 1992.

_____. *The French Socialist and Communist Party under the Fifth Republic.* New York: Irvington Publisher, 1985.

Parti socialiste. *Changer la vie: Programme de gouvernement du Parti socialiste.* Preface by François Mitterrand. Paris: Flammarion, 1972.

_____. *Programme commun de gouvernement de la gauche: Propositions socialistes pour l'actualisation.* Paris: Flammarion, 1977.

_____. *Le Projet socialiste pour la France des années '80.* Paris: Club Socialiste du Livre, 1980.

Péan, Pierre. *Une Jeunesse française.* Paris: Fayard, 1994.

Penniman, Howard R., ed. *France at the Polls: The Presidential Election of 1974.* Washington, D.C.: American Enterprise Institute for Public Policy Research, 1975.

_____. *The French National Assembly Elections of 1978.* Washington, D.C.: American Enterprise Institute, 1980.

Pfister, Thierry. *Les Socialistes: Les Secrets de familles, les rites, le code et les hommes du premier parti de France.* Paris: Albin Michel, 1977.

Pingaud, Bernard. *Mitterrand: L'Homme, les idées.* Paris: Flammarion, 1974.

Poperen, Jean. *La Gauche française: Le Nouvel Age 1958–1965.* Paris: Fayard, 1972.

_____. *L'Unité de la gauche.* Paris: Fayard, 1975.

*Le Programme commun de gouvernement du Parti communiste et du Parti socialiste.* Preface by Georges Marchais. Paris: Editions Sociales, 1972.

Rocard, Michel. *Parler vrai.* Paris: Seuil, 1979.

Salomon, André. *PS: La Mise à nu.* Paris: Laffont, 1980.

Schwartzenberg, Roger-Gérard. *La Campagne présidentielle de 1965.* Paris: Presses Universitaires de France, 1967.

Suffert, Georges. *De Defferre à Mitterrand.* Paris: Seuil, 1966.

Verdier, Robert. *PS/PC: Une Lutte pour l'entente.* Paris: Seghers, 1976.

Williams, Philip. *Crisis and Compromise: Politics in the Fourth Republic.* Hamden: Archon Books, 1964.

_____. *Politics in Post-War France: Parties and the Constitution in the Fourth Republic.* London: Longmans, Green, 1954.

## JOURNAL ARTICLES AND ESSENTIAL PERIODICALS

Blumenfeld, York. "French Parliamentary Elections." *Editorial Research Reports,* March 3, 1978, pp. 163–80.

*L'Express,* various issues.

Hayward, J. E. S. "Presidentialism and French Politics." *Parliamentary Affairs,* no. 18 (Winter 1964–65): 23–39.

Hayward, Jack, and Vincent Wright, "'Les Deux France' and the French Presidential Election of May 1974." *Parliamentary Affairs,* no. 27 (Summer 1974): 208–36.

Macridis, Roy C. "Oppositions in France: An Interpretation." *Government and Opposition*, no. 7 (Spring 1972): 166–85.

Mitterrand, François, and Valéry Giscard d'Estaing. "Le Débat radio-télévisé entre les deux candidats." *Le Monde*, May 7, 1982, pp. 8–14.

*Le Monde*, various issues, 1965–1981.

*Le Nouvel Observateur*, various issues.

Rocard, Michel. "Perspectives de la gauche." *Preuves*, no. 3 (1973): 55–78.

Wright, Vincent, and Howard Machin. "The French Socialist Party in 1973: Performance Prospects." *Government and Opposition*, no. 9 (Spring 1974): 123–45.

———. "The French Socialist Party: Success and the Problems of Success." *Political Quarterly*, no. 46 (January–March 1975): 36–52.

———. "Why Mitterrand Won: The French Presidential Elections of April–May 1981." *West European Politics*, 5, no. 1 (January 1982): 5–35.

# Index

## ABOUT THE AUTHOR

SALLY BAUMANN-REYNOLDS received her A.B. in French from Indiana University and M.A. and Ph.D. from the University of Chicago. She taught for seven years at the University of North Carolina at Asheville and since then has been teaching and writing in the Raleigh area.

ISBN 0-275-94887-0